[The Electors shall meet in their respective ... *persons, of whom one at least shall not be an Inhabitant of the same State* ... *Votes for each* ... *they sh*... *sign and certify, and trans-*

WAR POWERS

UNDER THE

CONSTITUTION OF THE UNITED STATES.

PISCHEL YEARBOOKS, INC.
P.O. Box 36, Marceline, Missouri 64658

WAR POWERS

UNDER THE

CONSTITUTION OF THE UNITED STATES.

BY

WILLIAM WHITING.

TENTH EDITION.

The Rio Grande Press, Inc.
GLORIETA, NEW MEXICO · 87535

Rio Grande Press Legal Consultant
ARTHUR ROSENBLUM, LL.B., J.B.,
134 North LaSalle Street
Chicago, Ill. 60602

Tenth edition from which this edition
was reproduced was supplied by
Robert Shuhi, Books
P. O. Box 136
Bantam, Conn. 06750

A RIO GRANDE PRESS SPECIAL
First published in 1864

LIBRARY OF CONGRESS CARD CATALOG 70-17197
I.S.B.N. 87380-073-7

First Printing 1971

The Rio Grande Press, Inc.
GLORIETA, NEW MEXICO · 87535

Publisher's Preface

What are the war powers of the President? Of the Congress? Of the Courts? What are the collective powers of the federal government itself in time of war? These are questions much on the public mind in the waning days of the Viet Nam war (or is it the waxing days of World War III, or of a new civil war?).

Here is a book that should be read and studied by President Richard M. Nixon, by all of the justices of the Supreme Court and the subordinate federal courts, by every member of Congress, by every political figure on the national stage, by newspaper and magazine publishers, by editors, feature writers and syndicated columnists, by the news staffs of television and radio stations, by law scholars and students, by university and college faculty professors, by clergymen of all faiths.

And above all, by the ordinary U. S. citizen.

It should be studied especially carefully by those who say they would like to destroy America and its Constitutional form of government.

According to Allibone's *Critical Dictionary of English literature and British and American Authors:*

> "*. . .This work first formulated the war powers of the country. It was called for from all quarters, and more than one edition was sent for from England, France and other foreign countries. It has passed through ten editions in Boston and seventeen in New York, and is still the handbook of the American statesman. . .*"

The *Dictionary of American Biography, First Supplement,* says that author William Whiting was born March 3, 1813, in Concord, Mass., the son of Colonel William and Hannah (Conant) Whiting. Young Whiting prepared for college at Concord Academy. He graduated at Harvard with an A.B. degree in 1833, and received a law degree there in 1838. In October of that year, he was admitted to practice before the bar of Massachusetts.

As a lawyer, Mr. Whiting proved to be so thorough, industrious and adroit in analysis of mastered cases that the old Common Pleas was often termed "Whiting's court". He married Lydia Cushing Russell, of Plymouth, on October 28, 1840. A Unitarian and a reformer like his Abolitionist father, he was a man of large public interests with a talent for writing exceptionally clear and concise legal treatises.

Appointed Special Counselor of the War Department in November, 1862, and later its Solicitor (an office established in February 1863 by a law which was repealed in 1866), Mr. Whiting resigned in April 1865, and no successor was ever named.

In 1862 he compiled a brochure, *The War Powers of the President and the Legislative Powers of Congress in Relation to Rebellion, Treason and Slavery,* which under the modified title (of this book) went through forty-three editions in eight years. Equally useful were his pamphlets, *Military Arrests in Time of War*––which was the bible of federal law–enforcement officers, *The Return of the Rebellious States to the Union,* and *Military Government of Hostile Territory in Time of War.* His annotated *Opinions on "Slavery" and "Reconstruction of the Union" as Expressed by President Lincoln* was used as a campaign text in the national election of 1864. All of the foregoing pamphlets are incorporated into this book.

Mr. Whiting became a presidential elector in 1868, and voted for U.S. Grant. In 1872 he was elected to Congress from the 3rd district of Massachusetts by an overwhelming vote, but his death at Roxbury intervened to prevent his taking the seat for which he was so well qualified. He died June 29, 1873, and was buried at Sleepy Hollow Cemetery near Concord. He was the father of four children––Rose Standish, William St. John (who died in infancy), William Russell and Harold

The Rio Grande Press has heretofore reprinted source

books of American history, with emphasis on the great Southwest. We call such books the Beautiful Rio Grande Classics. We do not so call this title; we categorize it, rather, as a "Rio Grande Press Special", as it is somewhat out of our ordinary publishing scope. We are nationalist by conviction; we love the United States and everything it has historically represented. We wish the Constitution well. If what we do here, with the republication of this fine old book, lends a hand in any way to the restoration of peace and tranquility to our native land, we are pleased that we could help.

For the record, this is the 76th title published by The Rio Grande Press since the firm was founded in Chicago in 1962.

Robert B. McCoy

La Casa Escuela
Glorieta, New Mexico
September 1971

WAR POWERS

UNDER THE

CONSTITUTION OF THE UNITED STATES.

BY

WILLIAM WHITING.

TENTH EDITION.

BOSTON:
LITTLE, BROWN, & COMPANY.
1864.

PRINTED BY
GEO. C. RAND AND AVERY,

PREFACE TO THE SECOND EDITION.

WAR POWERS OF THE PRESIDENT, AND LEGISLATIVE POWERS OF CONGRESS, IN RELATION TO REBELLION, TREASON, AND SLAVERY.

The following pages were not originally intended for publication, but were written by the author for his private use. He has printed them at the request of a few friends, to whom the opinions therein expressed had been communicated; and he is not unaware of several errors of the press, and of some inaccuracies of expression, which, in one or two instances, at least, modify the sense of the statements intended to be made. The work having been printed, such errors can conveniently be corrected only in the "*errata*." This publication was principally written in the spring of 1862, the chapter on the operation of the Confiscation Act of July 17th, 1862, having been subsequently added. Since that time President Lincoln has issued his Emancipation Proclamation, and several military orders, operating in the Free States, under which questions have arisen of the gravest importance. The views of the author on these subjects have been expressed in several recent public addresses; and, if circumstances permit, these subjects may be discussed in a future addition to this pamphlet.

To prevent misunderstanding, the learned reader is requested to observe the distinction between emancipating or confiscating slaves, and abolishing the laws which sustain slavery in the Slave

States. The former merely takes away slaves from the possession and control of their masters; the latter deprives the inhabitants of those States of the lawful right of obtaining, by purchase or otherwise, or of holding slaves. Emancipation or confiscation operates only upon the slaves personally; but a law abolishing the right to hold slaves, in the Slave States, operates on all citizens residing there, and effects a change of local law. If all the horses now in Massachusetts were to be confiscated, or appropriated by government to public use, though this proceeding would change the legal title to these horses, it would not alter the laws of Massachusetts as to personal property; nor would it deprive our citizens of the legal right to purchase and use *other* horses.

The acts for confiscation or emancipation of enemy's slaves, and the President's Proclamation of the 22d of September, do not abolish slavery as a legal institution in the States; they act upon persons held as slaves; they alter no local laws in any of the States; they do not purport to render slavery unlawful; they merely seek to remove slaves from the control of rebel masters. If slavery shall cease by reason of the legal emancipation of slaves, it will be because slaves are removed; nevertheless, the laws that sanction slavery may remain in full force. The death of all the negroes on a plantation would result in a total loss to the owner of so much "property;" but that loss would not prevent the owner from buying other negroes, and holding them by slave laws. Death does not interfere with the local law of property. Emancipation and confiscation, in like manner, do not necessarily interfere with local law establishing slavery.

The right to liberate slaves, or to remove the condition or *status* of slavery, as it applies to all slaves living at any one time, or the right to abolish slavery in the sense of liberating all existing slaves, is widely different and distinct from the right of repealing or annulling the laws of States which sanction the holding of slaves. State slave laws may or may not be beyond the reach of the legislative powers of Congress; but if they are, that fact would not determine the question as to the right to emancipate, liberate, or to change the relation to their masters of slaves *now living;* nor the question as to the right of abolishing slavery, in the sense in which this expression is used when it signifies the liberation of persons now held as slaves, from the operation of slave laws; while these laws are still left to act on other persons who may be hereafter reduced to slavery under them.

It is not denied that the powers given to the various departments of government are in general *limited* and defined; nor is it to be forgotten that "the powers not delegated to the United States by the constitution, nor prohibited by it to the States, are reserved to the States respectively, or to the people." (Const. Amendment, Art. X.) But the powers claimed for the President and for Congress, in this essay, are believed to be delegated to them respectively under the constitution, expressly or by necessary implication.

The learned reader will also notice, that the positions taken in this pamphlet do not depend upon the adoption of the most liberal construction of the constitution, Art. I. Sect. 8, Cl. 1, which is deemed by eminent statesmen to contain a distinct, substantive power to pass all laws which Congress shall judge expedient "*to provide for the common defence and general welfare.*" This construction was held to be the true one by many of the original framers of the constitution and their associates; among them was George Mason of Virginia, who opposed the adoption of the constitution in the Virginia convention, because, among other reasons, he considered that the true construction. (See Elliott's Debates, vol. ii. 327, 328.) Thomas Jefferson says, (Jefferson's Correspondence, vol. iv. p. 306,) that this doctrine was maintained by the *Federalists as a party*, while the opposite doctrine was maintained by the Republicans as a party. Yet it is true that several Federalists did not adopt that view, but Washington, Adams, Jefferson, Madison, Monroe, Hamilton, Mason, and others, were quite at variance as to the true interpretation of that much contested clause. Southern statesmen, drifting towards the state-rights doctrines, as time passed on, have generally adopted the strictest construction of the language of that clause; but it has not yet been authoritatively construed by the Supreme Court. Whatever may be the extent or limitation of the power conveyed in this section, it is admitted by all that it contains the power of imposing taxes to an unlimited amount, and the right to appropriate the money so obtained to "the common defence and public welfare." Thus it is obvious, that the right to appropriate private property to public use, and to provide compensation therefor, as stated in Chapter I.; the power of Congress to confiscate enemy's property as a belligerent right; the power of the President, as commander-in-chief, as an act of war, to emancipate slaves; or the power of Congress to pass laws to aid the President, in executing his military duties, by abolishing slavery, or emancipating slaves, under Art. I. Sect. 8, Cl. 18, as *war measures*, essential to save the country from destruction, do not depend upon the construction given to the disputed clause above cited.

It will also be observed, that a distinction is pointed out in these pages between the legislative powers of Congress, in time of peace, and in time of war. Whenever the words "*the common defence*" are used, they are intended to refer to a time, not of constructive war, but of actual open hostility, which requires the nation to exert its naval and military powers in self-defence, to save the government and the country from destruction.

The Introduction, and Chapters I. and VIII., should be read in connection, as they relate to the same subject; and the reader will bear in mind that, in treating of the powers of Congress in the first chapter, it is not asserted that Congress have, *without any public necessity justifying it*, the right to appropriate private property of any kind to public use. There must always be a justifiable cause for the exercise of every delegated power of legislation.

It is not maintained in these pages that Congress, in time of peace, has the right to abolish slavery in the States, by passing laws rendering the *holding of any slaves* therein illegal, so long as slavery is merely a household or family, or domestic institution· and so long as its existence and operation are confined to the States where it is found, and concern *exclusively* the domestic affairs of the Slave States; and so long as it does not conflict with or affect the rights, interests, duties, or obligations which appertain to the *affairs of the nation*, nor impede the execution of the laws and constitution of the United States, nor conflict with the rights of citizens under them. Yet cases might arise in which, in time of peace, the abolishment of slavery might be necessary, and therefore would be lawful, in order to enable Congress to carry into effect some of the express provisions of the constitution, as for example, that contained in Art. IV. Sect. 4, Cl. 1, in which the United States guarantee to every State in this Union a republican form of government; or that contained in Art. IV. Sect. 2, Cl. 1, which provides that citizens of each State shall be entitled to all the privileges and immunities of citizens in the several States.

It is asserted in this essay that, when the institution of slavery no longer concerns only the household or family, and no longer continues to be a matter exclusively appertaining to the domestic affairs of the State in which it exists; when it becomes a potent, operative, and efficient instrument for carrying on war against the Union, and an important aid to the public enemy; when it opposes the national military powers now involved in a gigantic rebellion; when slavery has been developed into a vast, an overwhelming *war power*, which is actually used by armed traitors for the overthrow of government and of the constitution; when it has become the origin of civil war, and the means by which hostilities are maintained in the deadly struggle of the Union for its own existence; when a local institution is perverted so as to compel three millions of loyal colored subjects to become belligerent traitors because they are held as slaves of disloyal masters, — then indeed slavery has become an affair most deeply affecting the national welfare and common defence, and has subjected itself to the severest enforcement of those legislative and military powers, to which alone, under the constitution, the people must look to save themselves from ruin. In the last extremity of our contest, the question must be decided whether slavery shall be rooted up and extirpated, or our beloved country be torn asunder and given up to our conquerors, our Union destroyed, and our people dishonored? Are any rights of property, or any claims, which one person can assume to have over another, by whatever local law they may be sanctioned, to be held, by any just construction of the constitution, as superior to the nation's right of self-defence? And can the local usage or law of any section of this country override and break down the obligation of the people to maintain and perpetuate their own government? Slavery is no longer local or domestic after it has become an engine of war. The country demands, at the hands of Congress and of the President, the exercise of every power they can lawfully put forth for its destruction, not as an *object* of the war, but as a *means* of terminating the rebellion, if by destroying slavery the republic may be saved. These considerations and others have led the author to the conclusion stated in the following pages, "that Congress has the right to abolish slavery, when in time of war its abolishment is necessary to aid the commander-in-chief in maintaining the '*common defence*.'"

W. W.

NOTE. — The reader is referred to the Preface, pages iii. and iv., for remarks upon the Constitution, *Art. I.*, *Sect.* 8, *clause* 1. relating to the alleged power of Congress "to provide for the general welfare and common defence," and, in addition to the authorities there cited, reference may be had to the speeches of Patrick Henry, who fully sustains the views of Mr. Jefferson. See also Story on the Constitution, Sect. 1286.

CONTENTS OF THE "WAR POWERS," ETC.

CHAPTER I.

CHAPTER II.

CHAPTER III.

CHAPTER IV.

CHAPTER V.

CHAPTER VI.

CHAPTER VII.

CHAPTER VIII.

CONTENTS OF MILITARY ARRESTS.

CONTENTS

OF THE

RETURN OF REBELLIOUS STATES TO THE UNION.

CONTENTS

OF

MILITARY GOVERNMENT OF HOSTILE TERRITORY

IN TIME OF WAR.

CHAPTER IV.

CHAPTER V.

CHAPTER VI.

CHAPTER VII.

CHAPTER VIII.

APPENDIX.

CONSTITUTION

OF THE

UNITED STATES OF AMERICA.

INTRODUCTION.

THE PURPOSE FOR WHICH IT WAS FOUNDED.

The Constitution of the United States, as declared in the preamble, was ordained and established by the people, "in order to form a more perfect union, establish justice, insure domestic tranquillity, provide for the common defence, promote the general welfare, and secure the blessings of liberty to themselves and their posterity."

HOW IT HAS BEEN VIOLATED.

A handful of slave-masters have broken up that Union, have overthrown justice, and have destroyed domestic tranquillity. Instead of contributing to the common defence and public welfare, or securing the blessings of liberty to themselves and their posterity, they have waged war upon their country, and have attempted to establish, over the ruins of the Republic, an aristocratic government founded upon Slavery.

1

"THE INSTITUTION" *vs.* THE CONSTITUTION.

It is the conviction of many thoughtful persons, that slavery has now become practically irreconcilable with republican institutions, and that it constitutes, at the present time, the chief obstacle to the restoration of the Union. They know that slavery can triumph only by overthrowing the republic; they believe that the republic can triumph only by overthrowing slavery.

"THE PRIVILEGED CLASS."

Slaveholding communities constitute the only "*privileged class*" of persons who have been admitted into the Union. They alone have the right to vote for their *property* as well as for themselves. In the free States citizens vote only for themselves. The former are allowed to count, as part of their representative numbers, three fifths of all slaves. If this privilege, which was accorded only to the original States, had not been extended (contrary, as many jurists contend, to the true intent and meaning of the constitution) so as to include other States subsequently formed, the stability of government would not have been seriously endangered by the temporary toleration of this "institution," although it was inconsistent with the principles which that instrument embodied, and revolting to the sentiments cherished by a people who had issued to the world the Declaration of Independence, and had fought through the revolutionary war to vindicate and maintain the rights of man.

UNEXPECTED GROWTH OF SLAVERY.

The system of involuntary servitude, which had received, as it merited, the general condemnation of the leading southern and northern statesmen of the country, — of those who were most familiar with its evils, and of all fair-minded persons throughout the world, — seemed, at the time when our government was founded, about to vanish and disappear from this continent, when the spinning jenny of Crompton, the loom of Wyatt, the cotton gin of Whitney, and the manufacturing capital of England, combined to create a new and unlimited demand for that which is now the chief product of southern agriculture. Suddenly, as if by magic, the smouldering embers of slavery were rekindled, and its flames, like autumnal fires upon the prairies, have rapidly swept over and desolated the southern states; and, as that local, domestic institution, which seemed so likely to pass into an ignominious and unlamented grave, has risen to claim an unbounded empire, hence the present generation is called upon to solve questions and encounter dangers not foreseen by our forefathers.

SLAVERY ABOLISHED BY EUROPEAN GOVERNMENTS.

In other countries the scene has been reversed. France, with unselfish patriotism, abolished slavery in 1794; and though Napoleon afterwards reëstablished servitude in most of the colonies, it was finally abolished in 1848. England has merited and received her highest tribute of honor from the enlightened nations of the world for that great act of Parliament in 1833, whereby she proclaimed universal emancipation.

In 1844, King Oscar informed the Swedish states of his desire to do away with involuntary servitude in his dominions; in 1846 the legislature provided the pecuniary means for carrying that measure into effect; and now all the slaves have become freemen.

Charles VIII., King of Denmark, celebrated the anniversary of the birth of the Queen Dowager by abolishing slavery in his dependencies, on the 28th of July, 1847.

In 1862, Russia has consummated the last and grandest act of emancipation of modern times.*

While Europe has thus practically approved of the leading principle of the American constitution, as founded on justice, and as essential to public welfare, the United States, as represented by the more recent administrations, have practically repudiated and abandoned it. Europe, embarrassed by conservative and monarchical institutions, adopts the preamble to that instrument, as a just exposition of the true objects for which governments should be established, and accordingly abolishes slavery — while, in this country, in the mean time, slavery, having grown strong, seeks by open rebellion to break up the Union, and to abolish republican democracy.

SLAVERY IN 1862 NOT SLAVERY IN 1788.

However harmless that institution may have been in 1788, it is now believed by many, that, with few but honorable exceptions, the *slave-masters* of the present day, *the privileged class*, cannot, or will not, conduct themselves so as to render it longer possible, by peaceable association with them, to preserve "the Union," to "establish justice," "insure domestic tranquillity, the general welfare, the common defence, or the blessings of liberty to ourselves or our posterity." And since the wide-spread but secret conspiracies of traitors in the

* To the above examples we must add that of the Dutch West Indies, where the law emancipating the slaves goes into operation in July, 1863.

slave states for the last thirty years; their hatred of the Union, and determination to destroy it; their abhorrence of republican institutions, and of democratic government; their preference for an "oligarchy with slavery for its corner stone," have become known to the people, — their causeless rebellion; their seizure of the territory and property of the United States; their siege of Washington; their invasion of States which have refused to join them; their bitter, ineradicable, and universal hatred of the people of the free States, and of all who are loyal to the government, have produced a general conviction that slavery (which alone has caused these results, and by which alone the country has been brought to the verge of ruin) must itself be terminated; and that this "privileged class" *must be abolished;* otherwise the unity of the American people must be destroyed, the government overthrown, and constitutional liberty abandoned.

To secure domestic tranquillity is to make it certain by controlling power. It cannot be thus secured while a perpetual uncontrollable cause of civil war exists. The cause, the means, the opportunity of civil war must be removed; the perennial fountain of all our national woes must be destroyed; otherwise "it will be in vain to cry, Peace! peace! There is no peace."

ARE SLAVEHOLDERS ARBITERS OF PEACE AND WAR?

Is the Union so organized that the means of involving the whole country in ruin must be left in the hands of a small privileged class, to be used at their discretion? Must the blessing of peace and good government be dependent upon the sovereign will and pleasure of a handful of treasonable and unprincipled slave-masters?

Has the constitution bound together the peaceable citizen with the insane assassin, so that his murderous knife cannot lawfully be wrenched from his grasp even in self-defence?

If the destruction of slavery be necessary to save the country from defeat, disgrace, and ruin,—and if, at the same time, the constitution guarantees the perpetuity of slavery, whether the country is saved or lost, — it is time that the friends of the government should awake, and realize their awful destiny. If the objects for which our government was founded can lawfully be secured only so far as they do not interfere with the pretensions of slavery, we must admit that the interests of slave-masters stand first, and the welfare of the people of the United States stands last, under the guarantees of the constitution. If the Union, the constitution, and the laws, like Laocoön and his sons, are to be strangled and crushed, in order that the unrelenting serpent may live in triumph, it is time to determine which of them is most worthy to be saved. Such was not the Union formed by our forefathers. Such is not the Union the people intend to preserve. *They* mean to uphold a *Union, under the constitution, interpreted by common sense;* a *government* able to attain results worthy of a great and free people, and for which it was founded; a *republic*, representing the sovereign majesty of the whole nation, clothed with ample powers to maintain its supremacy forever. They mean that liberty and union shall be "one and inseparable."

WHY SLAVERY, THOUGH HATED, WAS TOLERATED.

It is true, that indirectly, and *for the purpose of a more equal distribution of direct taxes*, the framers of the constitution *tolerated*, while they condemned slavery; but they tolerated it because they believed that it would soon disappear. They even refused to allow the charter of their own liberties to be polluted by the mention of the word "slave." Having called the world to witness their heroic and unselfish sacrifices for the vindication of their own inalienable rights, they could not, consistently with honor or self-respect, transmit to future ages the evidence that some of them had trampled upon the inalienable rights of others.

RECOGNITION OF SLAVERY NOT INCONSISTENT WITH THE PERPETUITY OF THE REPUBLIC.

Though slavery was thus tolerated by being ignored, we should dishonor the memory of those who organized that government to suppose that they did not intend to bestow upon it the power to maintain its own authority — the right to overthrow or remove slavery, or whatever might prove fatal to its permanence, or destroy its usefulness. We should discredit the good sense of the great people who ordained and established it, to deny that they bestowed upon the republic, created by and for themselves, the right, the duty, and the powers of *self-defence*. For self-defence by the government was only maintaining, through the people's agents, the right of the people to govern themselves.

DISTINCTION BETWEEN THE OBJECTS AND THE MEANS OF WAR.

We are involved in a war of self-defence.

It is not the *object and purpose* of our hostilities to lay waste lands, burn bridges, break up railroads, sink ships, blockade harbors, destroy commerce, capture, imprison, wound, or kill citizens; to seize, appropriate, confiscate, or destroy private property; to interfere with families, or domestic institutions; to remove, employ, liberate, or arm slaves; to accumulate national debt, impose new and burdensome taxes; or to cause thousands of loyal citizens to be slain in battle. But, as *means of carrying on the contest,* it has become necessary and lawful to lay waste, burn, sink, destroy, blockade, wound, capture, and kill; to accumulate debt, lay taxes, and expose soldiers to the peril of deadly combat. Such are the ordinary results and incidents of war. If, in further prosecuting hostilities, the liberating, employing, or arming of slaves shall be deemed convenient for the more certain, speedy, and effectual overthrow of the enemy, the question will arise, whether the constitution prohibits those measures as acts of legitimate war against rebels, who, having abjured that constitution and having openly in arms defied the government, claim for themselves only the rights of belligerents.

It is fortunate for America that securing the liberties of a great people by giving freedom to four millions of bondmen would be in accordance with the dictates of justice and humanity. If the preservation of the Union required the enslavement of four millions of freemen, very different considerations would be presented.

LIBERAL AND STRICT CONSTRUCTIONISTS.

The friends and defenders of the constitution of the United States of America, ever since its ratification, have expressed widely different opinions regarding the limitation of the powers of government in time of peace, no less than in time of war. Those who have contended for the most narrow and technical construction, having stuck to the letter of the text, and not appreciating the spirit in which it was framed, are opposed to all who view it as only a *frame* of government, a *plan-in-outline,* for regulating the affairs of an enterprising and progressive nation. Some treat that frame of government as though it were a cast-iron mould, incapable of adaptation or alteration — as one which a blow would break in pieces. Others think it a hoop placed around the trunk of a living tree, whose growth must girdle the tree, or burst the hoop. But sounder judges believe that it more resembles the tree itself, — native to the soil that bore it, — waxing strong in sunshine and in storm, putting forth branches, leaves, and roots, according to the laws of its own growth, and flourishing with eternal verdure. Our constitution, like that of England, contains all that is required to adapt itself to the present and future changes and wants of a free and advancing people. This great nation, like a distant planet in the solar system, may sweep round a wide orbit; but in its revolutions it never gets beyond the reach of the central light. The sunshine of constitutional law illumines its pathway in all its changing positions. We have not yet arrived at the "dead point" where the hoop must burst — the mould be shattered — the tree girdled — or the sun shed darkness rather than light. By a liberal construction of the constitution, our government has passed through many storms unharmed. Slaveholding States, other than those whose inhabitants originally formed it, have found their way into the Union, notwithstanding the guarantee of equal rights to all. The territories of Florida and Louisiana have been purchased from European powers. Conquest has added a nation to our borders. The purchased and the conquered regions are now legally a part of the United States. The admission of new States containing a privileged class, the incorporation into our Union of a foreign people, are held to be lawful and valid by all the courts of the country. Thus far from the old anchorage have we sailed under the flag of "public necessity," "general welfare," or "common defence." Yet the great charter of our political rights "still lives;" and the question of to-day is, whether that instrument, which has not prevented America from acquiring one country by purchase, and another by conquest, will permit her to *save herself?*

POWERS WE SHOULD EXPECT TO FIND.

If the ground-plan of our government was intended to be more than a temporary expedient,—if it was designed, according to the declaration of its authors, for a *perpetual* Union, — then it will doubtless be found, upon fair examination, to contain whatever is essential to carry that design into effect. Accordingly, in addition to provisions for adapting it to great changes in the situation and circumstances of the people by *amendments*, we find that powers essential to its own perpetuity are vested in the executive and legislative departments, to be exercised *according to their discretion*, for the good of the country — powers which, however dangerous, must be intrusted to every government, to enable it to maintain its own existence, and to protect the rights of the people. Those who founded a goverment for themselves intended that it should never be overthrown; nor even altered, except by those under whose authority it was established. Therefore they gave to the President, and to Congress, the means essential to the preservation of the republic, but none for its dissolution.

LAWS FOR PEACE, AND LAWS FOR WAR.

Times of peace have required the passage of numerous statutes for the protection and development of agricultural, manufacturing, and commercial industry, and for the suppression and punishment of ordinary crimes and offences. A state of general civil war in the United States is, happily, new and unfamiliar. These times have demanded new and unusual legislation to call into action those powers which the constitution provides for times of war.

Leaving behind us the body of laws regulating the rights, liabilities, and duties of citizens, in time of public tranquillity, we must now turn our attention to the RESERVED and HITHERTO UNUSED powers contained in the constitution, which enable Congress to pass a body of laws to regulate the rights, liabilities, and duties of citizens in time of war. We must enter and explore the arsenal and armory, with all their engines of defence, enclosed, by our wise forefathers for the safety of the republic, within the old castle walls of that constitution; for now the garrison is summoned to surrender; and if there be any cannon, it is time to unlimber and run them out the port-holes, to fetch up the hot shot, to light the match, and hang out our banner on the *outer* walls.

THE UNION IS GONE FOREVER IF THE CONSTITUTION DENIES THE POWER TO SAVE IT.

The question whether republican constitutional government shall now cease in America, must depend upon the construction given to these *hitherto unused powers.* Those who desire to see an end of this government will deny that it has the ability to save itself. Many new inquiries have arisen in relation to the existence and limitation of its powers. Must the successful prosecution of war against rebels, the preservation of national honor, and securing of permanent peace,—if attainable only by rooting out the evil which caused and maintains the rebellion,—be effected by destroying rights solemnly guaranteed by the constitution we are defending? If so, the next question will be, whether the law of self-defence and overwhelming necessity will not justify the country in denying to rebels and traitors in arms whatever rights they or their friends may claim under a charter which they have repudiated, and have armed themselves to overthrow and destroy? Can one party break the contract, and justly hold the other party bound by it? Is the constitution to be so interpreted that rebels and traitors cannot be put down? Are we so hampered, as some have asserted, that even if war end in reëstablishing the Union, and enforcing the laws over all the land, the results of victory will be turned against us, and the conquered enemy may then treat us as though they had been victors? Will vanquished criminals be able to resume their rights to the same political superiority over the citizens of Free States, which, as the only "privileged class," they have hitherto enjoyed?

Have they who alone have made this rebellion, while committing treason and other high crimes against the republic, a protection, an immunity against punishment for these crimes, whether by forfeiture of life or property by reason of any clause in the constitution? Can government, the people's agent, wage genuine and effectual war against their enemy? or must the soldier of the Union, when in action, keep one eye upon his rifle, and the other upon the constitution? Is the power to make war, when once lawfully brought into action, to be controlled, baffled, and emasculated by any obligation to guard or respect rights set up by or for belligerent traitors?

THE LEADING QUESTIONS STATED.

What limit, if any, is prescribed to the war-making power of the President, as *Commander-in-Chief* of the army and navy of the United States? What authority has Congress to frame laws interfering with the ordinary civil rights of persons and property, of loyal or disloyal citizens, in peaceful or in rebellious districts; of the enemy who may be captured as spies, as pirates, as guerrillas or bush-whackers; as aiders and comforters of armed traitors, or as soldiers in the battle-field? What rights has Congress, or the President, in relation to *belligerent districts* of country; in relation to slaves captured or escaping into the lines of our army, or escaping into Free States; or slaves used by the enemy in military service; or those belonging to rebels, not so used? Whether they are contraband of war? and whether they may be released, manumitted, or emancipated, and discharged by the civil or military authority? or whether slaves may be released from their obligation to serve rebel masters? and whether slavery may be abolished with or without the consent of the masters, as a military measure, or as a legislative act, required by the public welfare and common defence? Where the power to abolish it resides, under the constitution?

And whether there is any restraint or limitation upon the power of Congress to punish treason? What are the rights of government over the private property of loyal citizens? What are the rights and liabilities of traitors? These and similar inquiries are frequently made among the plain people; and it is for the purpose of explaining some of the doctrines of law applicable to them, that the following suggestions have been prepared.

CHAPTER I.

THE CONSTITUTIONAL RIGHT OF THE GOVERNMENT TO APPROPRIATE PRIVATE PROPERTY TO PUBLIC USE, EITHER IN TIME OF PEACE OR IN TIME OF WAR.

The general government of the United States has, in time of peace, a legal right, under the constitution, to appropriate to public use the private property of any subject, or of any number of subjects, owing it allegiance.

Each of the States claims and exercises a similar right over the property of its own citizens.

THE RIGHT IS FOUNDED IN REASON.

All permanent governments in civilized countries assert and carry into effect, in different ways, the claim of "eminent domain;" for it is essential to their authority, and even to their existence. The construction of military defences, such as forts, arsenals, roads, navigable canals, however essential to the protection of a country in war, might be prevented by private interests, if the property of individuals could not be taken by the country, through its government. Internal improvements in time of peace, however important to the interests of the public, requiring the appropriation of real estate belonging to individuals, might be interrupted, if there were no power to *take*, without the consent of the owner, what the public use requires. And as it is the government which protects all citizens in their rights to life, liberty, and property, they are deemed to hold their property subject to the claim of the supreme protector to take it from them when demanded by "public welfare." It is under this quasi *sovereign* power that the State of Massachusetts seizes by law the private estates of her citizens; and she even authorizes several classes of corporations to seize land, against the will of the proprietor, for public use and benefit. Railroads, canals, turnpikes, telegraphs, bridges, aqueducts, could never have been constructed were the existence of this great right denied. And the TITLE to that interest in real estate, which is thus acquired by legal seizure, is deemed by all the courts of this commonwealth to be as legal, and as *constitutional*, as if purchased and conveyed by deed, under the hand and seal of the owner.

INDEMNITY IS REQUIRED.

But, when individuals are called upon to give up what is their own for the advantage of the community, justice requires that they should be fairly compensated for it: otherwise public burdens would be shared unequally. To secure the right to indemnification, which was omitted in the original constitution of the United States, an amendment was added, which provides, (Amendments, Art. V, last clause,) "*Nor shall private property be taken for public use without just compensation.*"*

The language of this *amendment* admits the right of the United States to take private property for public use. This amendment, being now a part of the constitution, leaves that right no longer open to question, if it ever was questioned.

* Similar provisions are found in the constitution of Massachusetts, and several other states.

In guarding against the abuse of the right to take private property for public use, it is provided that the owner shall be entitled to be fairly paid for it; and thus he is not to be taxed *more than his due share* for public purposes.

It is not a little singular that the framers of the constitution should have been *less* careful to secure equality in distributing the burden of taxes. Sect. 8 requires *duties, imposts, and excises* to be *uniform* throughout the United States, but it does not provide that *taxes* should be uniform. Although Art. I., Sect. 9, provides that no *capitation* or other *direct tax* shall be laid unless in proportion to the census, yet far the most important subjects of taxation are still unprotected, and may be UNEQUALLY assessed, without violating any clause of that constitution, which so carefully secures equality of public burdens by providing compensation for private property appropriated to the public benefit.

"PUBLIC USE."

What is "*public use*" for which private property may be taken?

Every appropriation of property for *the benefit* of the United States, either for a national public improvement, or to carry into effect any valid law of Congress for the maintenance, protection, or security of national interests, is "public *use*." *Public use* is contradistinguished from *private use.* That which is for the *use of the country*, however applied or appropriated, is for public use.

Public use does not require that the property taken shall be actually *used.* It may be *disused, removed,* or *destroyed.* And destruction of private property may be the best public use it can be put to.

Suppose a bridge, owned by a private corporation, were so located as to endanger a military work upon the bank of a river. The *destruction* of that bridge to gain a military advantage would be appropriating it to *public use.*

So also the blowing up or demolition of buildings in a city, for the purpose of preventing a general conflagration, would be an appropriation of them to public use. The *destruction* of arms, or other munitions of war, belonging to private persons, in order to prevent their falling into possession of the enemy, would be applying them to *public use.* Congress has power to pass laws providing for the common defence and general welfare, under Art. I. Sect. 8 of the constitution; and whenever, in their judgment, the common defence or general welfare requires them to authorize the appropriation of private property to public use, — whether that use be *the employment or destruction of the property taken,* — they have the right to pass such laws; to appropriate private property in that way; and whatever is done with it is "public use," and entitles the owner to just compensation therefor.

ALL KINDS OF PROPERTY, INCLUDING SLAVES, MAY BE SO APPROPRIATED.

There is no restriction as to the kind or *character* of private property which may be lawfully thus appropriated, whether it be real estate, personal estate, rights in action or in possession, *obligations for money, or for labor and service.* Thus the obligations of minor children to their parents, of apprentices to their masters, and of other persons owing labor and service to their masters, may lawfully be appropriated to public use, or discharged and destroyed, for public benefit, by Congress, with the proviso that just compensation shall be allowed to the parent or master.

Our government, by treaty, discharged the claims of its own citizens against France, and thus appropriated private property to public use. At a later date the United States discharged the claims of certain slave owners to labor and service, whose slaves had been carried away by the British contrary to their treaty stipulations. In both cases indemnity was promised by our government to the owners; and in case of the slave masters it was actually paid. By abolishing slavery in the District of Columbia, that which was considered for the purposes of the act as private property was appropriated to public use, with just compensation to the owners; Congress, in this instance, having the right to pass the act as a local, municipal law; but the compensation was from the treasury of the United States.

During the present rebellion, many minors, apprentices, and slaves have been relieved from obligation to their parents and masters, the claim for their services having been appropriated to public use, by employing them in the military service of the country.

That Congress should have *power* to appropriate *every description* of private property for public benefit in time of war, results from the *duty* imposed on it by the constitution to pass laws "providing for the common defence and general welfare."

Suppose that a large number of apprentices desired to join the army as volunteers in time of sorest need, but were restrained from so doing only by reason of their owing labor and service to their employers, who were equally with them citizens and subjects of this government; would any one doubt or deny the right of government to accept these apprentices as soldiers, to discharge them from the obligation of their indentures, providing just compensation to their employers for loss of their services? Suppose that these volunteers owed labor and service for life, as slaves, instead of owing it for a term of years; what difference could it make as to the right of government to use their services, and discharge their obligations, or as to the liability to indemnify the masters? The right to use the services of the minor, the apprentice, and the slave, for public benefit, belongs to the United States. The claims of all American citizens upon their services, whether by local law, or by common law, or by indentures, can be annulled by the same power, for the same reasons, and under the same restrictions that govern the appropriation of any other private property to public use.

THE UNITED STATES MAY REQUIRE ALL SUBJECTS TO DO MILITARY DUTY.

Slaves, as well as apprentices and minors, are equally *subjects* of the United States, whether they are or are not *citizens* thereof. The government of the United States has the right to call upon all its subjects to do *military duty*. If those who owe labor and service to others, either by contract, by indenture, by common or statute law, or by local usage, could not be lawfully called upon to *leave* their employments to serve their country, no inconsiderable portion of the able-bodied men would thus be exempt, and the constitution and laws of the land providing for calling out the army and navy would be set at nought. But the constitution makes no such exemptions from military duty. Private rights cannot be set up to overthrow the claims of the country to the services of every one of its subjects who owes it allegiance.

How far the United States is under obligation to compensate parents, masters of apprentices, or masters of slaves, for the loss of service and labor of those subjects who are enlisted in the army and navy, has not been yet decided.* The constitution recognizes slaves as "*persons held to labor or service.*" So also are apprentices and minor children "persons held to labor and service." And, whatever other claims may be set up, by the laws of either of the slave states, to any class of "persons," the constitution recognizes *only* the claim of individuals to *the labor and service* of other individuals. It seems difficult, therefore, to state any sound principle which should require compensation in one case and not in the other.

WILL SLAVEHOLDERS BE ENTITLED TO INDEMNITY IF THEIR SLAVES ARE USED FOR MILITARY PURPOSES?

It is by no means improbable, that, in the emergency which we are fast approaching, the right and duty of the country to call upon *all* its *loyal subjects* to aid in its military defence *will be deemed paramount to the claims of any private person upon such subjects*, and that the

* If an apprentice enlist in the army, the courts will not, upon a *habeas corpus*, issued at the relation of the master, *remand* the apprentice to his custody, if he be *unwilling* to return, but will leave the master to his suit against the officer, who, by Stat. 16 Mar. 1802, was forbidden to enlist him without the master's consent. *Commonwealth* v. *Robinson*, 1 S. & R. 353; *Commonwealth* v. *Harris*, 7 Pa. L. J. 283.

loss of *labor and service* of certain citizens, like the loss of life and property, which always attends a state of war, must be borne by those upon whom the misfortune happens to fall. It may become one of the great political questions hereafter, whether, if slavery should as a civil act in time of peace, or by treaty in time of war, be wholly or partly abolished, for *public benefit*, or *public defence*, such abolishment is *an appropriation* of *private property* for public use, *within the meaning of the constitution.*

INDEMNITY TO MORMONS.

The question has not yet arisen in the courts of the United States, whether the act of Congress, which, under the form of a statute against polygamy abolishes Mormonism, a domestic institution, sustained like slavery only by local law, is such an appropriation of the claims of Mormons to the labor and service of their wives as requires just compensation under the constitution? A decision of this question may throw some light on the point now under consideration.

EFFECT OF NATURALIZATION AND MILITIA LAWS ON THE QUESTION OF INDEMNITY TO SLAVE-MASTERS.

A further question may arise as to the application of the "compensation" clause above referred to. Congress has the power to pass naturalization laws, by Art. I. Sect. 8. This power has never been doubted. The only question is, whether this power is not exclusive.* Congress may thus give the privileges of citizenship to

* See *Chirac* v. *Chirac*, 2 Whea. 269; *U. S.* v. *Villato*, 2 Dall. 372; *Thirlow* v. *Mass.*, 5 How. 585; *Smith* v. *Turner*, 7 ib. 556; *Golden* v. *Prince*, 3 W. C. C. Reports, 314.

any persons whatsoever, black or white. Colored men, having been citizens in *some* of the *States* ever since they were founded, having acted as citizens prior to 1788 in various civil and military capacities, are therefore citizens of the United States.*

Under the present laws of the United States, according to the opinion of the attorney-general of Massachusetts, *colored men are equally with white men required to be enrolled in the militia of the United States*,† although such was not the case under the previous acts of 1792 and 1795. "The general government has authority to determine who shall and who may not compose the militia of the United States; and having so determined, the state government has no legal authority to prescribe a different enrolment.‡ If, therefore, Congress exercise either of these undoubted powers to grant *citizenship* to all colored persons residing or coming within either of the States, or to pass an act requiring *the enrolment* of all able-bodied persons within a prescribed age, whether owing labor and service or not, § as *part of the militia of the United States*, and thereby giving to all, as they become soldiers or seamen, their freedom from obligations of labor and service, except *military* labor and service, then the question would arise, whether government, by calling its own subjects and citizens into the military service of the country, in case of overwhelming necessity, could be required by the constitution to recognize the private relations in which the soldier might stand, by *local* laws, to persons setting up

* See case of *Dred Scott;* which in no part denies that if colored men *were* citizens of either of the states which adopted the constitution, they were citizens of the United States.

† See Stat. U. S. July 17, 1862.

‡ 8 Gray's R. 615.

§ See Act approved February 24, 1864.

claims against him? If white subjects or citizens, owe labor and service, even by formal indentures, such obligations afford no valid excuse against the requisition of government to have them drafted into the militia to serve the country. The government does not compensate those who claim indemnity for the loss of such "labor and service." Whether the *color* of the debtor, or the *length* of time during which the obligation (to labor and service) has to run, or the *evidence* by which the *existence* of the obligation is proved, can make an essential difference between the different kinds of labor and service, remains to be seen. The question is, whether the soldier or seaman, serving his country in arms, can be deemed *private property*, as recognized in the constitution of the United States?

DOES THE WAR POWER OF SEIZURE SUPERSEDE THE CIVIL POWER OF CONGRESS TO APPROPRIATE PRIVATE PROPERTY TO PUBLIC USE?

That the property of any citizen may, under certain circumstances, be seized in time of war, by *military officers*, for public purposes, is not questioned, just compensation being offered, or provided for; but the question has been asked, whether this power does not supersede the right of Congress, in war, to pass laws to take away what martial law leaves unappropriated?

This inquiry is conclusively answered by reference to the amendment of the constitution, above cited, which admits the existence of that power in CONGRESS;* but in addition to this, there are other clauses which devolve powers and duties on the legislature, giving them a large and important share in instituting, organizing, carrying on, regulating, and ending war; and these duties could not, under all circumstances, be discharged

* Amendments, Art. V. last clause.

in war, without exercising the right to take for public use the property of the subject. It would seem strange if private property could not be so taken, while it is undeniable that in war the government can call into the military service of the country every able-bodied citizen, and tax his property to any extent.

REFERENCES AS TO THE CONSTITUTION, SHOWING THE WAR POWERS OF CONGRESS.

The powers of the *legislative* department in relation to war are contained chiefly in the following sections in the constitution: —

Art. I., Sect. 8, Cl. 11. *Congress* may *institute* war by declaring it against an enemy. The President alone cannot do so. Also, Congress may make laws concerning *captures on land*, as well as *on water*.

Art. I., Sect. 8, Cl. 12. Congress may *raise and support armies*: and provide and maintain a navy.

Art. I., Sect. 8, Cl. 14. Congress may make laws for the *government* of land and naval forces.

Art. I., Sect. 8, Cl. 15. Congress may provide for *calling forth* the militia to execute the laws of the Union, suppress insurrection, and repel invasion.

Art. I., Sect. 8, Cl. 16: And may provide for organizing, arming, and disciplining the militia, and for *governing* such part of them as may be employed in the service of the United States.

The preamble to the constitution declares the objects for which it was framed to be these: "to form a more perfect Union; establish justice; *insure domestic tranquillity*; provide for *the common defence*; promote the general welfare, and secure the blessings of liberty to ourselves and our posterity." In Art. I., Sect. 8, Cl. 1, the *first power* given to Congress is to lay and collect taxes, duties, imposts, and excises, to pay the debts, and provide for the *common defence and general welfare of the United States.* And in the same article (the eighteenth clause) express power is given to Congress *to make all laws which shall be necessary and proper for carrying into execution the foregoing and all other powers vested by the constitution in the government of the United States, or in any department or officer thereof.*"

SLAVE PROPERTY SUBJECT TO THE SAME LIABILITY AS OTHER PROPERTY TO BE APPROPRIATED FOR WAR PURPOSES.

If the *public welfare* and *common defence*, in time of war, require that the claims of masters over their apprentices or slaves should be cancelled or abrogated, against their consent, and if a general law carrying into execution such abrogation, is, in the judgment of Congress, "a necessary and proper measure for accomplishing that object," there can be no question of the constitutional power and right of Congress to pass such laws. The only doubt is in relation to the right to compensation. If it should be said that the release of slaves from their servitude would be tantamount to impairing or destroying the obligation of contracts, it may be said, that though states have no right to pass laws impairing the obligation of contracts, Congress is at liberty to pass such laws. It will be readily perceived that the right to abrogate and cancel the obligations of apprentices and slaves does not rest solely upon the power of Congress to appropriate private property to public use; but it may be founded upon their power and obligation to accomplish one of the chief objects for which the Union was formed, viz., to provide for the *common defence* and *general welfare* of the United States.

IMPORTANCE AND DANGER OF THIS POWER.

The powers conveyed in this 18th clause of Art. I., Sect. 8, are of *vast* importance and extent. It may be said that they are, in one sense, unlimited and discretionary. They are more than imperial. But it was intended by the framers of the constitution, or, what is of more importance, by the *people* who made and adopted it, that the powers of government in dealing with civil rights in time of peace, should be *defined* and limited; but the powers "to provide for the *general welfare* and the *common defence*" in time of war, should be *unlimited.* It is true that such powers may be temporarily abused; but the remedy is always in the hands of the people, who can unmake laws and select new representatives and senators.

POWERS OF THE PRESIDENT NOT IN CONFLICT WITH THOSE OF CONGRESS.

It is not necessary here to define the extent to which congressional legislation may justly control and regulate the conduct of the army and navy in service; or where falls the dividing line between civil and martial law. But the power of Congress to pass laws on the subjects expressly placed in its charge by the terms of the constitution cannot be taken away from it, by reason of the fact that the President, as commander-in-chief of the army and navy, also has powers, equally constitutional, to act upon the same subject-matters. It does not follow that because Congress has power to abrogate the claims of Mormons or slaveholders, the President, as commander, may not also do the same thing.

These powers are not *inconsistent,* or conflicting. Congress may pass laws concerning *captures* on land

and on the water. If slaves are *captured*, and are treated as "captured property," Congress should determine what is to be done with them;* and it will be the President's duty to see that *these* as well as other laws of the United States are *executed*.

CONGRESS HAS POWER UNDER THE CONSTITUTION TO ABOLISH SLAVERY.

Whenever, in the judgment of Congress, the common defence and public welfare, in time of war, require the removal of the condition of slavery, it is within the scope of their constitutional authority to pass laws for that purpose.

If such laws are deemed to take private property for public use, or to destroy private property for public benefit, as has been shown, that may be done under the constitution, by providing just compensation; otherwise, no compensation can be required. It has been so long the habit of those who engage in public life to disclaim any intention to interfere with slavery in the States, that they have of late become accustomed to deny the *right of Congress* to do so. But *the constitution contains no clause or sentence prohibiting the exercise by Congress of the plenary power of abrogating involuntary servitude.* The only prohibition contained in that instrument relating to persons held to labor and service, is in Art. IV., which provides that, "No person held to labor and service in one state, *under the laws thereof*, escaping into another, shall, in consequence of any *law* or *regulation* "*therein*," be discharged from such service or labor; but shall be delivered up on claim of the party to whom such service or labor may be due." Thus, if a slave or appren-

* Constitution, Art. I., Sect. 8, Cl. 11.

tice, owing service to his employer in Maryland, escapes to New York, the legislature of New York cannot, by any law or regulation, legally discharge such apprentice or slave from his liability to his employer. *This restriction is, in express terms, applicable only to State legislatures, and not to Congress.*

Many powers given to Congress are denied to the States; and there are obvious reasons why the supreme government alone should exercise so important a right. That a power is withdrawn from the States, indicates, by fair implication, that *it belongs to the United States,* unless expressly prohibited, if it is embraced within the scope of powers necessary to the safety and preservation of the government, in peace or in civil war.

It will be remarked that the provision as to slaves in the constitution relates only to fugitives from labor escaping from one state into another; not to the *status* or *condition* of slaves in any of the states where they are held, while another clause in the constitution relates to *fugitives* from justice.* Neither clause has any application to citizens or persons who are not *fugitives.* And it would be a singular species of reasoning to conclude that, because the constitution prescribed certain rules of conduct towards persons *escaping from one State into another,* therefore there is no power to make rules relating *to other persons who do not escape from one State into another.* If Congress were expressly empowered to pass laws relating to persons *when escaping* from justice or labor by fleeing from their own States, it would be absurd to infer that there could be no power to pass laws relating to these same persons when staying at home. The govern-

* Constitution, Art. IV. Sect. 2.

ment may pass laws requiring the return of fugitives: they may pass other laws punishing their crimes, or relieving them from penalty. The power to do the one by no means negatives the power to do the other. If Congress should discharge the obligations of slaves to render labor and service, by passing a law to that effect, such law would supersede and render void all rules, regulations, customs, or laws of either State to the contrary, for the constitution, treaties, and laws of the United States are the supreme law of the land. If slaves were released by act of Congress, or by the act of their masters, there would be no person *held to labor* as a slave by the laws of *any State*, and therefore there would be no person to whom the clause in the constitution restraining State legislation could apply. This clause, relating to fugitive slaves, has often been misunderstood, as it has been supposed to limit the power of *Congress*, while in fact *it applies in plain and express terms only to the States*, controlling or limiting *their* powers, but having no application to the general government. If the framers of the constitution intended to take from Congress the power of passing laws relating to slaves in the States or elsewhere, they would have drafted a clause to that effect. They did insert in that instrument a proviso that Congress should pass no law prohibiting the "importation of such persons as any of the States should think proper to admit" (meaning slaves) "prior to 1808."* And if they did not design that the legislature should exercise control over the subject of domestic slavery, whenever it should assume such an aspect as to involve *national* interests, the introduction of the proviso relating to the slave

* Constitution, Art. I. Sect. 9.

trade, and of several other clauses in the plan of government, makes the omission of any prohibition of legislation on slavery unaccountable.

CONCLUSION.

Thus it has been shown that the government have the right to appropriate to public use *private property* of every description; that "public use" may require the employment or the destruction of such property; that if the "right to the labor and service of others," as slaves, be recognized in the broadest sense as "property," there is nothing in the constitution which deprives Congress of the power to appropriate "that description of property" to public use, by terminating slavery, as to all persons now held in servitude, whenever laws to that effect are required by "the public welfare and the common defence" in time of war; that this power is left to the discretion of Congress, who are the sole and exclusive judges as to the occasions when it shall be exercised, and from whose judgment there is no appeal. The right to "just compensation" for private property so taken, depends upon the circumstances under which it is taken, and the loyalty and other legal conditions of the claimant.

NOTE. — As to the use of discretionary powers in *other* departments, see *Martin* v. *Mott*, 12 Wheat. 29–31; *Luther* v. *Borden*, 7 How. 44, 45.

INTRODUCTION TO CHAPTER II.

THE Constitution, *Art. I., Sect.* 8, *clause* 18, gives Congress power ' to make *all laws* which shall be necessary and proper for carrying into execution the foregoing powers, and *all other powers* vested by this Constitution in the Government of the United States, or in any Department *or officer thereof.*"

Art. II., Sect. 2, *clause* 1, provides that "the President shall be *Commander-in-chief* of the Army and Navy of the United States, and of the Militia of the several States, when called into the actual service of the United States."

Art. I., Sect. 8, declares that "Congress shall have power to provide for calling forth the Militia to execute the laws of the Union, suppress insurrections, and repel invasions."

As the President is, within the sense of *Art. I., Sect.* 8, *clause* 18, "*an officer of government;*" and by virtue of *Art. II., Sect.* 2, *clause* 1, he is *Commander-in-chief of the Army and Navy;* and as, by virtue of *Art. II., Sect.* 2, *clause* 1, and *Art. I., Sect.* 8, the *power is vested in him as* "*an officer of the government*" to suppress rebellion, repel invasion, and to maintain the Constitution by force of arms, in time of war, and for that purpose to overthrow, conquer, and subdue the enemy of his country, so completely as to "*insure* domestic tranquillity,"—it follows by *Art. I., Sect.* 8, *clause* 18, that Congress may, in time of war, pass all laws which shall be necessary and proper to enable the President to carry into execution" all his military powers.

It is *his* duty to break down the enemy, and to deprive them of their means of maintaining war: Congress is therefore bound to pass such laws as will *aid* him in accomplishing that object.

If it has power to make laws for carrying on the government in time of peace, it has the power and duty to make laws to preserve it from destruction in time of war.

CHAPTER II.

WAR POWERS OF CONGRESS.*

CONGRESS has power to frame statutes not only for the punishment of crimes, but also for the purpose of aiding the President, as commander-in-chief of the army and navy, in suppressing rebellion, and in the final and permanent conquest of a public enemy. "It may pass such laws as it may deem necessary," says Chief Justice Marshall, "to carry into execution the great powers granted by the constitution;" and "necessary means, in the sense of the constitution, does not import an absolute physical necessity, so strong that one thing cannot exist without the other. It stands for any means calculated to produce the end."

RULES OF INTERPRETATION.

The constitution provides that Congress shall have power to pass "all laws necessary and proper" for carrying into execution all the powers granted to the government of the United States, or any department or officer thereof. The word "necessary," as used, is not limited by the additional word "proper," but enlarged thereby.

"If the word *necessary* were used in the strict, rigorous sense, it would be an extraordinary departure from the usual course of the human mind, as exhibited in solemn instruments, to add another word, the only possible effect of which is to qualify that strict and rigorous meaning, and to present clearly the idea of a choice of means in the course of legislation. If no means are to be resorted to but such as

* For references to the clauses of the Constitution containing the war powers of Congress, see *ante*, pp. 27, 28.

are *indispensably* necessary, there can be neither sense nor utility in adding the word '*proper*,' for the *indispensable necessity* would shut out from view all consideration of the *propriety* of the means." *

Alexander Hamilton says, —

"The authorities essential to the care of the common defence are these: To raise armies; to build and equip fleets; to prescribe rules for the government of both; to direct their operations; to provide for their support. These powers ought to exist WITHOUT LIMITATION, because it is impossible to foresee or to define the extent and variety of national exigencies, and the correspondent extent and variety of the means necessary to satisfy them. The circumstances which endanger the safety of nations are infinite; and for this reason no constitutional shackles can wisely be imposed on the power to which the care of it is committed. . . . This power ought to be under the direction of the same councils which are appointed to preside over the *common defence*. . . . It must be admitted, as a necessary consequence, that there can be no limitation of that authority which is to provide for the defence and protection of the community in any matter essential to its efficacy — that is, in any matter essential to the *formation*, *direction*, or *support* of the NATIONAL FORCES."

This statement, Hamilton says, —

"Rests upon two axioms, simple as they are universal: the *means* ought to be proportioned to the *end;* the persons from whose agency the attainment of the *end* is expected, ought to possess the *means* by which it is to be attained." †

The doctrine of the Supreme Court of the United States, announced by Chief Justice Marshall, and approved by Daniel Webster, Chancellor Kent, and Judge Story, is thus stated: —

"The government of the United States is one of enumerated powers, and it can exercise only the powers granted to it; but though limited in its powers, it is supreme within its sphere of action. It is the government of the people of the United States, and emanated from them. Its powers were delegated by all, and it represents all, and acts for all.

"There is nothing in the constitution which excludes *incidental* or

* 3 Story's Commentaries, Sec. 122. † Federalist, No. 23, pp. 95, 96.

implied powers. The Articles of Confederation gave nothing to the United States but what was expressly granted; but the new constitution dropped the word *expressly*, and left the question whether a particular power was granted to depend on a fair construction of the whole instrument. No constitution can contain an accurate detail of all the subdivisions of its powers, and all the *means* by which they might be carried into execution. It would render it too prolix. Its nature requires that only the great outlines should be marked, and its important objects designated, and all the minor ingredients left to be deduced from the nature of those objects. The sword and the purse, all the external relations, and no inconsiderable portion of the industry of the nation, were intrusted to the general government; and a government intrusted with such ample powers, on the due execution of which the happiness and prosperity of the people vitally depended, must also be intrusted with *ample means of their execution.* Unless the words imperiously require it, we ought not to adopt a construction which would impute to the framers of the constitution, when granting great powers for the public good, the intention of impeding their exercise by withholding a *choice of means.* The powers given to the government imply the ordinary means of execution; and the government, in all sound reason and fair interpretation, must have the choice of the means which it deems the most convenient and appropriate to the execution of the power. The constitution has not left the right of Congress to employ the necesssary means for the execution of its powers to general reasoning. Art. I, Sect. 8, of the constitution, expressly confers on Congress the power 'to make all laws that may be necessary and proper to carry into execution the foregoing powers.'

"Congress may employ such means and pass such laws as it may deem necessary to carry into execution great powers granted by the constitution; and *necessary* means, in the sense of the constitution, does not import an absolute physical necessity, so strong that one thing cannot exist without the other. It stands for any means calculated to produce the end. The word *necessary* admits of all degrees of comparison. A thing may be necessary, or very necessary, or absolutely or indispensably necessary. The word is used in various senses, and in its construction the subject, the context, the intention, are all to be taken into view. The powers of the government were given for the welfare of the nation. They were intended to endure for ages to come, and to be adapted to the various *crises* in human affairs. To prescribe the specific means by which government should in all future time execute its power, and to confine the choice of means to such narrow limits as should not leave it in the power of Congress to adopt any which might be appropriate and conducive to the end, would be most unwise and pernicious, because it would be an attempt to provide, by immutable rules, for exigencies which, if foreseen at all, must have been foreseen dimly, and would deprive the legislature of the capacity to avail itself of experience, or to exercise its reason, and accommodate its legislation to circumstances. If the end be legitimate, and within the scope of the constitution, all means which are appropriate, and plainly adapted to this end, and which are not prohibited by the constitution, are lawful." *

Guided by these principles of interpretation, it is obvious that if the confiscation of property, or the liberation of slaves of rebels, be " plainly adapted to the end," — that is, to the suppression of rebellion, — it is within the power of Congress to pass laws for those purposes. Whether they are adapted to produce that result is for the legislature alone to decide. But, in considering the war powers conferred upon that department of government, a broad distinction is to be observed between confiscation or emancipation laws, passed in time of peace, for the punishment of crime, and similar laws, passed in time of war, to aid the President in suppressing rebellion, in carrying on a civil war, and in securing "the public welfare" and maintaining the "common defence" of the country. Congress may pass such laws in peace or in war as are within the general powers conferred on it, unless they fall within some express prohibition of the constitution. If confiscation or emancipation laws are enacted under the war powers of Congress, we must determine, in order to test their validity, whether, in suppressing a rebellion of colossal proportions, the United States are, within the meaning of

* On the interpretation of constitutional power, see 1 Kent's Com. 351, 352; *McCulloch* v. *The State of Maryland,* 4 Wheat. R. 413–420.

the constitution, *at war* with its own citizens? whether confiscation and emancipation are sanctioned as belligerent rights by the law and usage of civilized nations? and whether our government has full belligerent rights against its rebellious subjects?

ARE THE UNITED STATES AT WAR?

War may originate in either of several ways. The navy of a European nation may attack an American frigate in a remote sea. Hostilities then commence without any invasion of the soil of America, or any insurrection of its inhabitants. A foreign power may send troops into our territory with hostile intent, and without declaration of war; yet war would exist solely by this act of invasion. Congress, on one occasion, passed a resolution that "war existed by the act of Mexico;" but no declaration of war had been made by either belligerent. Civil war may commence either as a general armed insurrection of slaves, a servile war; or as an insurrection of their masters, a rebellion; or as an attempt, by a considerable portion of the subjects, to overthrow their government—which attempt, if successful, is termed a revolution. Civil war, within the meaning of the constitution, exists also whenever any combination of citizens is formed to resist generally the execution of any one or of all the laws of the United States, if accompanied with overt acts to give that resistance effect.

DECLARATION OF WAR NOT NECESSARY ON THE PART OF THE GOVERNMENT TO GIVE IT FULL BELLIGERENT POWERS.

A state of war may exist, arising in either of the modes above mentioned, without a declaration of war by either of the hostile parties. Congress has the sole power, under the constitution, to make that declaration, and to sanction or authorize the commencement of *offensive* war. If the United States commence hostilities against a foreign nation, such commencement is by proclamation, which is equivalent to a declaration of war. But this is quite a different case from a defensive or a civil war. The constitution establishes the mode in which this government shall *commence* wars, and what authority shall ordain, and what declarations shall precede, any act of hostility; but it has no power to prescribe the manner in which others should begin war against us. Hence it follows, that when war is commenced against this country, by aliens or by citizens, no declaration of war by the government is necessary.* The fact that war is levied against the United States, makes it the duty of the President to call out the army or navy to subdue the enemy, whether foreign or domestic. The chief object of a declaration of war is to give notice thereof to neutrals, in order to fix their rights, and liabilities to the hostile powers, and to give to innocent parties reasonable time to withdraw their persons and property from danger. If the commander-in-chief could not call out his forces to repel an invasion until Congress should have made a formal declaration of war, a foreign army might march from Canada to the Gulf before such declaration could be made, if it should commence the campaign while Congress was not in session. Before a majority of its members could be convened, our navy might be swept from the seas. The constitution, made as it was by men of sense, never leaves the nation powerless for self-defence. That instrument, which gives the legislature authority to declare war, whenever war is *initiated* by the United States, also makes it the duty of the President, as com-

* See opinion of the Supreme Court of the U. S. on this subject, pronounced since the 4th edition of this work was published. Appendix, p. 141.

mander-in-chief, to engage promptly and effectually in war; or, in other words, to make the United States a belligerent nation, without declaration of war, or any other act of Congress, whenever he is legally called upon to suppress rebellion, repel invasion, or to execute the laws against armed and forcible resistance thereto. The President has his duty, Congress have theirs; they are separate, and in some respects independent. Nothing is clearer than this, that when such a state of hostilities exists as justifies the President in calling the army into actual service, without the authority of Congress, no declaration of war is requisite, either in form or substance, for any purpose whatsoever. Hence it follows, that government, while engaged in suppressing a rebellion, is not deprived of the rights of a *belligerent against rebels,* by reason of the fact that no formal declaration of war has been made against them, as though they were an alien enemy, — nor by reason of the circumstance that this great civil war originated, so far as we are parties to it, in an effort to resist an armed attack of citizens upon the soldiers and the forts of the United States. It must not be forgotten that by the law of nations and by modern usage, no formal *declaration* of war *to the enemy* is made or deemed necessary.* All that is now requisite is for each nation to make suitable declarations or proclamations to its own citizens, to enable them to govern themselves accordingly. These have been made by the President.

HAS GOVERNMENT FULL WAR POWERS AGAINST REBEL CITIZENS?

Some persons have questioned the right of the United States to make and carry on war against citi-

* See 1 Kent's Com. p. 54.

zens and subjects of this country. Conceding that the President may be authorized to call into active service the navy and army "to repel invasion, or suppress rebellion," they neither admit that suppressing rebellion places the country in the attitude of making war on rebels, nor that the commander-in-chief has the constitutional right of conducting his military operations as he might do if he were actually at war (in the ordinary sense of the term) against an alien enemy. Misapprehension of the meaning of the constitution on this subject has led to confusion in the views of some members of Congress during the last session, and has in no small degree emasculated the efforts of the majority in dealing with the questions of emancipation, confiscation, and enemy's property.

Some have assumed that the United States are not *at war* with rebels, and that they have no authority to exercise the rights of war against them. They admit that the army has been lawfully called into the field, and may kill those who oppose them; they concede that rebels may be taken captive, their gunboats may be sunk, and their property may be seized; that martial law may be declared in rebellious districts, and its pains and penalties may be enforced; that every armed foe may be swept out of the country by military power. Yet they entertain a vague apprehension that something in the constitution takes away from these military proceedings, in suppressing rebellion and in resisting the attacks of the rebels, the quality and character of warfare. All these men in arms are not, they fancy, "*making war*." When the citizens of Charleston bombarded Fort Sumter, and captured property exclusively owned by the United States, it is not denied that *they* were "*waging war*" upon the government. When Major Anderson returned the enemy's fire and attempted to defend the fort and the guns from capture, it is *denied* that the *country* was "waging war." While other nations, as well as our own, had formally or informally conceded to the rebels the character and the rights usually allowed to belligerents, — that is, to persons making war *on us*, — *we*, according to the constitutional scruple above stated, were not entitled to the rights of belligerents against them. It therefore becomes important to know what, according to the constitution, the meaning of the term "levying war" really is; and as the military forces of this country are in actual service to suppress rebellion, whether such military service is *making war* upon its own citizens; and if war actually exists, whether there is any thing in the constitution that limits or controls the full enjoyment and exercise by the government of the rights of a belligerent against the belligerent enemy?

IS "SUPPRESSING REBELLION" BY ARMS MAKING WAR ON THE CITIZENS OF THE UNITED STATES, IN THE SENSE OF THE CONSTITUTION?

To "repel invasion" by arms, all admit, is entering upon defensive war against the invader. War exists wherever and whenever the army or navy is in active service against a public enemy.

When *rebels* are organized into armies in large numbers, overthrow the government, invade the territory of States not consenting thereto, attack, and seize, and confiscate the property not of the government only, but of all persons who continue loyal, such proceedings constitute war in all its terrors — a war of subjugation and of conquest, as well as of rebellion. Far *less* than these operations constitutes the *levying of war*, as those terms are explained in the language of the constitution.

"*War is levied*" on the United States wherever and whenever the crime of *treason* is committed, (see Constitution, Art. III., Sect. 3, Cl. 3,) and under that clause, as interpreted by the Supreme Court, "*war is levied*" when there exists a combination resorting to overt acts to oppose generally the execution of any law of the United States, even if no *armed* force be used. The language of the constitution is clear and express. "Treason shall consist only in levying war upon the United States, or in giving aid and comfort to the enemy." If, therefore, any person, or collection of persons, have committed the crime of treason, the constitution declares them to have *levied war*. As *traitors* they have become belligerent, or war levying enemies.

War may be waged *against* the government or *by* the government; it may be either offensive or defensive. Wherever war exists there must be two parties to it. If traitors (belligerents by the terms of the constitution) are one party, the government is the other party. If, when treason is committed, any body is at war, then it follows that the United States are at war. The inhabitants of a section of this country have issued a manifesto claiming independence; they have engaged in open war on land and sea to maintain it; they have invaded territory of peaceful and loyal sections of the Union; they have seized and confiscated ships, arsenals, arms, forts, public and private property of our government and people, and have killed, captured, and imprisoned soldiers and private citizens. Of the million of men in arms, are those on one side levying war, and are those opposed to them *not* levying war?

As it takes two parties to carry on war, either party may begin it. That party which begins usually declares war. But when it is actually begun, the party attacked is as much at war as the party who made the attack. The United States are AT WAR with rebels, in the strictly legal and constitutional sense of the term, and have therefore all the rights against them which follow from a state of *war*, in addition to those which are derived from the fact that the rebels are also subjects.

REBELS MAY BE TREATED AS BELLIGERENTS AND AS SUBJECTS.

Wars may be divided into two classes, foreign and civil. In all civil wars the government claims the belligerents, on both sides, as subjects, and has the legal right to treat the insurgents both as subjects and as belligerents; and they therefore may exercise the full and untrammelled powers of war against their subjects, or they may, in their discretion, relieve them from any of the pains and penalties attached to either of these characters. The right of a country to treat its rebellious citizens *both as belligerents and as subjects* has long been recognized in Europe, and by the Supreme Court of the United States.* In the civil war between St. Domingo and France, such rights were exercised, and were recognized as legitimate in *Rose* v. *Himely*, 4 Cranch, 272. So in *Cherriot* v. *Foussatt*, 3 Binney, 252. In *Dobrie* v. *Napier*, 3 Scott R. 225, it was held that a blockade of the coast of Portugal, by the Queen of that country, was lawful, and a vessel was condemned as a *lawful prize* for running the blockade. The cases

* See note A. page 215.

of the *Santisima Trinidad,* 7 Wheat. 306, and *United States* v. *Palmer,* 3 W. 635, confirm this doctrine. By the terms of the constitution defining treason, a traitor *must be a subject and a belligerent,* and none but a belligerent subject can be a traitor.

The government have in fact treated the insurgents *as belligerents* on several occasions, without recognizing them in express terms as such. They have received the capitulation of rebels at Hatteras, as prisoners of war, *in express terms,* and have exchanged prisoners of war as such, and have blockaded the coast by military authority, and have officially informed other nations of such blockade, and of their intention to make it effective, under the present law of nations. They have not exercised their undoubted right to repeal the laws making either of the blockaded harbors ports of entry. They have relied solely on their *belligerent* rights, under the law of nations.

Having thus the full powers and right of making and carrying on war against rebels, both as subjects and as belligerents, this *right* frees the President and Congress from the difficulties which might arise if rebels could be treated *only* as SUBJECTS, and if *war* could not be waged upon them. If conceding to rebels the privileges of belligerents should relieve them from some of the harsher penalties of treason, it will subject them to the liabilities of the belligerent character. The privileges and the disadvantages are correlative. But it is by no means conceded that the government may not exercise the right of treating the same rebels both as subjects and as belligerents. The constitution defines a rebel who commits treason as one who "levies war" on the United States; and the laws punish this highest of crimes with death, thus expressly treating the same person *as subject and as belligerent.* Those who save their necks from the halter by claiming to be treated as prisoners of war, and so to protect themselves under the shield of belligerent rights, must bear the weight of that shield, and submit to the legal consequences of the character they claim. They cannot sail under two flags at the same time. But a rebel does not cease to be a subject because he has turned traitor. The constitution expressly authorizes Congress to pass laws to punish traitor—that is, belligerent—subjects; and suppressing rebellion by armed force is making war. Therefore the war powers of government give full belligerent rights against rebels in arms.

THE LAW OF NATIONS IS ABOVE THE CONSTITUTION.

Having shown that the United States being actually engaged in civil war,—in other words, having become a belligerent power, without formal declaration of war,—it is important to ascertain what some of the *rights* of *belligerents* are, according to the law of nations. It will be observed that the law of nations is above the constitution of any government; and no people would be justified by its peculiar constitution in violating the rights of other nations. Thus, if it had been provided in the Articles of Confederation, or in the present constitution, that all citizens should have the inalienable right to practise the profession of *piracy* upon the ships and property of foreign nations, or that they should be lawfully empowered to make incursions into England, France, or other countries, and seize by force and bring home such men and women as they should select, and, if these privileges should be put in practice, England

and France would be justified in treating us as a nest of pirates, or a band of marauders and outlaws. The whole civilized world would turn against us, and we should justly be exterminated. An association or agreement on our part to violate the rights of others, by whatever name it may be designated, whether it be called a constitution, or league, or conspiracy, or a domestic institution, is no justification, under the law of nations, for illegal or immoral acts.

INTERNATIONAL BELLIGERENT RIGHTS ARE DETERMINED BY THE LAW OF NATIONS.

To determine what are the rights of different nations when making war upon each other, we look only to the law of nations. The peculiar forms or rights of the subjects of one of these war-making parties under their own government give them no rights over their enemy other than those which are sanctioned by international law. In the great tribunal of nations, there is a "higher law" than that which has been framed by either one of them, however sacred to each its own peculiar laws and constitution of government may be.

But while this supreme law is in full force, and is binding on all countries, softening the asperities of war, and guarding the rights of neutrals, it is not conceded that the government of the United States, in a civil war for the suppression of rebellion among its own citizens, is subject to the same limitations as though the rebels were a foreign nation, owing no allegiance to the country.

With this caveat, it will be desirable to state some of the rights of belligerents.

BELLIGERENT RIGHT OF CONFISCATION OF PERSONAL ESTATE.

Either belligerent may seize and confiscate all the property of the enemy, on land or on the sea, including real as well as personal estate.

PRIZE COURTS.

As the property of all nations has an equal right upon the high seas, (the highway of nations,) in order to protect the commerce of neutrals from unlawful interference, it is necessary that ships and cargoes seized on the ocean should be brought before some prize court, that it may be judicially determined whether the captured vessel and cargo were, in whole or in part, enemy's property or contraband of war. The decision of any prize court, according to the law of nations, is conclusive against all the world. Where personal property of the enemy is captured from the enemy, on land, in the enemy's country, no decision of any court is necessary to give a title thereto. Capture passes the title. This is familiar law as administered in the courts of Europe and America.*

TITLE BY CAPTURE.†

Some persons have questioned whether title passes in this country by capture or confiscation, by reason of some of the limiting clauses of the constitution; and others have gone so far as to assert that all the proceedings under martial law, such as capturing enemy's property, imprisonment of spies and traitors, and seizures of articles contraband of war, and suspending the *habeas corpus,* are in violation of the constitution, which declares that no man shall be deprived of life, liberty, or

* *Alexander* v. *Duke of Wellington,* 2 Russ. & Mylne, 35. Lord Brougham said that military prize rests upon the same principles of law as prize at sea, though in general no statute passes with respect to it. See 1 Kent's Comm. 357.

† See the prize cases, Appendix, p. 141.

property without due process of law;* that private property shall not be taken for public use without just compensation;† that unreasonable searches and seizures shall not be made;‡ that freedom of speech and of the press shall not be abridged;§ and that the right of the people to keep and bear arms shall not be infringed.||

THESE PROVISIONS NOT APPLICABLE TO A STATE OF WAR.

If these rules are applicable to a state of war, then capture of property is illegal, and does not pass a title; no defensive war can be carried on; no rebellion can be suppressed; no invasion can be repelled; the army of the United States, when called into the field, can do no act of hostility. Not a gun can be fired *constitutionally*, because it might deprive a rebel foe of his life without *due process of law*—firing a gun not being deemed "due process of law."

Sect. 4 of Art. IV. says, that "the United States shall guarantee to every State in this Union a republican form of government, and shall protect each of them against invasion, and, on application of the legislature, or of the Executive, when the legislature cannot be convened, against domestic violence."

Art. I. Sect. 8, gives Congress power to declare war, raise and support armies, provide and maintain a navy; to provide for calling forth the militia to execute the laws of the Union, suppress insurrection and repel invasion; to provide for organizing, arming, and disciplining the militia, and for governing such part of them as may be in the service of the United States.

* Constitutional Amendments, Art. V. † Ibid. Art. V.
‡ Ibid. Art. IV. § Ibid. Art. I. || Ibid. Art. II.

If these rules above cited have any application in a time of war, the United States *cannot protect* each of the States from invasion by citizens of other States, nor against domestic violence; nor can the army, or militia, or navy be used for any of the purposes for which the constitution authorizes or requires their employment. If all men have the right to "keep and bear arms," what right has the army of the Union to take them away from rebels? If "no one can constitutionally be deprived of life, liberty, or property, without due process of law," by what right does government seize and imprison traitors? By what right does the army kill rebels in arms, or burn up their military stores? If the only way of dealing constitutionally with rebels in arms is to go to law with them, the President should convert his army into lawyers, justices of the peace, and constables, and serve "summonses to appear and answer to complaints," instead of a summons to surrender. He should send "GREETINGS" instead of sending rifle shot. He should load his caissons with "pleas in abatement and demurrers," instead of thirty-two pound shell and grape shot. In short, he should levy writs of execution, instead of levying war. On the contrary, the commander-in-chief proposes a different application of the due process of law. His summons is, that rebels should lay down their arms; his pleas are batteries and gunboats; his arguments are hot shot, and always "to the point;" and when his fearful execution is "levied on the body," all that is left will be for the undertaker.

TRUE APPLICATION OF THESE CONSTITUTIONAL GUARANTEES.

The clauses which have been cited from the amendments to the constitution were intended as declarations of the rights of peaceful and loyal citizens, and safeguards in the administration of justice by the civil tribunals; but it was necessary, in order to give the government the means of defending itself against domestic or foreign enemies, to maintain its authority and dignity, and to enforce obedience to its laws, that it should have unlimited war powers; and it must not be forgotten that the same authority which provides those safeguards, and guarantees those rights, also imposes upon the President and Congress the duty of so carrying on war as of necessity to supersede and hold in temporary suspense such civil rights as may prove inconsistent with the complete and effectual exercise of such war powers, and of the belligerent rights resulting from them. The rights of war and the rights of peace cannot coexist. One must yield to the other. Martial law and civil law cannot operate at the same time and place upon the same subject matter. Hence the constitution is framed with full recognition of that fact; it protects the citizen in peace and in war; but his rights enjoyed under the constitution, in time of peace are different from those to which he is entitled in time of war.

WHETHER BELLIGERENTS SHALL BE ALLOWED CIVIL RIGHTS UNDER THE CONSTITUTION DEPENDS UPON THE POLICY OF GOVERNMENT.

None of these rights, guaranteed to peaceful citizens, by the constitution belong to them after they have become belligerents against their own government. They thereby forfeit all protection under that sacred charter which they have thus sought to overthrow and destroy. One party to a contract cannot break it and at the same time hold the other to perform it. It is true that if the government elects to treat them as subjects and to hold them liable only to penalties for violating statutes, it must concede to them all the legal rights and privileges which other citizens would have when under similar accusations; and Congress must be limited to the provisions of the constitution in legislation against them as citizens. But the fact that war is waged by these miscreants releases the government from all obligation to make that concession, or to respect the rights to life, liberty, or property of its enemy, because the constitution makes it the duty of the President to prosecute war against them in order to suppress rebellion and repel invasion.

THE CONSTITUTION ALLOWS CONFISCATION.

Nothing in the constitution interferes with the belligerent right of confiscation of enemy property. The right to confiscate is derived from a state of war. It is one of the rights of war. It originates in the principle of self-preservation. It is the means of weakening the enemy and strengthening ourselves. The right of confiscation belongs to the government as the necessary consequence of the power and duty of making war—offensive or defensive. Every capture of enemy ammunition or arms is, in substance, a confiscation, without its formalities. To deny the right of confiscation is to deny the right to make war, or to conquer an enemy.

If authority were needed to support the right of confiscation, it may be found in 3 Dallas, 227; Vat. lib. iii., ch. 8, sect. 188; lib. iii., ch. 9, sect. 161; *Smith* v. *Mansfield*, Cranch, 306–7; *Cooper* v. *Telfair*, 4 Dallas; *Brown* v. *U. S.*, 8 Cranch, 110, 228, 229.

The following extract is from 1 Kent's Com., p. 59: —

" But however strong the current of authority in favor of the modern and milder construction of the rule of national law on this subject, the point seems to be no longer open for discussion in this country; and it has become definitively settled in favor of the ancient and sterner rule by the Supreme Court of the United States. *Brown* v. *United States*, 8 Cranch, 110; ibid. 228, 229.

" The effect of war on British property found in the United States on land, at the commencement of the war, was learnedly discussed and thoroughly considered in the case of Brown, and the Circuit Court of the United States at Boston decided as upon a settled rule of the law of nations, that the goods of the enemy found in the country, and all vessels and cargoes found afloat in our ports at the commencement of hostilities, were liable to seizure and confiscation; and the exercise of the right vested in the discretion of the sovereign of the nation.

" When the case was brought up on appeal before the Supreme Court of the United States, the broad principle was assumed that war gave to the sovereign the full right to take the persons and confiscate the property of the enemy wherever found; and that the mitigations of this rigid rule, which the wise and humane policy of modern times had introduced into practice, might, more or less, affect the exercise of the right, but could not impair the right itself.

" Commercial nations have always considerable property in possession of their neighbors; and when war breaks out, the question, What shall be done with enemy property found in the country? is one rather of policy than of law, and is one properly addressed to the consideration of the legislature, and not to the courts of law.

" The strict right of confiscation of that species of property existed in Congress, and without a legislative act authorizing its confiscation it could not be judicially condemned; and the act of Congress of 1812 declaring war against Great Britain was not such an act. Until some statute directly applying to the subject be passed, the property would continue under the protection of the law, and might be claimed by the British owner at the restoration of peace.

" Though this decision established the right contrary to much of modern authority and practice, yet a great point was gained over the rigor and violence of the ancient doctrine, by making the exercise of the right depend upon a special act of Congress."

From the foregoing authorities, it is evident that the

government has a right, as a belligerent power, to capture or to confiscate any and all the personal property of the enemy; that there is nothing in the constitution which limits or controls the exercise of that right; and that capture in war, or confiscation by law, passes a complete title to the property taken; and that, if *judicial* condemnation of enemy property be sought, in order to pass the title to it by formal decree of courts, by mere seizure, and without capture, the confiscation must have been declared by act of Congress, a mere declaration of war not being *ex vi termini* sufficient for that purpose. The army of the Union, therefore, have the right, according to the law of nations, and of the constitution, to obtain by capture a legal title to all the personal property of the enemy they get possession of, whether it consist of arms, ammunition, provisions, slaves, or any other thing which the law treats as personal property. No judicial process is necessary to give the government full title thereto, and when once captured, the government may dispose of the property as absolute owner thereof, in the same manner as though the title passed by bill of sale: and Congress have plenary authority to pass such confiscation laws against belligerent enemies as they deem for the public good.

MILITARY GOVERNMENT UNDER MARTIAL LAW.

In addition to the right of *confiscating personal property* of the enemy, a state of war also confers upon the government other not less important belligerent rights, and among them, the right to seize and hold conquered territory by military force, and of instituting and maintaining military government over it, thereby suspending in part, or in the whole, the ordinary civil administration. The exercise of this right has been sanctioned by the decision of the Supreme Court of the United States, in the case of California.* And it is founded upon well-established doctrines of the law of nations. Without the right to make laws and administer justice in conquered territory, the inhabitants would be plunged into anarchy. The old government being overthrown, and no new one being established, there would be none to whom allegiance would be due — none to restrain lawlessness, none to secure to any persons any civil rights whatever. Hence, from the necessity of the case, the conqueror has power to establish a quasi military civil administration of government for the protection of the innocent, the restraint of the wicked, and the security of that conquest for which war has been waged.†

It is under this power of holding and establishing military rule over conquered territory, that all provisional governments are instituted by conquerors. The President, as commander-in-chief, has formally appointed Andrew Johnson governor of Tennessee, with all the powers, duties, and functions pertaining to that office, during the pleasure of the President, or until the *loyal* inhabitants of that State shall organize a civil government in accordance with the constitution of the United States. To legalize these powers and duties, it became expedient to give him a military position; hence he was nominated as a brigadier general, and his nomination was confirmed by the Senate. Mr. Stanley acts as provisional military governor of North Carolina, under similar authority. All acts of military government which are within the scope of their authority, are as legal and constitutional as any other military

* *Cross* v. *Harrison*, 16 How. 164–190.

† See *Fleming* v. *Page*, 9 How. 615. *Leitensdorfer* v. *Webb*, 20 How. 177. As to California, see Stat. at Large, Vol. ix. p. 452. New Mexico, Stat. at Large, ibid. 446. Halleck on International Law, 781. Story on Const., Sect. 1324. *Amer. Ins. Co.* v. *Canter*, 1 Pet. S. C. R. 542–3.

proceeding. Hence any section of this country, which, having joined in a general rebellion, shall have been *subdued* and conquered by the military forces of the United States, may be subjected to military government, and the rights of citizens in those districts are subject to martial law, so long as the war lasts. Whatever of their rights of property are *lost* in and by the war, are lost forever. No citizen, whether loyal or rebel, is deprived of any right guaranteed to him in the constitution by reason of his subjection to *martial law*, because *martial law*, when in force, is *constitutional law*. The people of the United States, through their lawfully chosen commander-in-chief, have the constitutional right to seize and hold the territory of a belligerent enemy, and to govern it by martial law, thereby superseding the local government of the place, and all rights which rebels might have had as citizens of the United States, if they had not violated the laws of the land by making war upon the country.

By martial law, loyal citizens may be for a time debarred from enjoying the rights they would be entitled to in time of peace. Individual rights must always be held subject to the exigencies of national safety.

In war, when *martial law is in force*, the laws of war are the laws which the constitution expressly authorizes and requires to be enforced. The constitution, when it calls into action martial law, for the time changes *civil* rights, or rights which the citizen would be entitled to in peace, because the rights of persons in one of these cases are totally incompatible with the obligations of persons in the other. Peace and war cannot exist together; the laws of peace and of war cannot operate together; the rights and procedures of peaceful times are incompatible with those of war. It is an obvious but pernicious error to suppose that in a *state of war*, the rules of martial law, and the consequent modification of the rights, duties, and obligations of citizens, private and public, are not *authorized* strictly under the *constitution*. And among the rights of martial law, none is more familiar than that of seizing and establishing a military government over territory taken from the enemy; and the duty of thus protecting such territory is imperative, since the United States are obligated to guarantee to each State a republican form of government.* That form of government having been overthrown by force, the country must take such steps, military and civil, as may tend to restore it to the loyal citizens of that State, if there be any; and if there be no persons who will submit to the constitution and laws of the United States, it is their duty to hold that State by military power, and under military rule, until loyal citizens shall appear there in sufficient numbers to entitle them to receive back into their own hands the local government.

A SEVERE RULE OF BELLIGERENT LAW.

"Property of persons residing in the enemy's country is deemed, in law, hostile, and subject to condemnation without any evidence as to the opinions or predilections of the owner." If he is the subject of a neutral, or a citizen of one of the belligerent States, and has expressed no disloyal sentiments towards his country, still his residence in the enemy's country impresses upon his property, engaged in commerce and found upon the ocean, a hostile character, and subjects it to

* Constitution, Art. IV., Sect. 4., Cl. 1.

8

condemnation. This familiar principle of law is sanctioned in the highest courts of England and of the United States, and has been decided to apply to cases of *civil* as well as of foreign war.*

Thus personal property of every kind, ammunition, provisions, contraband, or slaves, may be lawfully seized, whether of *loyal* or *disloyal* citizens, and is by law *presumed hostile*, and liable to *condemnation*, if *captured within the rebellious districts.* This right of seizure and condemnation is harsh, as all the proceedings of war are harsh, in the extreme, but it is nevertheless lawful. It would be harsh to kill in battle a loyal citizen who, having been impressed into the ranks of the rebels, is made to fight against his country; yet it is lawful to do so.

Against all persons in arms, and against all property situated and seized in rebellious districts, the laws of war give the President full belligerent rights; and when the army and navy are once lawfully called out, there are no limits to the war-making power of the President, other than the law of nations, and such rules as Congress may pass for their regulation.

"The statute of 1807, chap. 39," says a learned judge,† "provides that whenever it is lawful for the President to call forth the militia to suppress an insurrection, he may employ the land and naval forces for that purpose. The authority to use the army is thus expressly confirmed, but the *manner* in which they are to be used is not prescribed. That is left to the discretion of the President, guided by the usages and principles of civilized war."

* *The Venus*, 8 Cranch Rep.; *The Hoop*, 1 Robinson, 196,—and cases there cited. *The Amy Warwick*, opinion of Judge Sprague.

† Judge Sprague.

As a matter of expediency, Congress may direct that *no* property of *loyal citizens*, residing in *disloyal* States, should be seized by military force, without compensation. This is an act of grace, which, though not required by the *laws of war*, may well be granted. The commander-in-chief may also grant the same indulgence. But the military commanders are always at liberty to seize, in an enemy's country, whatever property they deem necessary for the sustenance of troops, or military stores, whether it is the property of friend or enemy; it being usual, however, to pay for all that is taken from friends. These doctrines have been carried into effect in Missouri.

The President having adopted the policy of protecting loyal citizens wherever they may be found, all seizure of their property, and all interference with them, have so far been forborne. But it should be understood that such forbearance is optional, not compulsory. It is done from a sense of justice and humanity, not because law or constitution renders it inevitable. And this forbearance is not likely to be carried to such an extent as to endanger the success of the armies of the Union, nor to despoil them of the legitimate fruits of victory over rebels.

CIVIL RIGHTS OF LOYAL CITIZENS IN LOYAL DISTRICTS ARE MODIFIED BY THE EXISTENCE OF WAR.

While war is raging, many of the rights held sacred by the constitution — rights which cannot be violated by any acts of Congress — may and must be suspended and held in abeyance. If this were not so, the government might itself be destroyed; the army and navy might be sacrificed, and one part of the constitution would NULLIFY the rest.

If *freedom of speech* cannot be suppressed, spies cannot be caught, imprisoned, and hung.

If *freedom of the press* cannot be interfered with, all our military plans may be betrayed to the enemy.

If no man can be *deprived of life without trial by jury,* a soldier cannot slay the enemy in battle.

If *enemy's property* cannot be taken without "due process of law," how can the soldier disarm his foe and seize his weapons?

If no person can be arrested, sentenced, and shot, without *trial by jury* in the county or State where his crime is alleged to have been committed, how can a *deserter be shot,* or a *spy be hung,* or an *enemy be taken prisoner?*

It has been said that "*amidst arms* the *laws are silent.*" It would be more just to say, that while war rages, the *rights,* which in peace are sacred, must and do give way to the higher right—the right of *public safety*—the right which the COUNTRY, *the whole country, claims* to be protected from its enemies, domestic and foreign—from spies, from conspirators, and from traitors.* The sovereign and almost dictatorial powers—existing only in actual war; ending when war ends—to be used in self-defence, and to be laid down when the occasion has passed, are, while they last, as *lawful,* as *constitutional,* as *sacred,* as the administration of justice by judicial courts in times of peace. They may be dangerous; war itself is dangerous; but danger does not make them *unconstitutional.* If the commander-in-chief orders the army to seize the arms and ammunition of the enemy; to capture their persons; to shell out their batteries; to hang spies or shoot deserters; to destroy the armed enemy in open battle; to send traitors to

* "Among absolute international rights, one of the most essential and important, and that which lies at the root of all the rest, is the right of self-preservation. It is not only a right in respect to other states, but it is a duty in respect to its own members, and the most solemn and important which a state owes to them." Wheaton, p. 115, 116.

forts and prisons; to stop the press from aiding and comforting the enemy by betraying our military plans; to arrest within our lines, or wherever they can be seized, persons against whom there is reasonable evidence of their having aided or abetted the rebels, or of intending so to do, — the pretension that in so doing he is violating the constitution is not only erroneous, but it is a plea in behalf of treason. To set up the rules of civil administration as overriding and controlling the laws of war, is to aid and abet the enemy. It falsifies the clear meaning of the constitution, which not only gives the power, but makes it the plain duty of the President, to go to war with the enemy of his country. And the restraints to which he is subject *when in war*, are not to be found in the municipal regulations, which can be administered only in peace, but in the laws and usages of nations regulating the conduct of war.

BELLIGERENT RIGHT TO CONFISCATE ENEMY'S REAL ESTATE.

The *belligerent right* of the government to confiscate *enemy's real estate, situated in this country*, can hardly admit of a question. The title to no inconsiderable part of the real estate in each of the original States of the Union, rests upon the validity of confiscation acts, passed by our ancestors against loyal adherents to the crown. Probably none of these States failed to pass and apply these laws. English and American acts of confiscation were recognized by the laws of both countries, and their operation modified by treaties; their *validity never was denied.* The *only* authority which either of the States or colonies ever had for passing such laws was derived from the fact that they were *belligerents.*

It will be observed that the question as to the belligerent right to confiscate enemy's real estate situated in the United States, is somewhat different from the question whether in conquering a foreign country it will be lawful to confiscate the private real estate of the enemy.

It is *unusual*, in case of *conquest* of a foreign country, for the conqueror to do more than to displace its sovereign, and assume dominion over the country. On a *mere* change of *sovereignty* of the country, it would be harsh and severe to confiscate the private property and annul the private rights of citizens generally. And *mere* conquest of a country does not *of itself* operate as confiscation of enemy's property; nor does the cession of a country by one nation to another destroy private rights of property, or operate as confiscation of personal or real estate.* So it was held by the Supreme Court in the case of the transfer by treaty of Florida to the United States; but it was specially provided in that treaty that private property should not be interfered with. The forbearance of a conqueror from confiscating the entire property of a conquered people is usually founded in good policy, as well as in humanity. The object of foreign conquest is to acquire a permanent addition to the power and territory of the conqueror. This object would be defeated by stripping his subjects of every thing. The case is very different where confiscation will only break up a nest of traitors, and drive them away from a country they have betrayed.

Suppose that certain Englishmen owned large tracts

* *United States* v. *Juan Richmond*, 7 Peters, 51.

of real estate in either of the United States or territories thereof, and war should break out; would any one doubt the right of Congress to pass a law confiscating such estate?

The laws of nations allow either belligerent to seize and appropriate whatever property of the enemy it can gain possession of; and, of all descriptions of property which government could safely permit to be owned or occupied by an alien enemy, real estate within its own dominion would be the last.

No distinction can be properly or legally made between the different kinds of enemy property, whether real, personal, or mixed, so far as regards their liability to confiscation by the war power. Lands, money, slaves, debts, may and have been subject to this liability. The methods of appropriating and holding them are different — the result is the same. And, considering the foundation of the right, the object for which it is to be exercised, and the effects resulting from it, there is nothing in law, or in reason, which would indicate why one can and the other cannot be taken away from the enemy.

In *Brown* v. *United States*, 8 Cranch, p. 123, the Supreme Court of the United States say, —

> "Respecting the power of government, no doubt is entertained. That war gives to the sovereign the full right to take the persons and confiscate the property of the enemy, wherever found, is conceded. The mitigations of this rule, which the humane and wise policy of modern times has introduced into practice, will more or less affect the exercise of this right, but cannot impair the right itself — that remains undiminished; and when the sovereign authority shall choose to bring it into operation, the judicial department must give effect to its will."

> "It may be considered," they say, "as the opinion of all who have written on the *jus belli*, that war gives the *right* to confiscate," &c.

Chancellor Kent says, —

"When war is duly declared, it is not merely a war between this and the adverse government in their political characters. Every man is, in judgment of law, a party to the acts of his own government, and a war between the government of two nations is a war between all the individuals of the one and all the individuals of which the other nation is composed. Government is the representative of the will of the people, and acts for the whole society. This is the theory of all governments, and the best writers on the law of nations concur in the doctrine, that when the sovereign of a state declares war against another sovereign, it implies that the whole nation declares war, and that all the subjects of the one are enemies to all the subjects of the other."

"Very important consequences concerning the obligations of subjects are deducible from this principle. When hostilities have commenced, the first objects that present themselves for detention and capture are the persons and property of the enemy found within the territory on the breaking out of war. According to strict authority, a state has a right to deal as an enemy with persons and property so found within its power, and to confiscate the property and detain the persons as prisoners of war." *

We thus see, that by the law of nations, by the practice of our own States, by the decisions of courts, by the highest authority of legal writers, and by the deductions of reason, there can be no question of the constitutional right of confiscation of enemy real estate of which we may gain possession. And the legal presumption that real estate situated in rebellious districts is enemy property, would seem to be as well founded as it is in case of personal property.†

It is for the government to decide how it shall use its belligerent right of confiscation. The number of slaveholders in the rebellious States, who

* 1 Kent's Com., p. 55. See also Grotius, B. III. ch. 3, sect. 9; ch. 4, sect. 8. Burlamaqui, Part IV. ch. 4, sect. 20. Vattel, B. III. ch. 5, sect. 70.

† See page 57.

are the principal land owners in that region, and who are the chief authors and supporters of this rebellion, constitute, all told, less than *one in one hundred and twenty eight* of the people of the United States, and less than *one fiftieth* part of the inhabitants of their own districts, being far less in proportion to the whole population of the country than the *old tories* in the time of the revolution were to the colonists.*

* In confirmation of these views of the War Powers of Congress, see the chapter on the War Powers of the President, and NOTES thereon.

CHAPTER III.

WAR POWER OF THE PRESIDENT TO EMANCIPATE SLAVES.

The power of the President, as commander-in-chief of the army and navy of the United States, when in actual service, to emancipate the slaves of any belligerent section of the country, if such a measure becomes necessary to save the government from destruction, is not, it is presumed, denied by any respectable authority.*

WHY THE POWER EXISTS.

The liberation of slaves is looked upon as a means of embarrassing or weakening the enemy, or of strengthening the military power of our army. If slaves be treated as contraband of war, on the ground that they may be used by their masters to aid in prosecuting war, as employees upon military works, or as laborers furnishing by their industry the means of carrying on hostilities; or if they be treated as, in law, belligerents, following the legal condition of their owners; or if they be deemed loyal subjects having a just claim upon the government to be released from their obligations to give aid and service to disloyal and belligerent masters, in order that they may be free to perform their higher duty of allegiance and loyalty to the United States; or if they be regarded as subjects

* It has been shown in a previous chapter that the government has a right to treat *rebels* either as *belligerents* or as subjects, and to subject them to the severities of international belligerent law.

of the United States, liable to do military duty; or if they be made citizens of the United States, and soldiers; or if the authority of the masters over their slaves is the means of aiding and comforting the enemy, or of throwing impediments in the way of the government, or depriving it of such aid and assistance in successful prosecution of the war, as slaves would and could afford, if released from the control of the enemy, — or if releasing the slaves would embarrass the enemy, and make it more difficult for them to collect and maintain large armies; in either of these cases, the taking away of these slaves from the "aid and service" of the enemy, and putting them to the aid and service of the United States, is justifiable as an act of war. The ordinary way of depriving the enemy of slaves is by declaring emancipation.

THE PRESIDENT IS THE SOLE JUDGE.

"It belongs exclusively to the President to judge when the exigency arises in which he has authority, under the constitution, to call forth the militia, and his decision is conclusive on all other persons." *

The constitution confers on the Executive, when in actual war, full belligerent powers. The emancipation of enemy's slaves is a belligerent right. It belongs exclusively to the President, as commander-in-chief, to judge whether he shall exercise his belligerent right to emancipate slaves in those parts of the country which are in rebellion. If exercised in fact, and while the war lasts, his act of emancipation is conclusive and

* Such is the language of Chief Justice Taney, in delivering the opinion of the Supreme Court, in *Martin* v. *Mott*, 12 Wheaton, 19.

binding forever on all the departments of government, and on all persons whatsoever.

POWERS OF THE PRESIDENT NOT INCONSISTENT WITH POWERS OF CONGRESS TO EMANCIPATE SLAVES.

The right of the Executive to strike this blow against his enemy does not deprive Congress of the concurrent right or duty to emancipate enemy's slaves, if in *their judgment* a civil act for that purpose is required by public welfare and common defence, for the purpose of aiding and giving effect to such war measures as the commander-in-chief may adopt.

The military authority of the President is not incompatible with the peace or war powers of Congress; but both coexist, and may be exercised upon the same subject. Thus, when the army captures a regiment of soldiers, the legislature may pass laws relating to the captives. So may Congress destroy slavery by abolishing the laws which sustain it, while the commander of the army may destroy it by capture of slaves, by proclamation, or by other means.

IS LIBERATION OF ENEMY'S SLAVES A BELLIGERENT RIGHT?

This is the chief inquiry on this branch of the subject. To answer it we must appeal to the law of nations, and learn whether there is any commanding authority which forbids the use of an engine so powerful and so formidable — an engine which may grind to powder the disloyalty of rebels in arms, while it clears the avenue to freedom for four millions of Americans. It is only the law of nations that can decide this question, because the constitution, having given authority to government to make war, has placed no limit whatever to the war powers. There is, therefore, no legal control over the war powers except the law of nations, and no moral control except the usage of modern civilized belligerents.

THE LAW OF NATIONS SANCTIONS EMANCIPATION OF ENEMY'S SLAVES.

It is in accordance with the law of nations and with the practice of civilized belligerents in modern times, to liberate enemy's slaves in time of war by military power. In the revolutionary war, England exercised that unquestioned right by not less than three of her military commanders — Sir Henry Clinton, Lord Dunmore, and Lord Cornwallis. That General Washington recognized and feared Lord Dunmore's appeal to the slaves, is shown by his letter on that subject.

"His strength," said Washington, "will increase as a snow-ball by rolling faster and faster, if some expedient cannot be hit upon to convince the slaves and servants of the impotency of his designs."

The right to call the slaves of colonists to the aid of the British arms was expressly admitted by Jefferson, in his letter to Dr. Gordon. In writing of the injury done to his estates by Cornwallis, he uses the following language: —

"He destroyed all my growing crops and tobacco; he burned all my barns, containing the same articles of last year. Having first taken what corn he wanted, he used, *as was to be expected,* all my stock of cattle, sheep, and hogs, for the sustenance of his army, and carried off all the horses capable of service. *He carried off also about thirty slaves. Had this been to give them freedom, he would have done right.* . . . From an estimate made at the time on the best information I could collect, I suppose the State of Virginia lost under Lord Cornwallis's hands, that year, about thirty thousand slaves."

Great Britain, for the second time, used the same right against us in the war of 1812. Her naval and military commanders invited the slaves, by public proclamations, to repair to their standard, promising them freedom.* The slaves who went over to them were liberated, and were carried away contrary to the express terms of the treaty of Ghent, in which it was stipulated that they should not be carried away. England preferred to become liable for a breach of the treaty rather than to break faith with the fugitives. Indemnity for this violation of contract was demanded and refused. The question was referred to the decision of the Emperor of Russia, as arbitrator, who decided that indemnity should be paid by Great Britain, not because she had violated the law of nations in emancipating slaves, but because she had broken the terms of the treaty.

In the arguments submitted to the referee, the British government broadly asserted the belligerent right of liberating enemy's slaves, even if they were treated as private property. Mr. Middleton was instructed by Mr. J. Q. Adams, then, in 1820, Secretary of State, to deny that right, and to present reasons for that denial. But that in this instance he acted in obedience to the instructions of the President and cabinet, and against his own opinions on the law of nations, is shown by his subsequent statement in Congress to that effect.† The question of international law was left undecided by the Emperor; but the assertion of England, that it is a

* For Admiral Cochrane's Proclamation, instigating the slaves to desert their masters, see Niles's Register, vol. vi. p. 242.

† "It was utterly against my judgment and wishes; but I was obliged to submit, and prepared the requisite despatches." See Congressional Globe, XXVII. Cong., 2d sess., 1841–2; vol. ii. p. 424.

legitimate exercise of belligerent rights to liberate enemy's slaves, — a right which had previously been enforced by her against the colonies, and by France against her, and again by her against the United States, — was entitled to great weight, as a reiterated and authentic reaffirmance of the well-settled doctrine.

In speeches before the House of Representatives on the 25th of May, 1836, on the 7th of June, 1841, and on the 14th and 15th of April, 1842, Mr. Adams explained and asserted in the amplest terms the powers of Congress, and the authority of the President, to free enemy's slaves, as a legitimate act of war.* Thus leading statesmen of England and America have concurred in the opinion that emancipation is a belligerent right.

St. Domingo, in 1793, contained more than five hundred thousand negroes, with many mulattoes and whites, and was held as a province of France. Intestine commotions had raged for nearly three years between the whites and mulattoes, in which the negroes had remained neutral. The Spaniards having effected an alliance with the slaves who had revolted in 1791, invaded the island and occupied several important military points. England, also, was making a treaty with the planters to invade the country; and thus the possession seemed about to be wrested from France by the efforts of one or the other of its two bitterest foes. One thousand French soldiers, a few mulattoes and loyal slaveholders, were all the force which could be mustered in favor of the government, for the protection of this precious island, situated so far away from France.

* For extracts from these speeches, see *postea*.

Sonthonax and Polverel, the French commissioners, on the 29th of August, 1793, issued a proclamation, under martial law, wherein they declared all the slaves free, and thereby brought them over *en masse* to the support of the government. The English troops landed three weeks afterwards, and were repulsed principally by the slave army.

On the 4th of February, 1794, the National Convention of France confirmed the act of the commissioners, and also abolished slavery in the other French colonies.

In June, 1794, Toussaint L'Ouverture, a colored man, admitted by military critics to be one of the great generals of modern times, having until then fought in favor of Spain, brought his army of five thousand colored troops to the aid of France, forced entrance into the chief city of the island in which the French troops were beleaguered, relieved his allies, and offered himself and his army to the service of that government, which had guaranteed to them their freedom. From that hour the fortunes of the war changed. The English were expelled from the island in 1798; the Spaniards also gave it up; and in 1801 Toussaint proclaimed the republic in the Spanish portion of the island which had been ceded to France by the treaty of 1795; thus extending the practical operation of the decree of emancipation over the whole island, and liberating one hundred thousand more persons who had been slaves of Spaniards.

The island was put under martial law; the planters were recalled by Toussaint, and permitted to hire their former slaves; and his government was enforced by military power; and from that time until 1802, the progress of the people in commerce, industry, and general prosperity was rapid and satisfactory. But in 1802 the influence of emigrant planters, and of the Empress Josephine, a creole of Martinique, induced Napoleon to send a large army to the island, to reëstablish the slave trade and slavery in all the other islands except St. Domingo, with the design of restoring slavery there after he should have conquered it. But war, sickness, and disasters broke up his forces, and the treacherous Frenchmen met the due reward of their perfidy, and were, in 1804, totally driven from the island. The independence of St. Domingo was actually established in 1804. The independence of Hayti was recognized by the United States in 1862.

From this brief outline it is shown, that France recognizes the right, under martial law, to emancipate the slaves of an enemy — having asserted and exercised that right in the case of St. Domingo.* And the slaves thus liberated have retained their liberty, and compose, at this day, the principal population of a government who have entered into diplomatic relations with the United States.

In Colombia slavery was abolished, first by the Spanish General Morillo, and secondly by the American General Bolivar. "It was abolished," says John Quincy Adams, "by virtue of a military command given at the head of the army, and its abolition continues to this day. It was abolished by the laws of war, and not by the municipal enactments; the power was exercised

* For the decree of the French Assembly, see *Choix de Rapports — Opinions et Discours prononcés à la Tribune Nationale depuis* 1789. Paris, 1821, t. xiv. p. 425. — See *Abolition d'Esclavage, (Colonies Francaises,) par Augustin Cochin.* Paris, 1861. Vol. i. pp. 14, 15, &c.

by military commanders, under instructions, of course, from their respective governments."

AUTHORITY AND USAGE CONFIRM THE RIGHT.

It may happen that when belligerents on both sides hold slaves, neither will deem it expedient, through fear of retaliation, to liberate the slaves of his adversary; but considerations of policy do not affect questions of international rights; and forbearance to exercise a power does not prove its non-existence. While no authority among eminent ancient writers on the subject has been found to deny the right of emancipation, the fact that England, France, Spain, and the South American republics have actually freed the slaves of their enemies, conclusively shows that the law and practice of modern civilized nations sanction that right.

HOW FAR THE GOVERNMENT OF THE UNITED STATES UNDER FORMER ADMINISTRATIONS HAVE SANCTIONED THE BELLIGERENT RIGHT OF EMANCIPATING SLAVES OF LOYAL AND OF DISLOYAL CITIZENS.

The government of the United States, in 1814, recognized the right of their military officers, in time of war, to appropriate to public use the slaves of loyal citizens without compensation therefor; also, in 1836, the right to reward slaves who have performed public service, by giving freedom to them and to their families; also, in 1838, the principle that slaves of loyal citizens, captured in war, should be emancipated, and not returned to their masters; and that slaves escaping to the army of the United States should be treated as prisoners of war, and not as property of their masters. These propositions are supported by the cases of General Jackson, General Jessup, General Taylor, and General Gaines.

"In December, 1814," says a distinguished writer and speaker, "General Jackson impressed a large number of slaves at and near New Orleans, and set them at work erecting defences, behind which his troops won such glory on the 8th of January, 1815. The masters remonstrated. Jackson disregarded their remonstrances, and kept the slaves at work until many of them were killed by the enemy's shot; yet his action was approved by Mr. Madison, the cabinet, and by the Congress, which has ever refused to pay the masters for their losses. In this case, the masters were professedly friends to the government; and yet our Presidents, and cabinets, and generals have not hesitated to emancipate their slaves, whenever in time of war it was supposed to be for the interest of the country to do so. This was done in the exercise of the war power to which Mr. Adams referred, and for which he had the most abundant authority."

"In 1836 General Jessup engaged several fugitive slaves to act as guides and spies, agreeing, if they would serve the government faithfully, to secure to them the freedom of themselves and families. They fulfilled their engagement in good faith. The general gave them their freedom, and sent them to the west. Mr. Van Buren's administration sanctioned the contract, and Mr. Tyler's administration approved the proceeding of the general in setting the slaves and their families free."

The writer above quoted says,—

"Louis, the slave of a man named Pacheco, betrayed Major Dade's battalion, in 1836, and when he had witnessed their massacre, he joined the enemy. Two years subsequently he was captured. Pacheco claimed him; General Jessup said if he had time, he would try him before a court martial and hang him, but would not deliver him to any man. He, however, sent him west, and the fugitive slave became a free men. General Jessup reported his action to the War Department, and Mr. Van Buren, then President, with his cabinet, approved it. Pacheco then appealed to Congress, asking that body to pay him for the loss of his slave. The House of Representatives voted against the bill, which was rejected. All concurred in the opinion that General Jessup did right in emancipating the slave, instead of returning him to his master.

"In 1838 General Taylor captured a number of negroes said to be fugitive slaves. Citizens of Florida, learning what had been done, immediately gathered around his camp, intending to secure the slaves who had escaped from them. General Taylor told them that he had no prisoners but 'prisoners of war.' The claimants then desired to look at them, in order to determine whether he was holding their slaves as prisoners. The veteran warrior replied that no man should examine his prisoners for such a purpose; and he ordered them to depart. This action, being reported to the War Department, was approved by the Executive. The slaves, however, were sent west, and set free.

"In 1838 many fugitive slaves and Indians, captured in Florida, had been ordered to be sent west of the Mississippi. Some of them were claimed at New Orleans by their owners, under legal process. General Gaines, commander of the military district, refused to deliver them up to the sheriff, and appeared in court and stated his own defence.

"His grounds of defence were, 'that these men, women, and children were captured in war, and held as prisoners of war; that as commander of that military department he held them subject only to the order of the national Executive; that he could recognize no other power in time of war, or by the laws of war, as authorized to take prisoners from his possession. He asserted that in time of war all slaves were belligerents as much as their masters. The slave men cultivate the earth, and supply provisions. The women cook the food and nurse the sick, and contribute to the maintenance of the war, often more than the same number of males. The slave children equally contribute whatever they are able to the support of the war. The military officer, he said, can enter into no judicial examination of the claim of one man to the bone and muscle of another, as property; nor could he, as a military officer, know what the laws of Florida were while engaged in maintaining the federal government by force of arms. In such case he could only be guided by the laws of war, and whatever may be the laws of any State, they must yield to the safety of the federal government. He sent the slaves west, and they became free.'" *

On the 26th of May, 1836, in a debate in the House of Representatives upon the joint resolution for *distributing rations* to the distressed fugitives from Indian hostilities

* This defence of General Gaines may be found in House Document No. 225 of the 2d session of the 25th Congress.

in the states of Alabama and Georgia, JOHN QUINCY ADAMS expressed the following opinions: —

"Sir, in the authority given to Congress by the constitution of the United States to *declare war*, all the powers incidental to war are, by necessary implication, conferred upon the *government* of the United States. Now, the powers incidental to war are derived, not from their internal municipal source, *but from the laws and usages of nations.*

"There are, then, Mr. Chairman, in the *authority of Congress and of the Executive, two classes of powers, altogether different in their nature, and often incompatible with each other — the war power and the peace power.* The peace power is limited by regulations and restricted by provisions prescribed within the Constitution itself. *The war power* is limited only by the laws and usages of nations. This power is tremendous; *it is strictly constitutional, but it breaks down every barrier so anxiously erected for the protection of liberty, of property, and of life.* This, sir, is the power which authorizes you to pass the resolution now before you, and, in my opinion, no other."

After an interruption, Mr. Adams went on to say, —

"There are, indeed, powers of peace conferred upon Congress which also come within the scope and jurisdiction of the laws of nations, such as the negotiation of treaties of amity and commerce, the interchange of public ministers and consuls, and all the personal and social intercourse between the individual inhabitants of the United States and foreign nations, and the Indian tribes, which require the interposition of any law. *But the powers of war are all* regulated by the laws of nations, and *are subject to no other limitation.* . . . It was upon this principle that I voted *against* the resolution reported by the slavery committee, 'that Congress possess no constitutional authority to interfere, *in any way*, with the institution of slavery in any of the States of this confederacy,' to which resolution most of those with whom I usually concur, and even my own colleagues in this house, gave their assent. *I do not admit that there is, even among the peace powers of Congress, no such authority; but in war, there are many ways by which Congress not only have the authority, but* ARE BOUND TO INTERFERE WITH THE INSTITUTION OF SLAVERY IN THE STATES. The *existing law prohibiting the importation of slaves* into the United States from foreign countries is itself an *interference with the insti-*

tution of slavery in the States. It was so considered by the founders of the constitution of the United States, in which it was stipulated that Congress should not interfere, in that way, with the institution, prior to the year 1808.

"During the late war with Great Britain, the military and naval commanders of that nation issued proclamations inviting the slaves to repair to their standard, with promises of freedom and of settlement in some of the British colonial establishments. This surely was an interference with the institution of slavery in the States. By the treaty of peace, Great Britian stipulated to evacuate all the forts and places in the United States, without carrying away any slaves. If the government of the United States had no power to interfere, *in any way*, with the institution of slavery in the States, they would not have had the authority to require this stipulation. It is well known that this engagement was not fulfilled by the British naval and military commanders; that, on the contrary, they did carry away all the slaves whom they had induced to join them, and that the *British government inflexibly refused to restore any of them to their masters;* that a claim of indemnity was consequently instituted in behalf of the owners of the slaves, and was successfully maintained. All that series of transactions was an interference by Congress with the institution of slavery in the States in one way — in the way of protection and support. It was by the institution of slavery alone that the restitution of slaves, enticed by proclamations into the British service, could be claimed as *property.* But for the institution of slavery, the British commanders could neither have allured them to their standard, nor restored them otherwise than as liberated prisoners of war. But for the institution of slavery, there could have been no stipulation that they should not be carried away as property, nor any claim of indemnity for the violation of that engagement."

Mr. Adams goes on to state how the war power may be used: —

"But the war power of Congress over the institution of slavery in the States is yet far more extensive. Suppose the case of a servile war, complicated, as to some extent it is even now, with an Indian war; suppose Congress were called to raise armies, *to supply money from the whole Union to suppress a servile insurrection:* would they have no authority to interfere with the institution of slavery? The issue of a servile war may be disastrous; it may become necessary for the master of the slave to recognize his emancipation by a treaty of peace: can it for an instant be pretended that Congress, in such a contingency, would have no authority to interfere with the institution of slavery, *in any way*, in the States? Why, it would be equivalent to saying that Congress have no constitutional authority to make peace. I suppose a more portentous case, certainly within the bounds of possibility — I would to God I could say, not within the bounds of probability — "

"Do you imagine," he asks, "that your Congress will have no constitutional authority to interfere with the institution of slavery, in any way, in the States of this confederacy? Sir, they must and will interfere with it — perhaps to sustain it by war, perhaps to abolish it by treaties of peace; and they will not only possess the constitutional power so to interfere, but they will be bound in duty to do it, by the express provisions of the constitution itself. From the instant that your slaveholding States become the theatre of a war, *civil, servile, or foreign war*, from that instant the war powers of Congress extend to interference with the institution of slavery, in every way by which it can be interfered with, from a claim of indemnity for slaves taken or destroyed, to the cession of States burdened with slavery to a foreign power."

Extracts from the speech of John Quincy Adams, delivered in the United States House of Representatives, April 14th and 15th, 1842, on war with Great Britain and Mexico: —

"What I say is involuntary, because the subject has been brought into the house from another quarter, as the gentleman himself admits. I would leave that institution to the exclusive consideration and management of the States more peculiarly interested in it, just as long as they can keep within their own bounds. So far, I admit that Congress has no power to meddle with it. As long as they do not step out of their own bounds, and do not put the question to the people of the United States, whose peace, welfare, and happiness are all at stake, so long I will agree to leave them to themselves. But when a member from a free State brings forward certain resolutions, for which, instead of reasoning to disprove his positions, you vote a censure upon him, and that without hearing, it is quite another affair. At the time this was done, I said that, as far as I could understand the resolutions proposed by the gentleman from Ohio, (Mr. Giddings,) there were some of them for which I was ready to vote, and some which I must vote against; and I will now tell this house, my constituents, and the whole of mankind, that the resolution against which I would have voted was that in which he declares that what are called the slave States have the exclusive right of consultation on the subject of slavery. For that resolution I never would vote, because I believe that it is not just, and does not contain constitutional doctrine. I believe that, so long as the slave States are able to sustain their institutions without going abroad or calling upon other parts of the Union to aid them or act on the subject, so long I will consent never to interfere. I have said this, and I repeat it; but if they come to the free States, and say to them, You must help us to keep down our slaves, you must aid us in an insurrection and a civil war, then I say that with that call comes full and plenary power to this house and to the Senate over the whole subject. It is a war power. I say it is a war power; and when your country is actually in war, whether it be a war of invasion or a war of insurrection, Congress has power to carry on the war, and must carry it on, according to the laws of war; and by the laws of war, an invaded country has all its laws and municipal institutions swept by the board, and martial law takes the place of them. This power in Congress has, perhaps, never been called into exercise under the present constitution of the United States. But when the laws of war are in force, what, I ask, is one of those laws? It is this: that when a country is invaded, and two hostile armies are set in martial array, *the commanders of both armies have power to emancipate all the slaves in the invaded territory.* Nor is this a mere theoretic statement. The history of South America shows that the doctrine has been carried into practical execution within the last thirty years. Slavery was abolished in Colombia, first, by the Spanish General Morillo, and, secondly, by the American General Bolivar. It was abolished by virtue of a military command given at the head of the army, and its abolition continues to be law to this day. It was abolished by the laws of war, and not by the municipal enactments; the power was exercised by military commanders, under instructions, of course, from their respective governments. And here I recur again to the example of General Jackson. What are you now about in Congress? You are about passing a grant to refund to General Jackson the amount of a certain fine imposed upon him by a judge, under the laws of the State of Louisiana. You are going to refund him the money, with interest; and this you are going to do because the imposition of the fine was unjust. And why was it unjust? Because General Jackson was acting under the laws of war, and because the moment you place a military commander in a district which is the theatre of war, the laws of war apply to that district.

* * * * * * *

"I might furnish a thousand proofs to show that the pretensions of gentlemen to the sanctity of their municipal institutions under a state of actual invasion and of actual war, whether servile, civil, or foreign, is wholly unfounded, and that the laws of war do, in all such cases, take the precedence. I lay this down as the law of nations. I say that military authority takes, for the time, the place of all municipal institutions, *and slavery among the rest;* and that, under that state of things, so far from its being true that the States where slavery exists have the exclusive management of the subject, not only the President of the United States, but the commander of the army, has power to order the universal emancipation of the slaves. I have given here more in detail a principle which I have asserted on this floor before now, and of which I have no more doubt than that you, sir, occupy that chair. I give it in its development, in order that any gentleman from any part of the Union may, if he thinks proper, deny the truth of the position, and may maintain his denial; not by indignation, not by passion and fury, but by sound and sober reasoning from the laws of nations and the laws of war. And if my position can be answered and refuted, I shall receive the refutation with pleasure; I shall be glad to listen to reason, aside, as I say, from indignation and passion. And if, by the force of reasoning, my understanding can be convinced, I here pledge myself to recant what I have asserted.

"Let my position be answered; let me be told, let my constituents be told, let the people of my State be told, — a State whose soil tolerates not the foot of a slave, — that they are bound by the constitution to a long and toilsome march, under burning summer suns and a deadly southern clime, for the suppression of a servile war; that they are bound to leave their bodies to rot upon the sands of Carolina, to leave their wives widows and their children orphans; that those who cannot march are bound to pour out their treasures while their sons or brothers are pouring out their blood to suppress a servile, combined with a civil or a foreign war; and yet that there exists no power beyond the limits of the slave State where such war is raging to emancipate the slaves. I say, let this be proved — I am open to conviction; but till that conviction comes, I put it forth, not as a dictate of feeling, but as a settled maxim of the laws of nations, that, in such a case, the military supersedes the civil power; and on this account I should have been obliged to vote, as I have said, against one of the resolutions of my excellent friend from Ohio, (Mr. Giddings,) or should at least have required that it be amended in conformity with the constitution of the United States."

CONCLUSION.

It has thus been proved, that by the law and usage of modern civilized nations, confirmed by the judgment of eminent statesmen, and by the former practice of this government, that the President, as commander-in-chief, has the authority, as an act of war, to liberate the slaves of the enemy, that the United States have in former times sanctioned the liberation of slaves even of loyal citizens, by military commanders, in time of war, without compensation therefor; and have deemed slaves captured in war from belligerent subjects as entitled to their freedom.*

* GENERAL WAR POWERS OF THE PRESIDENT. It is not intended in this chapter to explain the *general* war powers of the President. They are principally contained in the Constitution, Art. II. Sect. 1, Cl. 1 and 7; Sect. 2, Cl. 1; Sect. 3, Cl. 1; and in Sect. 1, Cl. 1, and by necessary implication in Art. I. Sect. 9, Cl. 2. By Art. II. Sect. 2, the President is made commander-in-chief of the army and navy of the United States, and of the militia of the several States when called into the service of the United States. This clause gives ample powers of war to the President, when the army and navy are lawfully in "actual service." His military authority is supreme, under the constitution, while governing and regulating the land and naval forces, and treating captures on land and water in accordance with such rules as Congress may have passed in pursuance of Art. I. Sect. 8, Cl. 11, 14. Congress may effectually control the military power, by refusing to vote supplies, or to raise troops, and by impeachment of the President; but for the military movements, and measures essential to overcome the enemy, — for the general conduct of the war, — the President is responsible to and controlled by no other department of government. His duty is to uphold the constitution and enforce the laws, and to respect whatever rights loyal citizens are entitled to enjoy in time of civil war, to the fullest extent that may be consistent with the performance of the military duty imposed on him. The effect of a state of war, in changing or modifying civil rights, has been explained in the preceding chapters.

What is the extent of the military power of the President over the persons and property of citizens at a distance from the seat of war — whether he or the war department may lawfully order the arrest of citizens in loyal states on reasonable proof that they are either enemies or aiding the enemy — or that they are spies or emissaries of rebels sent to gain information for their use, or to discourage enlistments — whether martial law may be extended over such places as the commander deems it necessary to guard, even though distant from any battle field, in order to enable him to prosecute the war effectually — whether the writ of *habeas corpus* may be suspended as to persons under military arrest, by the President, or only by Congress, (on which point judges of the United States courts disagree); whether, in time of war, all citizens are liable to military arrest, on reasonable proof of their aiding or abetting the enemy — or whether they are entitled to practise treason until indicted by some grand jury — thus, for example, whether Jefferson Davis, or General Lee, if found in Boston, could be arrested by military authority and sent to Fort Warren? Whether, in the midst of wide-spread and terrific war, those persons who violate the laws of war and the laws of peace, traitors, spies, emissaries, brigands, bush-whackers, guerrillas, persons in the free States supplying arms and ammunition to the enemy, must all be proceeded against by civil tribunals only, under due forms and precedents of law, by the tardy and ineffectual machinery of arrests by *marshals*, (who can rarely have means of apprehending them,) and of grand *juries*, (who meet twice a year, and could seldom if ever seasonably secure the evidence on which to indict them)? Whether government is not entitled by military power to PREVENT the traitors and spies, by arrest and imprisonment, from doing the intended mischief, as well as to punish them after it is done? Whether war can be carried on successfully, without the power to save the army and navy from being betrayed and destroyed, by *depriving* any citizen temporarily of the power of acting as an enemy, whenever there is reasonable cause to suspect him of being one? Whether these and similar proceedings are, or are not, in violation of any civil rights of citizens under the constitution, are questions to which the answers depend on the construction given to the war powers of the Executive. Whatever any commander-in-chief, in accordance with the usual practice of carrying on war among civilized nations, may order his army and navy to do, is within the *power* of the President to order and to execute, because the constitution, in express terms, gives him the supreme command of both. If he makes war upon a foreign nation, he should be governed by the law of nations; if lawfully engaged in civil war, he may treat his enemies as subjects and as belligerents.

The constitution provides that the government and regulation of the land and naval forces, and the treatment of captures, should be according to law; but it imposes, in express terms, no other qualification of the war power of the President. It does not prescribe any territorial limits, within the United States, to which his military operations shall be restricted; nor to which the picket guard, or military guards (sometimes called *provost marshals*) shall be confined. It does not exempt any person making war upon the country, or aiding and comforting the enemy, from being *captured*, or arrested, wherever he may be found, whether within or out of the lines of any division of the army. It does not provide that public enemies, or their abettors, shall find safe asylum in any part of the United States where military power can reach them. It requires the President, as an executive magistrate, in time of peace to see that the laws existing in time of peace are faithfully executed — and as commander-in-chief, in time of war, to see that the laws of war are executed. In doing both duties he is strictly obeying the constitution.

CHAPTER IV.

BILLS OF ATTAINDER.

After the authority of government shall have been reëstablished over the rebellious districts, measures may be taken to punish individual criminals.

The popular sense of outraged justice will embody itself in more or less stringent legislation against those who have brought civil war upon us. It would be surprising if extreme severity were not demanded by the supporters of the Union in all sections of the country. Nothing short of a general bill of attainder, it is presumed, will fully satisfy some of the loyal people of the slave States.

BILLS OF ATTAINDER IN ENGLAND.

By these statutes, famous in English political history, tyrannical governments have usually inflicted their severest revenge upon traitors. The irresistible power of law has been evoked to annihilate the criminal, as a citizen of that State whose majesty he had offended, and whose existence he had assailed. His life was terminated with horrid tortures; his blood was corrupted, and his estates were forfeited to the king. While still living, he was deemed, in the language of the law, as "*civiliter mortuus.*"

PUNISHMENT BY ATTAINDER.

The refined cruelty which characterized the punishment of treason, according to the common law of England, would have been discreditable to the barbarism of North American savages in the time of the Georges, and has since been equalled only by some specimens of chivalry in the secession army. The mode of executing these unfortunate political offenders was this: —

1. The culprit was required to be dragged on the ground or over the pavement to the gallows; he could not be allowed, by law, to walk or ride. Blackstone says, that *by connivance*, at last ripened into law, he was allowed to be dragged upon a hurdle, to prevent the extreme torment of being dragged on the ground or pavement.

2. To be hanged by the neck, and then cut down alive.

3. His entrails to be taken out and burned while he was yet alive.

4. His head to be cut off.

5. His body to be divided into four parts.

6. His head and quarters to be at the king's disposal.*

Blackstone informs us that these directions were, in former times, literally and studiously executed. Judge Story observes, they "indicate at once a savage and ferocious spirit, and a degrading subserviency to royal resentments, real or supposed." †

ATTAINDERS PROHIBITED AS INCONSISTENT WITH CONSTITUTIONAL LIBERTY.

Bills of attainder struck at the root of all civil rights and political liberty. To declare single individuals, or

* 4 Bla. Com. 92.

† Lord Coke undertakes to justify the severity of this punishment by examples drawn from Scripture.

a large class of persons, criminals, in time of peace, merely upon the ground that they entertained certain opinions upon questions of church or state; to do this by act of Parliament, without a hearing, or after the death of the alleged offender; to involve the innocent with the guilty in indiscriminate punishment, — was an outrage upon the rights of the people not to be tolerated in our constitution as one of the powers of government.

BILLS OF ATTAINDER ABOLISHED.

The constitution provides expressly,* that "no bill of attainder, or *ex post facto* law, shall be passed by Congress; and that no State shall pass any bill of attainder, *ex post facto* law, or law impairing the obligation of contracts." † There is, therefore, no power in this country to pass any bill of attainder.

WHAT IS A BILL OF ATTAINDER?

Wherein does it differ from other statutes for the punishment of criminals?

A "bill of attainder," in the technical language of the law, is a statute by which the offender becomes "attainted," and is liable to punishment without having been convicted of any crime in the ordinary course of judicial proceedings.

If a person be expressly named in the bill, or comes within the terms thereof, he is liable to punishment. The legislature undertakes to pronounce upon the guilt of the accused party. He is entitled to no hearing, when living, and may be pronounced guilty when ab-

* Art. I. Sect. 9. † Art. I. Sect. 10.

sent from the country, or even long after his death. Lord Coke says that the reigning monarch of England, who was slain at Bosworth, is said to have been attainted by act of Parliament a few months after his death, notwithstanding the absurdity of deeming him at once in possession of a throne and a traitor.*

A question has been raised, whether any statute can be deemed a bill of attainder if it inflicts a degree of punishment less than that of death?

In technical law, statutes were called bills of attainder only when they inflicted the penalty of death or outlawry; while statutes which inflicted only forfeitures, fines, imprisonments, and similar punishments, were called bills of "pains and penalties." This distinction was practically observed in the legislation of England. No bill of attainder can probably be found which did not contain the marked feature of the death penalty, or the penalty of outlawry, which was considered as equivalent to a judgment of death. Judgment of outlawry on a capital crime, pronounced for absconding or fleeing from justice, was founded on that which was in law deemed a tacit confession of guilt.†

BILLS OF PAINS AND PENALTIES.

It has been said that within the sense of the constitution, bills of attainder include bills of pains and penalties; and this view seemed to derive support from a remark of a judge of the Supreme Court. "A bill of attainder may affect the life of an individual, or may confiscate his property, or both." ‡

* See Story on the Constitution, B. III. Sect. 678.

† Standf. Pl. Co. 44, 122, 182. ‡ *Fletcher* v. *Peck*, 6 Cranch, R.

It is true that a bill of attainder may affect the life of an individual; but if the individual attainted were dead before the passage of the act, as was the case with Richard III., the bill could not affect his life; or if a bill of attainder upon outlawry were passed against persons beyond seas, the life of the party would not be in fact affected, although the outlawry was equivalent in the eye of the law to civil death. There is nothing in this dictum inconsistent with the ancient and acknowledged distinction between bills of attainder and bills of pains and penalties; nothing which would authorize the enlargement of the technical meaning of the words; nothing which shows that Judge Marshall deemed that bills of attainder included bills of pains and penalties within the sense of the constitution. This dictum is quoted by Judge Story,* who supposed its meaning went beyond that which is now attributed to it. But he does not appear to sanction such a view of the law. This is the only authority to which he refers; and he introduces the proposed construction of this clause by language which is used by lawyers who have little confidence in the result which the authority indicates, viz., "it seems." No case has been decided by the Supreme Court of the United States which shows that "bills of attainder," within the sense of the constitution, include any other statutes than those which were technically so considered according to the law of England.

EX POST FACTO LAWS PROHIBITED. BILLS OF PAINS AND PENALTIES, AS WELL AS ATTAINDERS, UNCONSTITUTIONAL.

It does not seem important whether the one or the other construction be put upon the language of this

* Com. Const. III. Ch. 32, Sect. 3.

clause, nor whether bills of pains and penalties be or be not included within the prohibition; for Congress can pass no *ex post facto* law; and it was one of the invariable characteristics of bills of attainder, and of bills of pains and penalties, that they were passed for the punishment of supposed crimes which had been committed before the acts were passed.

The clause prohibiting Congress from passing any *ex post facto* law would doubtless have prevented their passing any bill of attainder; but this prohibition was inserted from greater caution, and to prevent the exercise of constructive powers against political offenders. No usurpation of authority in the worst days of English tyranny was more detested by the framers of our constitution than that which attempted to ride over the rights of Englishmen to gratify royal revenge against the friends of free government. Hence in that respect they shut down the gate upon this sovereign power of government. They forbade any punishment, under any form, for crime not against some standing law, which had been enacted before the time of its commission. They prevented Congress from passing any attainder laws, whereby the accused might be deprived of his life, or his estate, or both, without trial by jury, and by his political enemies; and whereby also his relatives would suffer equally with himself.

ATTAINDERS IN THE COLONIES AND STATES.

Bills in the nature of bills of attainder were familiar to our ancestors in most of the colonies and in the States which subsequently formed the Union. And several of these acts of attainder have been pronounced valid by the highest courts in these States. By the act of the State of New York, October 22, 1779, the real and personal property of persons adhering to the enemy was forfeited to the State; and this act has been held valid,* and proceedings under acts of attainder were, as the court held, to be construed according to the rules in cases of attainder, and not by the ordinary course of judicial proceedings;† and these laws applied to persons who were dead at the time of the proceedings.‡

"Bills of attainder," says the learned judge, (in 2 Johnson's Cases,) "have always been construed in this respect with more latitude than ordinary judicial proceedings, for the purpose of giving them more certain effect, and that the intent of the legislature may prevail." "They are extraordinary acts of sovereignty, founded on public policy § and the peace of the community." "The attainted person," says Sir Matthew Hale, "is guilty of the execrable murder of the king." The act of New York, October 22, 1779, attainted, among others, Thomas Jones of the offence of adhering to the enemies of the State. This was a specific offence, and was not declared or understood to amount to treason, because many of the persons attainted had never owed allegiance to the State. ||

Bills of attainder were passed not only in New York, but in several other colonies and States, inflicting the penalties of attainder for other crimes than treason, actual or constructive. And the harsh operation of such laws, their injustice, and their liability to be abused

* *Sleight* v. *Kane*, 2 Johns. Cas. 236, decided in April, 1801.

† *Jackson* v. *Sands*, 2 Johns. 267.

‡ *Jackson* v. *Stokes*, 3 Johns. 15.

§ Foster, 83, 84.

|| *Jackson* v. *Catlin*, 2 Johns. R. 260.

in times of public excitement, were understood by those who laid the foundations of this government too well to permit them to disregard the dangers which they sought to avert, by depriving Congress, as well as the several States, of all power to enact such cruel statutes.

If bills of attainder had been passed only for the punishment of treason, in the sense of making war upon the government, or aiding the enemy, they would have been less odious and less dangerous; but the regiment of crimes which servile Parliaments had enrolled under the title of "treason," had become so formidable, and the brutality of the civil contests in England had been so shocking, that it was thought unsafe to trust any government with the arbitrary and irresponsible power of condemning by statute large classes of their opponents to death and destruction for that which only want of success had made a crime.

BILLS OF ATTAINDER, HOW RECOGNIZED.

The consequences of attainder to the estate of the party convicted will be more fully stated hereafter; but it is essential to observe that there are certain characteristics which distinguish bills of attainder from all other penal statutes.

1. They always inflict the penalty of death upon the offender, or of outlawry, which is equivalent to death.

2. They are always *ex post facto* laws, being passed after the crime was committed which they are to punish.

3. They never allow the guilt or innocence of the persons attainted to be ascertained by trial; but the guilt is attributed to them by act of Parliament.

4. They always inflicted certain penalties, among

which were corruption of blood and forfeiture of estate. The essence of attainder was in corruption of blood, and without the corruption of blood no person was by the English law attainted.

Unless a law of Congress shall contain these four characteristics — penalty of death, or outlawry, corruption of blood, and the legislative, not judicial condemnation — embodied in a law passed after the commission of the crime it seeks to punish, it is not a bill of attainder under the sense of the constitution.

INTRODUCTION TO CHAPTER V.

UNDER the English law, prior to the Revolution, there had been three modes of punishing the crime of Treason. First, by bills of attainder. Second, by judicial attainder. Third, by statutes of the realm against treason, actual and constructive. Bills of attainder were acts of Parliament, which declared one or more persons, whether living or dead, or absent beyond seas, guilty of the crime of actual or constructive treason. Judicial attainder was effected in the courts of law by process issued against persons accused of treason, whether living or dead, or absent beyond seas. The effect of attainder by judicial process was substantially the same as that of attainder by act of Parliament, in effecting corruption of blood, and working forfeiture of estates during the life of the offender, and after he was dead.

Persons accused of treason were punishable under statutes, by death and total forfeiture of estates; but no one could be convicted, sentenced, and punished for treason, under statutes, "unless during his life," that is to say, while alive, nor unless he had received a trial in court, conducted according to the usual forms of procedure.

By our Constitution, all power is taken from the General Government, and from all the States, to punish treason by passing any bill of attainder, as is shown in Chapter IV.

Congress has power to authorize courts to punish treason by judicial attainder; but the Constitution has limited the time during which such process may be applied, and its effect, in these words:

"No attainder of treason shall work corruption of blood, nor forfeiture of estate, except during the life of the offender."

These provisions apply only to judicial attainder, and not to punishments of treason under ordinary statutes of Congress, which provide for no attainder.

The constitutional power of Congress to authorize proceedings for judicial attainder of persons who have committed treason, has not been, thus far, carried into effect.

No process of attainder of treason is now known in our municipal law.

To guard against abuse, under which our forefathers in England suffered, by reason of unjust and arbitrary definitions of treason, the Constitution prescribes certain rules for the definition, proof, and punishment of offences under statute law, which Congress may pass for the punishment of that crime. It defines treason to be "a levying of war against the United States," thus cutting off all the other descriptions of treason known to the English law. It requires, in proof of treason, that there shall be two witnesses to each overt act with which the accused is charged. A trial by jury in open court, and in the presence of witnesses, is secured, but when one is convicted he is liable to such punishment as may have been prescribed by the statute, and there is no limit in the Constitution to the penalty which Congress may provide.

Thus the traitor may be subjected to punishment by death, and to the forfeiture of all his estate, or to fine to an unlimited amount. The criminal, however, may not be, and by existing laws is not, attainted, or subject to any of the effects of attainder, by these proceedings. The limitations of the Constitution are inapplicable to statutes which do not provide for attainder, but only for penalties of death and confiscation.

CHAPTER V.

RIGHT OF CONGRESS TO DECLARE BY STATUTE THE PUNISHMENT OF TREASON, AND ITS CONSTITUTIONAL LIMITATIONS.

TREASON.

THE highest crime known to the law is *treason.* It is "the sum of all villanies;" its agents have been branded with infamy in all countries where fidelity and justice have respect. The name of one who betrays his friend becomes a byword and a reproach. How much deeper are the guilt and infamy of the criminal who betrays his country! No convict in our State prisons can have fallen so low as willingly to associate with a TRAITOR. There is no abyss of crime so dark, so horrible, as that to which the traitor has descended. He has left forever behind him conscience, honor, and hope.

ANCIENT ENGLISH DOCTRINE OF CONSTRUCTIVE TREASON.

Treason, as defined in the law of England, at the date of the constitution, embraced many misdemeanors which are not now held to be crimes. Offences of a political character, not accompanied with any intention to subvert the government; mere words of disrespect to the ruling sovereign; assaults upon the king's officers at certain times and places; striking one of the judges in court; and many other acts which did not partake of the nature of treason, were, in ancient times, declared treason by Parliament, or so construed by judges, as to constitute that crime. Indeed, there was nothing to prevent Parliament from proclaiming any act of a subject to be treason, thereby subjecting him to all its terrible penalties. The doctrine of *constructive treasons*, created by servile judges, who held their office during the pleasure of the king, was used by them in such a way as to enable the sovereign safely to wreak vengeance upon his victims under the guise of judicial condemnation. If the king sought to destroy a rival, the judges would pronounce him guilty of constructive treason; in other words, they would so construe the acts of the defendant as to make them treason. Thus the king could selfishly outrage every principle of law and justice, while avoiding responsibility. No man's life or property was safe. The wealthier the citizen, the greater was his apprehension that the king would seize and confiscate his estates. The danger lay in the fact that the nature and extent of the legal crime of treason was indeterminate, or was left to arbitrary determination. The power to *define* treason, to declare from time to time who should be deemed in law to be traitors, was in its nature an *arbitrary* power. No government having that power would fail to become oppressive in times of excitement, and especially in civil war. As early as the reign of Edward III., Parliament put an end to these judge-made-treasons by declaring and defining all the different acts which should be deemed treason; and, although subsequent statutes have added to or modified the law, yet treason has at all times since that reign been defined by statute.

POWER OF CONGRESS TO DEFINE AND PUNISH TREASON LIMITED.

It was with full knowledge of the history of judicial usurpation, of the tyranny of exasperated governments, and of the tendency of rival factions in republics to seek revenge on each other, that the convention which framed the constitution, having given no power to the judiciary, like that possessed by English judges, to make constructive crimes, introduced several provisions limiting the power of Congress to define and punish the political crime of treason, as well as other offences.

The various clauses in the constitution relating to this subject, in order to a clear exposition of their meaning, should be taken together as parts of our system.

ATTAINDER AND EX POST FACTO LAWS.

The first and most important limitation of the power of Congress is found in Art. I. Sect. 9: "No bill of attainder, or *ex post facto* law, shall be passed." By prohibiting bills of attainder, no subject could be made a criminal, or be deprived of life, liberty, or property, by mere *act of legislation*, without trial or conviction. The power to enact *ex post facto* laws having been withheld, Congress could not pass "a statute which would render an act punishable in a manner in which it was not punishable when it was committed." No man's life could be taken, his liberty abridged, nor his estate, nor any part of it, seized for an act which had not, previously to the commission thereof, been declared by some law as a crime, and the manner and extent of punishment prescribed.* Hence no law of Congress can make that deed a crime which was not so before the deed was done. Every man may know what are the

* See *Fletcher* v. *Peck*, 6 Cranch, 138.

laws to which he is amenable in time of peace by reading the statutes. There can be no retrospective criminal legislation by any State, or by the United States.

TREASON DEFINED BY STATUTE.

These points having been secured, the next step was to *define* the CRIME OF TREASON. Countless difficulties and dangers were avoided by selecting from the English statutes *one crime only*, which should be deemed to constitute that offence.

The constitution provides that, "Treason against the United States shall consist only in levying war against them, or in adhering to their enemies, giving them aid and comfort." * Hence many acts are not treasonable which were so considered according to the law of England, and of the colonies and States of this country. Each State still retains the power to define and punish treason against itself in its own way.

Nothing but *overt acts* are treasonable by the laws of the United States; and these overt acts must be overt acts of war.† These acts must be proved either by confession in open court, or by two witnesses to the same act. ‡ Our ancestors took care that no one should be convicted of this infamous crime, unless his guilt is made certain. So odious was the offence that even a senator or representative could be arrested on *suspicion* of it. § All civil officers were to be removed from office on impeachment and conviction thereof. || And a person charged with treason against a State, and fleeing from that State to another, was to be delivered

* Art. III. Sect. 3. † Ibid. ‡ Ibid.
§ Art. I. Sect. 6. || Art. II. Sect. 4.

up, on demand, to the State having jurisdiction.* The crime being defined, and the nature of the testimony to establish it being prescribed, and conviction being possible only in "open court," the constitution then provides, — that "Congress shall have power to declare the *punishment* of treason, but no attainder of treason shall work corruption of blood, or forfeiture, except during the life of the person attainted." †

CONGRESS HAVE UNLIMITED POWER TO DECLARE THE PUNISHMENT OF TREASON.

By this article, the constitution has in express terms given to Congress the power to declare the *punishment* of treason; and the nature and extent of the punishment which they may declare are not limited. Congress may impose the penalty of fine, or imprisonment, or outlawry, or banishment, or forfeiture, or death, or of death and forfeiture of property, personal and real. Congress might have added to all these punishments the more terrible penalty which followed, *as a consequence of attainder of treason*, under the law of England, had the constitution not limited the effect and operation of that species of attainder.

A COMMON ERROR.

Some writers have supposed that this article in the constitution, which qualifies the *effect* of an attainder of treason, was *a limitation* of the power of Congress to declare the *punishment* of treason. This is an error. A careful examination of the language used in the in-

* Constitution, Art. IV. Sect. 6. † Art. III. Sect. 3.

strument itself, and of the history of the English law of attainder, will make it evident that the framers of the constitution, in drafting Sect. 3 of Art. III. did not design to restrain Congress from declaring against the traitor himself, his person or estate, such penalties as it might deem sufficient to atone for the highest of crimes.

Whenever a person had committed high treason in England, and had been duly indicted, tried, and convicted, and when final judgment of guilty, and sentence of death or outlawry, had been pronounced upon him, the immediate and inseparable consequence, by common law, of the sentence of death or outlawry of the offender for treason, and for certain other felonies, was *attainder*. Attainder means, in its original application, the staining or corruption of the blood of a criminal who was in the contemplation of law dead. He then became "*attinctus* — stained, blackened, attainted."

CONSEQUENCES OF ATTAINDER.

Certain legal results followed *attainder*, among which are the following: The convict was no longer of any credit or reputation. He could not be a witness in any court. He was not capable of performing the legal functions of any other man; his power to sell or transfer his lands and personal estate ceased. By anticipation of his punishment he was already dead in law,* except when the fiction of the law would protect him from some liability to others which he had the power to discharge. It is true that the attainted felon could not be murdered with impunity,† but the law preserved

* 3 Inst. 213.

† Foster, 73.

his physical existence only to vindicate its own majesty, and to inflict upon the offender an ignominious death.

CORRUPTION OF BLOOD.

Among the most important consequences of *attainder of felony*, were those *resulting from "corruption of blood,"* which is the *essence of attainder.** Blackstone says,† —

"Another immediate consequence of attainder is the corruption of blood, both upwards and downwards; so that an attainted person can neither inherit lands or other hereditaments from his ancestors, nor retain those he is already in possession of, nor transmit them by descent to any heir; but the same shall escheat to the lord of the fee, subject to the king's superior right of forfeiture; and the person attainted shall also obstruct all descents to his posterity whenever they are obliged to derive a title through him, to a remote ancestor."

The distinctions between escheat and forfeiture it is not necessary now to state, ‡ because, whether the forfeiture enured to the benefit of the lord or of the king, the effect was the same upon the estate of the criminal. § By this legal fiction of *corruption of blood*, the offender was deprived of all his estate, personal and real; his children or other heirs could not inherit any thing from him, nor through him from any of his ancestors. "If a father be seized in fee, and the son commits treason and is attainted, and then the father dies, then the lands shall escheat to the lord." ||

SAVAGE CRUELTY OF ENGLISH LAW.

By the English system of escheats to the lord and forfeitures to the king, the innocent relatives of the offender were punished, upon the theory that it was

* See Co. Litt. 391. † 4 Com. b. 388. ‡ See Co. Litt. 13.
§ Co. Litt. p. 391. Bla. Com. Vol. II. p. 254 || Co. Litt. p. 13.

the duty of every family to secure the loyalty of all its members to the sovereign; and upon failure to do so, the whole family should be plunged into lasting disgrace and poverty. A punishment which might continue for twenty generations, was indeed inhuman, and received, as it merited, the condemnation of liberal men in all countries; * but aristocratic influence in England had for centuries resisted the absolute and final abandonment of these odious penalties. The framers of the constitution have deprived Congress of the power of passing bills of attainder. They might have provided that no person convicted of treason should be held to be attainted, or be liable to suffer any of the common law penalties which resulted from attainder, but only such penalties as Congress should prescribe by statute. They have, however, not in terms, abolished attainders, but have modified their effect, by declaring that attainder shall not work corruption of blood.

FORFEITURES.

By the law of England, forfeiture of estates was also one of the necessary legal consequences of attainder of felony. Real estate was forfeited upon attainder, personal estate upon conviction before attainder. By these forfeitures all the property, rights, and claims, of every name and nature, went to the lord or the king. But forfeiture of lands related back to the time when the felony was committed, so as to avoid all subsequent sales and encumbrances, but forfeiture of goods took effect at the date of conviction, so that sales of personal property, prior to that time, were valid, unless col-

* See 4 Bla. Com. p. 388.

lusive.* The estates thus forfeited were not mere estates for life, but the whole interest of the felon, whatever it might be. Thus forfeiture of property was a consequence of attainder; attainder was a consequence of the sentence of death or outlawry; and these penal consequences of attainder were over and above, and in addition to, the penalties expressed in the terms of *the judgment* and *sentence of the court*.† The punishment, and in many instances the only punishment, to which the sentence of the court condemned the prisoner, was death or outlawry. The disabilities which resulted from that sentence were like the disabilities which in other cases result from the sentence of a criminal for infamous crimes. Disability to testify in courts, or to hold offices of trust and honor, sometimes follows, not as part of the punishment prescribed for the offence, but as a consequence of the condition to which the criminal has reduced himself.

There is a clear distinction between the punishment of treason by specific penalties and those consequential damages and injuries which follow by common law as the result or technical effect of a sentence of death or outlawry for treason, viz., attainder of treason, and corruption of blood and forfeiture of estates.‡ To set this subject in a clearer light, the learned reader will recollect that there were different kinds of attainder:

* See Stat. 13 Eliz. ch. 5; 2 B. & A. 258; 2 Hawkins's P. C. 454; 3 Ins. 232; 4 Bla. 387; Co. Litt. 391, b.

† See 2 Greenleaf's Cruise on Real Property, p. 145, and note; 2 Kent, 386; 1 Greenleaf's Cruise, p. 71, sect. 1, and note.

‡ There is a provision in the new constitution of Maryland, (1851,) that "no conviction shall work corruption of blood or forfeiture of estate." (Decl. of Rights, Art. 24.) The constitution of Ohio (1851) contains the same words in the 12th sect. of the Decl. of Rights. The constitutions of

1. *Attainders in a præmunire;* in which, "from the conviction, the defendant shall be out of the king's protection, his lands, tenements, goods, and chattels forfeited to the king, and his body remain in prison during the king's pleasure, or during life."* But the offences punishable under the statutes of præmunire were not felonies, for the latter are punishable only by common law, and not by statute.† 2. *Attainder by bill.* 3. *Attainders of* FELONY and treason; and the important distinction between attainders in treason and attainders in præmunire is this: that in the former the forfeitures are consequences of the judgment, in the latter they are part of the judgment and penalty. Blackstone‡ recognizes fully this distinction. "I here omit the particular forfeitures created by the statutes of præmunire and others, because I look upon them rather as a part of the judgment and penalty inflicted by the respective statutes, than as consequences of such judgment, as in treason and felony they are." Lord Coke expresses the

Kentucky, Delaware, and Pennsylvania declare that attainder of treason shall not work forfeiture beyond the lifetime of the offender. In Alabama, Connecticut, Indiana, Illinois, Maine, Missouri, New Jersey, Rhode Island, and Tennessee, all forfeitures for crime are abolished, either by statutes or constitutions.

"In New Hampshire, Massachusetts, Virginia, Georgia, Michigan, Mississippi, and Arkansas, there are statutes providing specifically for the punishment of treason and felonies; but no mention is made of corruption of blood or forfeiture of estate; and inasmuch as these offences are explicitly legislated upon, and a particular punishment provided in each case, it may be gravely doubted whether the additional common law punishment of forfeiture of estate ought not to be considered as repealed by implication." 1 Greenleaf's Cruise Dig. 196, note.

* 1 Inst. 129; 3 Bla. p. 118; and for the severity of the penalties, see 1 Hawk. P. C. 55.

† 4 Bla. 118.

‡ 4 Com. p. 386.

same opinion.* And statutes of præmunire and attainders of treason are both different in law from *bills of pains and penalties;* of which English history affords, among many other examples, that against the Bishop of Rochester;† in the latter the pains and penalties are all expressly declared by statute, and not left as consequences of judgment. That clause in the constitution which gives power to Congress to make laws for the punishment of treason, limits and qualifies the effect of attainder of treason, in case such attainder should be deemed by the courts as a legal consequence of such sentence as the statute requires the court to impose on traitors. This limitation applies, in terms, *only* to the effect of attainders of treason.

CHARACTERISTICS OF ATTAINDER OF TREASON.

There is no attainder of treason known to the law of England, unless, 1. The judgment of death or outlawry has been pronounced against the traitor.‡ 2. Where the crime was a *felony*, and punishable according to common law;§ and, 3. Where the attainder was a consequence of the judgment, and not part of the judgment and penalty.|| Congress may pass a law condemning every traitor to death, and to the consequential punishment of "attainder;" but such attainder will not of itself operate to corrupt blood or forfeit estate, except during the life of the offender. But unless Congress pass a law expressly *attainting* the criminal of

* Co. Litt. 391, b.
† Stat. 9 Geo. I. ch. 17.
‡ 4 Bla. 387.
§ 4 Bla. 387.
|| Ib; Co. Litt. 391, b.; 4 Bla. 386.

treason, there is not, under the laws of the United States, any "attainder." The criminal laws of the United States are all embraced in specific statutes, defining crimes and all their penalties. No consequential penalties of this character are known to this law. And if a person is convicted and sentenced to death for treason, there can be no corruption of blood, nor forfeiture of estate except by express terms of the statute. The leading principles of the constitution forbid the making of laws which should leave the penalty of crime to be determined by ancient or antiquated common law proceedings of English courts. Forfeiture of estate, by express terms of statute, may be in the nature of forfeiture by a bill of pains and penalties, or præmunire, but is not forfeiture by attainder; nor is it such forfeiture as is within the sense of the constitution, which limits the operation of attainders of treason. This distinction was well known to the framers of the constitution. They thought it best to guard against the danger of those constructive and consequential punishments, giving full power to Congress, in plain terms, to prescribe by statute what punishment they should select; but in case of resort to attainder of treason, as one of those punishments, that form of punishment should not be so construed as, *ex vi termini*, to corrupt blood nor forfeit estate except during the life of the person attainted.

TECHNICAL LANGUAGE TO BE CONSTRUED TECHNICALLY.

The language of the constitution is peculiar; it is technical; and it shows on the face of it an intention to limit the technical operation of attainders, not to limit the scope or extent of legislative penalties. If the authors of the constitution meant to say that Congress should pass no law punishing treason by attainder, or by its consequences, viz., forfeiture of estate, or corruption of blood, they would, in plain terms, have said so; and there would have been an end to the penalties of attainder, as there was an end to bills of attainder. Instead of saying, "Congress shall have power to declare the punishment of treason, but shall not impose the penalties of attainder upon the offender," they said, "Congress shall have power to declare the punishment of treason, but no attainder of treason shall work corruption of blood, or forfeiture, except during the life of the person attainted."

This phraseology has reference only to the technical effect of attainder. The "working of forfeitures" is a phrase used by lawyers to show the legal result or effect which arises from a certain state of facts. If a traitor is convicted, judgment of death is passed upon him; by that judgment he becomes attainted. Attainder works forfeitures and corruption of blood; forfeitures and corruption of blood are, in the ordinary course of common law, followed by certain results to his rights of property. But the constitution provides, if the traitor is attainted, that attainder shall not, *ex vi termini*, and of its own force, and without statute to that effect, "work" forfeiture or corruption of blood. The convict may still retain all those civil rights of which he has not been deprived by the strict terms of the statute which shall declare the punishment of treason.

The punishment of treason, by the statute of the United States of April 30, 1790, is death, and nothing more. Can any case be found, since the statute was enacted, in which a party convicted and adjudged guilty of treason and sentenced to death, has been held to be "attainted" of treason, so that the attainder has worked forfeiture of any of his estate, real or personal? Would not any lawyer feel astonishment if a court of the United States, having sentenced a traitor to death under the law of 1790, should announce as a further penalty the forfeiture of the real and personal estate of the offender, "worked" by the attainder of felony, notwithstanding no such penalty is mentioned in that statute?

If Congress should pass an act punishing a traitor by a fine of five dollars, and imprisonment for five years, who would not feel amazed to learn that by the English doctrine of forfeitures worked by attainders, by operation of law, the criminal might be stripped of property worth thousands of dollars, over and above the penalty prescribed by statute?

TRUE MEANING OF ART. III. SECT. III. CL. II.

The constitution means that if traitors shall be attainted, unlimited forfeitures and corruption of blood shall not be worked by attainders. It means to leave untrammelled the power of Congress to cause traitors to be attainted or otherwise; but if attainted Congress must provide by statute for the attainder; and the constitution settles how far that attainder shall operate constitutionally; and when the legislature has awarded one punishment for treason, the court shall not evoke the doctrine of forfeitures worked by attainder, and thus, by technical implication, add punishments not specifically set down in the penal statute itself; or if this implication exist, the results of the technical effect of attainder shall not be corruption of blood, or forfeiture, except during the life of the offender. The third article does not limit the power of Congress to punish, but it limits the technical consequences of a special kind of punishment, which may or may not be adopted in the statutes.

From the foregoing remarks it is obvious that no person is attainted of treason, in the technical sense, who is convicted under the United States act of 1790. There can be no attainder of treason, within the meaning of the constitution, unless there be, first, a judgment of death, or outlawry; second, a penalty of attainder by express terms of the statute. A mere conviction of treason and sentence of death, or outlawry, and forfeitures of real and personal estate, do not constitute an attainder in form, in substance, nor in effect, when made under any of the present statutes of the United States.

IF CONGRESS MAY IMPOSE FINES, WHY NOT FORFEITURES?

No one doubts the power of Congress to make treason punishable with death, or by fines to any amount whatever. Nor would any reasonable person deem any fine too large to atone for the crime of involving one's own country in civil war. If the constitution placed in Congress the power to take life, and to take property of the offender in one form, why should it deny the power to take property in any other form? If the framers of the constitution were willing that a traitor should forfeit his life, how could they have intended to shelter his property? Was property, in their opinion, more sacred than life? Would all the property of rebels forfeited to the treasury of the country repair the injury of civil war?

FORFEITURES NOT LIMITED TO LIFE ESTATES.

Could the lawyers who drafted the constitution have intended to limit the pecuniary punishment of forfeiture to a life interest in personal estate, when every lawyer in the convention must have known than at common law there was no such thing as a life estate in personal property? Knowing this, did they mean to protect traitors, under all circumstances, in the enjoyment of personal property? If so, why did they not say so? If they meant to prevent Congress from passing any law that should deprive traitors of more than a life estate in real estate, the result would be, that the criminal would lose only the enjoyment of his lands for a few days or weeks, from the date of the judgment to the date of his execution, and then his lands would go to his heirs. Thus it is evident, that if the constitution cuts off the power of Congress to punish treason, and limits it to such forfeitures as are the consequence of attainder, and then cuts off from attainder its penal consequences of corruption of blood and forfeiture of estate, except during the life of the offender, then the framers of that instrument have effectually protected the personal and real estate of traitors, and have taken more care to secure them from the consequences of their crime than any other class of citizens. If so, they have authorized far more severity against many other felons than against them. If such were the purpose of the authors of the constitution, they would have taken direct and plain language to say what they meant. They would have said, "Congress may punish treason, but shall not deprive traitors of real or personal property, except for the time which may elapse between sentence of death and execution." Instead of such a provision, they gave full power to punish treason, including fines, absolute forfeitures, death, and attainder, only limiting the technical effect of the last-mentioned penalty, if that form of punishment should be adopted; and Congress has the power, under the constitution, to declare as the penalty for treason the forfeiture of all the real and personal estate of the offender, and is not limited, as has been supposed by some, to a forfeiture of real estate for life only.

NOTE. — Since the publication of the seventh edition, it has been decided by UNDERWOOD, J., in the Eastern District Court of the U. S. for Virginia, in the case of *U. S.* v. *Latham*, *first*, that the Confiscation Act above cited is authorized by the Constitution; *second*, that by the terms of that Act (dated July 17th, 1862, ch. 195), as modified by the joint resolution of July 27th, 1862 (No. 63), the punishment of treason is not limited to forfeiture of the life estate of the offender, and is not required to be so limited by the Constitution; but the forfeiture extends to the entire estate in fee simple.

CHAPTER VI.

STATUTES AGAINST TREASON. WHAT THEY ARE, AND HOW THEY ARE TO BE ADMINISTERED.

THE United States statute of April 30th, 1790, provides that, —

"If any person or persons, owing allegiance to the United States of America, shall levy war against them, or shall adhere to their enemies, giving them aid and comfort, within the United States or elsewhere, and shall be thereof convicted, on confession in open court, or on the testimony of two witnesses to the same overt act of the treason whereof he or they shall stand indicted, such person or persons shall be adjudged *guilty* of *treason* against the United States, and *shall suffer death.*"

Concealment of knowledge of treason (misprision of treason) is, by the same act, punished by fine not exceeding one thousand dollars, and imprisonment not exceeding seven years. By the statute of January 30th, 1799, corresponding with foreign governments, or with any officer or agent thereof, with intent to influence their controversies with the United States, or to defeat the measures of this government, is declared to be a high misdemeanor, though not called treason, and is punishable by fine not exceeding five thousand dollars, and imprisonment during a term not less than six months, nor exceeding three years. So the law has stood during this century, until the breaking out of the present rebellion.

The chief provisions of the law passed at the last session of Congress, and approved July, 17th, 1862, chap. 195. are these: —

Section 1. Persons committing treason shall suffer one of two punishments: 1. Either death, and freedom to his slaves; or, 2. Imprisonment not less than five years, fine not less than ten thousand dollars, and freedom of slaves; the fine to be collected out of any personal or real estate except slaves.

Sect. 2. Inciting rebellion, or engaging in it, or aiding those who do so, is punishable by imprisonment not more than ten years, fine not more than ten thousand dollars, and liberation of slaves.

Sect. 3 disqualifies convicts, under the preceding sections, from holding office under the United States.

Sect. 4 provides that former laws against treason shall not be suspended as against any traitor, unless he shall have been convicted under this act.

Sect. 5 makes it the duty of the President to cause the seizure of all the property, real and personal, of several classes of persons, and to apply the same to the support of the army, namely: 1. Rebel army and navy officers; 2. Government officers of Confederate States in their national capacity; 3. Confederate State officers; 4. United States officers turned traitor officers; 5. Any one holding any office or agency, national, state, or municipal, under the rebel government, *provided* persons enumerated in classes 3, 4, and 5 have accepted office since secession of the State, or have taken oath of allegiance to support the Confederate States; 6. Persons who, owning property in loyal States, in the territories, or in the District of Columbia, shall hereafter assist, aid, or comfort such rebellion. All transfers of property so owned shall be null, and suits for it by such persons shall be barred by proving that they are within the terms of this act.

Sect. 6. Any persons within the United States, not above named, who are engaged in armed rebellion, or aiding and abetting it, who shall not, within sixty days after proclamation by the President, "cease to aid, countenance, and abet said rebellion," shall be liable to have all their property, personal and real, seized by the President, whose duty it shall be to seize and use it, or the proceeds thereof. All transfers of such property, made more than sixty days after the proclamation, are declared null.

Sect. 7. To secure the condemnation and sale of seized property, so as to make it available, proceedings *in rem* shall be instituted in the name of the United States, in any District Court thereof, or in any territorial court, or in the United States District Court for the District of Columbia, within which district or territory the property, or any part of it, may be found, or into which, if movable, it may first be brought. Proceedings are to conform to those in admiralty or revenue cases. Condemnation shall be as of enemy's property, and it shall belong to the United States; the proceeds thereof to be paid into the treasury.

Sect. 8. Proper powers are given to the courts to carry the above proceedings into effect, and to establish legal forms and processes and modes of transferring condemned property.

Sect. 9. Slaves of rebels, or of those aiding them, escaping and taking refuge within the lines of our army; slaves captured from them; slaves deserted by them, and coming under the control of the United States government; slaves found in places occupied by rebel forces, and afterwards occupied by the United States army, shall be deemed captives of war, and shall be forever *free*.

Sect. 10. No fugitive slave shall be returned to a

person claiming him, nor restrained of his liberty, except for crime, or offence against law, unless the claimant swears that the person claiming the slave is his lawful owner, has not joined the rebellion, nor given aid to it. No officer or soldier of the United States shall surrender fugitive slaves.

Sect. 11. The President may employ, organize, and use as many persons of African descent as he pleases to suppress the rebellion, and use them as he judges for the public welfare.

Sect. 12. The President may make provisions for colonizing such persons as may choose to emigrate, after they shall have been freed by this act.

Sect. 13. The President is authorized by proclamation to pardon any persons engaged in the rebellion, on such terms as he deems expedient.

Sect. 14. Courts of the United States have full powers to institute proceedings, make orders, &c., to carry the foregoing measures into effect.

A resolution, explanatory of the above act, declares that the statute punishes no act done prior to its passage; and no judge or member of a State legislature, who has not taken the oath of allegiance to support the constitution of the Confederate States; nor shall any punishment or proceedings be so construed as to "work forfeiture of the real estate of the offender beyond his natural life."

The President's proclamation, in accordance with the above act, was issued July 25th, 1862. Thus all persons engaged in the rebellion, who come within the provisions of the sixth section, will be liable to the penalties after sixty days from July 25th. This is one of the most important penal acts ever passed by the Congress of the United States.

THE CONFISCATION ACT OF 1862 IS NOT A BILL OF ATTAINDER, NOR AN EX POST FACTO LAW.

This act is not a *bill of attainder*, because it does not punish the offender in any instance with corruption of blood, and it does not declare him, *by act of legislature*, guilty of treason, inasmuch as the offender's guilt must be duly proved and established by judicial proceedings before he can be sentenced. It is not an *ex post facto* law, as it declares no act committed prior to the time when the law goes into operation to be a crime, or to be punishable as such. It provides for no *attainder* of treason, and therefore for none of the penal consequences which might otherwise have followed from such attainder.

The resolution, which is to be taken as part of the act, or as explanatory of it, expressly provides that no punishment or proceedings under said act shall be so construed as to work a forfeiture of the real estate of the offender beyond his natural life. Thus, to prevent our courts from construing the sentence of death, under Sect. 1, as involving an attainder of treason, and its consequences, Congress has, in express terms, provided that no punishment or proceeding shall be so construed as to work forfeiture, as above stated. Thus this statute limits the constructive penalties which result from forfeitures worked by attainders, and perhaps may be so construed as to confine the punishments to those, and those only, which are prescribed in the plain terms of the statute. And this limitation is in accordance with the constitution, as understood by the President, although the forfeiture of rebels' real estate might have been made absolute and unlimited, without exceeding the constitutional power of Congress to punish treason.*

* See note to page 111.

CHAPTER VII.

THE RIGHT OF CONGRESS TO DECLARE THE PUNISHMENT OF CRIMES AGAINST THE UNITED STATES OTHER THAN TREASON.

THE NEW CRIMES OF REBELLION REQUIRE NEW PENAL LAWS.

Several crimes may be committed not defined as treason in the constitution, but not less dangerous to the public welfare. The prevention or punishment of such offences is essential to the safety of every form of government; and the power of Congress to impose penalties in such cases cannot be reasonably questioned. The rights guaranteed in express terms to private citizens cannot be maintained, nor be made secure, without such penal legislation; and, accordingly, Congress has, from time to time, passed laws for this purpose. The present rebellion has given birth to a host of crimes which were not previously punishable by any law. Among these crimes are the following: Accepting or holding civil offices under the Confederate government; violating the oath of allegiance to the United States; taking an oath of allegiance to the Confederate States; manufacturing, passing, or circulating a new and illegal currency; acknowledging and obeying the authority of a seceded State, or of the Confederate States; neglecting or refusing to return to allegiance and to lay down arms after due warning; attempting to negotiate treaties with foreign powers to intervene in our affairs; granting or taking letters of marque; conspiracy against the lawful government; holding public meetings to incite the people to the commission of treason; plotting treason; framing and passing ordinances of secession; organizing and forming new governments within any of the States, with the intent that they shall become independent of the United States, and hostile thereto; the making of treaties between the several States; refusal to take the oath of allegiance to the United States, when tendered by proper authority; resistance to civil process, or to civil officers of the United States, when such resistance is not so general as to constitute war. Each of these and many other public wrongs may be so committed as to avoid the penalty of treason, because they may not be overt acts of levying war, or of aiding and comforting the enemy, which the offender must have committed before he can have rendered himself liable to be punished for treason as defined in the constitution. These and other similar offences are perpetrated for the purpose of overthrowing government. Civil war must inevitably result from them. They might be deemed less heinous than open rebellion, if it were not certain that they are the fountain from which the streams of treason and civil war must flow, sweeping the innocent and the guilty with resistless tide onward to inevitable destruction.

ALL ATTEMPTS TO OVERTURN GOVERNMENT SHOULD BE PUNISHED.

Of the many atrocious misdeeds which are preliminary to or contemporaneous with treason, each and all may be and should be punishable by law. It is by no means desirable that the punishment of all of them should be by *death*, but rather by that penalty, which, depriving the criminal of the means of doing harm, will disgrace him in the community he has dishonored. Imprisonment, fines, forfeitures, confiscation, are the proper punishments for such hardened criminals, because imprisonment is a personal punishment, and fines, forfeitures, &c., merely transfer the property of the offender to the public, as a partial indemnity for the wrong he has committed.

When the terrible consequences of the crimes which foment civil war are considered, no penalty would seem too severe to expiate them. But it has been erroneously suggested that, as the levying of war — treason — itself is not punishable by depriving traitors of more than a life estate in their real estate, even though they are condemned to death, it could not have been the intention of the framers of the constitution to punish any of the crimes which may originate a civil war, by penalty equally severe with that to which they limited Congress, in punishing treason itself. A lower offence, it is said, should not be punished with more severity than a higher one. This objection would be more plausible if the power to punish treason were in fact limited. But, as has been shown in a previous chapter, such is not the fact.*

ACT OF 1862, SECTION VI., DOES NOT PURPORT TO PUNISH TREASON.

If the penalty of death be not inflicted on the guilty, and if he be not accused of treason, no question as to the validity of the statute could arise under this clause of the constitution limiting the effect of attainders of treason. No objection could be urged against its

* See Chap. V. page 93.

validity on the ground of its forfeiting or confiscating all the property of the offender, or of its depriving him of liberty by imprisonment, or of its exiling him from the country.

Section 6 of the act of 1862 does not impose the penalty of *death*, but it provides that if rebels in arms shall not, within sixty days after proclamation by the President, cease to aid and abet the rebellion, and return to their allegiance, they shall be liable to have all their property seized and used for the benefit of the country.

Suppose the rebels in arms refuse to obey the proclamation, and neglect or refuse to return to their allegiance; the mere non-performance of the requisition of this act is, *not levying war*, or aiding and comforting the enemy, technically considered, and so not treason — although, if they go on to perform overt acts in aid of the rebels, *those acts* will be treasonable. Will it be denied that the rebels in arms ought to be required by law to return to their allegiance and cease rebellion? If their refusal to do so is not technically treason, ought they not to be liable to punishment for violating the law? Is any degree of pecuniary loss too severe for those who will continue at war with their country after warning and proclamation, if their lives are not forfeited?

LEGAL CONSTRUCTION OF THE ACT OF 1862.

What will be the construction put upon section 6th of the Act of July 17, ch. 195, 1862, when taken in connection with the joint resolution which accompanied it, is not so certain as it should be. The language of the last clause in that resolution is, "Nor shall any punishment or proceedings, under said Act, be so construed as to work a 'forfeiture' of the real estate of the offender beyond his natural life." There is no forfeiture in express terms provided for in any part of the Act. The punishment of treason, in the first section, is either death and freedom of slaves, or imprisonment, fine, and freedom of slaves. The judgment of death for treason is the only one which could, even by the common law, have been so construed as to "work any forfeiture." It may have been the intention of Congress to limit the constructive effect of such a judgment. But the words of the resolution are peculiar; they declare that no "proceedings" under said act shall be so construed as to work a forfeiture, &c. Then the question will arise whether the "proceedings" (authorized by section 6, in which the President has the power and duty to seize and use all the property of rebels in arms who refuse, after warning, to return to their allegiance) are such that a sale of such real estate, under the provisions of sections 7 and 8, can convey any thing more than an estate for the life of the offender? But the crime punished by section 6 is not the *crime of treason;* and whether there be or be not a limitation to the power of the legislature to punish that crime, there is no limit to its power to punish the crime described in this section.*

Forfeiture and confiscation of real and personal estates for crimes, when there was and could have been no treason, were common and familiar penal statutes in several States or colonies when the constitution was framed. Many of the old tories, in the time of the revolution, were *banished,* and their real estate confiscated, without having been tried for or accused of

* See Note, page 111, United States v. Latham.

treason, or having incurred any forfeiture by the laws against treason. Such was the case in South Carolina in 1776.* In that State, one set of laws was in force against treason, the punishment of which was forfeiture *worked by attainder*. Another set of laws were confiscation acts against tory *refugees* who had committed no treason. These distinctions were familiar to those who formed the constitution, and they used language relating to these subjects with technical precision.

THE SEVERITY OF DIFFERENT PUNISHMENTS COMPARED.

Forfeiture and confiscation are, in the eye of the law, less severe punishments than death: they are in effect fines, to the extent to which the criminal is capable of paying them. It would not seem to be too severe a punishment upon a person who seeks, with arms in his hands, to destroy your life, to steal or carry away your property, to subvert your government, that he should be deprived of his property by confiscation or fine to any amount he could pay. Therefore, as the provisions of section 6, which would authorize the seizure and appropriation of rebel real estate to public use, are not within the prohibitions of Art. III. Sect. 3 of the constitution, it is much to be regretted that the joint resolution of Congress should have been so worded as to throw a doubt upon the construction of that part of the statute, if not to paralyze its effect upon the only class of rebel property which they cannot put out of the reach of government, viz., their real estate.

* See *Willis* v. *Martin*, 2 Bay 20. See also *Hinzleman* v. *Clarke and Al.*, Coxe N. J., 1795.

THE SIXTH SECTION OF THE CONFISCATION ACT OF 1862 IS NOT WITHIN THE PROHIBITION OF THE CONSTITUTION, ARTICLE III. SECTION III.

Congress cannot, by giving a new name to acts of treason, transcend the constitutional limits in declaring its punishment. Nor can legislation change the true character of crimes. Hence some have supposed that Congress has no right to punish the most flagrant and outrageous acts of civil war by penalties more severe than those prescribed, as they say, for treason. Since a subject must have performed some overt act, which may be construed by courts into the "levying of war," or "aiding the enemy," before he can be convicted of treason, it has been supposed that to involve a great nation in the horrors of civil war can be nothing more, and nothing else, than treason. This is a mistake. The constitution does not define the meaning of the phrase "levying war." Is it confined to the true, and genuine signification of the words, namely, "that to levy war is to raise or begin war; to take arms for attack;" or must it be extended to include the carrying on or waging war, after it has been commenced?* The crime committed by a few individuals by merely *levying* war, or beginning without prosecuting or continuing armed resistance to government, although it is treason, may be immeasurably less than that of carrying on a colossal rebellion, involving millions in a fratricidal contest. Though treason is the highest *political* crime known to the codes of law, yet wide-spread and savage rebellion

* To *levy war* is to *raise* or *begin war;* to take arms for attack; to attack. — Webster's Quarto Dict.

To *levy* is, 1. To *raise*, as a siege. 2. To raise or collect; to gather. 3. To *raise*, applied to *war*. — Worcester's Quarto Dict.

is a still higher crime against society; for it embraces a cluster of atrocious wrongs, of which the attack upon government — treason — is but one. Although there can be no treason unless the culprit levies war, or aids the enemy, yet it by no means follows that all acts of carrying on a war once levied are *only* acts of treason. Treason is the threshold of war; the traitor passes over it to new and deeper guilt. He ought to suffer punishment proportioned to his crimes.

It must also be remembered, that the constitution does not indicate that fines, forfeitures, confiscations, outlawry, or imprisonment are "severer penalties than death." The law has never so treated them. Nor is there any limit to the power of Congress to punish traitors, as has been shown in a previous chapter.* Who will contend that the crime of treason is in morals more wicked, in its tendencies more dangerous, or in its results more deadly than the conspiracy by which it was plotted and originated? Yet suppose the conspirator is artful enough not to commit any overt act in presence of two witnesses; he cannot be convicted of treason, though he may have been far more guilty than many thoughtless persons who have been put forward to execute the "overt acts," and have thereby become punishable as traitors. Suppose a person commit homicide; he may be accused of assault and battery, or assault with intent to kill, or justifiable homicide, or manslaughter, or murder in either degree. Suppose the constitution limited the punishment of wilful murder to the death of the criminal and forfeiture of his real and personal estate for life; would any person contend that neither of the other above-mentioned crimes could

* See Chap. V. p. 93.

be punished, unless the criminal were convicted of wilful murder? If he had committed murder, he must have committed all the crimes involved in murder. He must have made an assault with intent to kill; and he must have committed unjustifiable homicide, or manslaughter. If the government should, out of leniency, prosecute and convict him of manslaughter, and impose upon him a penalty of fine, or confiscation of his real and personal estate, instead of sentence of death, would any one say that the penalty imposed was severer than death? or that murder was legislated into any other crime? or that any other crime was legislated into murder? Many crimes of different grades may coexist, and culminate in one offence. It is no sign of undue severity to prosecute the offender for one less than the highest. The same course of crime may violate many of the duties the loyal citizen owes to his country. To pass laws declaring the penalty for each and all of these crimes does not transcend the true scope of the criminal legislation of Congress, where an offender has brought upon his country the horrors of civil war by destroying the lives of those who have given him no cause of offence, by violating the rights of the living and the dead, by heaping upon his guilty act the criminality of a thousand assassins and murderers, and by striking at the root of the peace and happiness of a great nation; it does not seem unduly severe to take from him his property and his life. The constitution does not protect him from the penalty of death; and it cannot be so interpreted as to protect him against confiscation of his real estate.

TREASON AND CONFISCATION LAWS IN 1862. THEIR PRACTICAL OPERATION.

To understand the practical operation of the statutes now in force for the punishment of treason and rebellion, and for the seizure and confiscation of rebel property, it is necessary to observe the effect of other statutes which regulate the modes of procedure in the United States courts. Section 1 of the act of 1862, which, as well as the act of 1790, prescribes the punishment of death for treason; section 2, which imposes fines and penalties; section 3, which adds disqualification for office; and, in fact, all the penal sections of this statute, — entitle the accused to a judicial trial. Before he can be made liable to suffer any penalty, he must have been "pronounced guilty of the offence charged," and he must have suffered "judgment and sentence on conviction." The accused cannot by law be subjected to a trial unless he has previously been indicted by a grand jury. He cannot be adjudged guilty unless upon a verdict of a petty jury, impanelled according to law, and by courts having jurisdiction of the person and of the alleged offence. A brief examination of the statutes regulating such proceedings will show that treason and confiscation laws will not be likely to prove effectual, unless they shall be amended, or unless other statutes shall be so modified as to adapt them to the present condition of the country.

LEGAL RIGHTS OF PERSONS ACCUSED OF TREASON.

All judicial convictions must be in accordance with the laws establishing the judiciary and regulating its proceedings. Whenever a person accused of crime is held by the government, not as a belligerent or prisoner of war, but merely as a citizen of the United States, then he is amenable to, and must be tried under and by virtue of, standing laws; and all rights guaranteed to other citizens in his condition must be conceded to him.

WILL SECESSIONISTS INDICT AND CONVICT EACH OTHER?

No person can lawfully be compelled to appear and answer to a charge for committing capital or otherwise infamous crimes, except those arising in the army and navy, when in actual service, in time of war or public danger, until he has been indicted by a grand jury.* That grand jury is summoned by the marshal from persons in the district where the crime was committed.

By the statute of September 24, 1789, section 29, "in all cases punishable with death, the trial shall be had in the county where the offence was committed; or where that cannot be done without great inconvenience, twelve petit jurors at least shall be summoned from thence." It has indeed been decided that the judges are not obliged to try these cases in the county where the crime was committed, but they are bound to try them within the district in which they were perpetrated.†

HOW THE JURIES ARE SELECTED, AND THEIR POWERS.

The juries are to be designated by lot, or according to the mode of forming juries practised in 1789, so far as practicable: the qualifications of jurors must be the same as those required by the laws of the State where

* Constitutional Amendment V.

† *United States* v. *Wilson*, Baldw. 117; *United States* v. *Cornell*, 2 Mass. 95–98; *United States* v. *The Insurgents*, 3 Dall. 518.

the trial is held, in order to qualify them to serve in the highest court of that State; and jurors shall be returned from such parts of the district, from time to time, as the court shall direct, so as to be most favorable to an impartial trial. And if so many jurors are challenged as to prevent the formation of a full jury, for want of numbers, the panel shall be completed from the bystanders.

STATE RIGHTS AND SECESSION DOCTRINES IN THE JURY ROOM.

The jury are by law judges of the law and the fact, according to the opinion of many eminent lawyers and judges. Whether this be so or not, their verdict, being upon the law and the fact, in a criminal case, they become in effect judges of law and fact. Suppose that the judge presiding at the trial is honest and loyal, and that the jury is composed of men who believe that loyalty to the State is paramount to loyalty to the United States; or that the States had, and have, a lawful right to secede from the Union. Whatever the opinions of the judge presiding in the United States court might be on these questions, he would have no power to root out from the jury their honest belief, that obedience to the laws of their own seceding State is not, and cannot be, treason. The first step towards securing a verdict would be to destroy the belief of the jury in these doctrines of State rights, paramount State sovereignty, and the right of secession. To decide the issue, according to the conscientious judgment of the jurymen upon the facts and the law, would require them to find a verdict against the United States.

SYMPATHY.

But this is not the only difficulty in the operation of this statute. The grand jurors and the petit jury are to be drawn from those who are neighbors, and possibly friends, of the traitors. The accused has the further advantage of knowing, before the time of trial, the names of all the jurors, and of all the witnesses to be produced against him; he has the benefit of counsel, and the process of the United States to compel the attendance of witnesses in his behalf.* How improbable is it that any jury of twelve men will be found to take away the lives or estates of their associates, when some of the jurymen themselves, or their friends and relatives or debtors, are involved in the same offence! Could any judge reasonably expect a jury of horse thieves to convict one of their own number, when either of the jurymen might be the next man required to take his turn in the criminal box? Under the present state of the law, it is not probable that there will ever be a conviction, even if laws against treason, and those which confiscate property, were not unpopular and odious in a community against whom they are enacted. When an association of traitors and conspirators can be found to convict each other, then these statutes will punish treason, but not sooner.

LAWS ARE MOST EFFECTIVE WHICH REQUIRE NO REBEL TO ADMINISTER THEM.

Those sections of the act of 1862, empowering government to seize rebel property, real, personal, and mixed, and to apply it to the use of the army, to secure the condemnation and sale of seized property, so as to

* Statute of April 30, 1790, Sect. 29.

make it available, and to authorize proceedings *in rem*, conformably to proceedings in admiralty or revenue cases, are of a different and far more effective character. Those clauses in the act which allow of the employment in the service of the United States of colored persons, so far as they may be serviceable, and the freeing of the slaves of rebels, whether captured, seized, fugitive, abandoned, or found within the lines of the army, may be of practical efficacy, because these measures do not require the aid of any secession jury to carry them into effect.

STATUTES OF LIMITATION WILL PROTECT TRAITORS.

The statutes limiting the time during which rebels and traitors shall be liable to indictment ought also to be considered. By the act of 1790, no person can be punished unless indicted for treason within three years after the treason was committed, if punishable capitally; nor unless indicted within two years from the time of committing any offence punishable with fine or forfeiture. Thus, by the provisions of these laws, if the war should last two years, or if it should require two or three years after the war shall have been ended to reëstablish regular proceedings in courts, all the criminals in the seceded States will escape by the operation of the statutes of limitations. It is true, that if traitors flee from justice these limitations will not protect them; but this exception will apply to few individuals, and those who flee will not be likely to be caught. Unless these statutes are modified, those who have caused and maintained the rebellion will escape from punishment.*

* Several bills have been introduced during the present session of Congress (1863–64) to remedy the difficulties here pointed out.

CHAPTER VIII.

INTERFERENCE OF GOVERNMENT WITH THE DOMESTIC AFFAIRS OF THE STATES.

PARTY PLATFORMS CANNOT ALTER THE CONSTITUTION.

POLITICAL parties, in times of peace, have often declared that they do not intend to interfere with slavery in the States. President Buchanan denied that government had any power to coerce the seceded States into submission to the laws of the country. When President Lincoln called into service the army and navy, he announced that it was not his purpose to interfere with the rights of loyal citizens, nor with their domestic affairs. Those who have involved this country in bloody war, all sympathizers in their treason, and others who oppose the present administration, unite in denying the right of the President or of Congress to interfere with slavery, even if such interference is the only means by which the Union can be saved from destruction. No constitutional power can be obliterated by any denial or abandonment thereof, by individuals, by political parties, or by Congress.

The war power of the President to emancipate enemy's slaves has been the subject of a preceding chapter. Congress has power to pass laws necessary and proper to provide for the defence of the country in time of war, by appropriating private property to public use, with just compensation therefor, as shown in Chapter I.; also laws enforcing emancipation, confiscation, and all other belligerent rights, as shown in Chapter II.; and it is the sole judge as to what legislation, to effect these objects, the public welfare and defence require;

it may enact laws abolishing slavery, whenever slavery, ceasing to be *merely* a private and domestic relation, becomes a matter of *national* concern, and the public welfare and defence cannot be provided for and secured without interfering with slaves. Laws passed for that purpose, in good faith, against belligerent subjects, not being within any express prohibition of the constitution, cannot lawfully be declared void by any department of government. Reasons and authority for these propositions have been stated in previous chapters.

DOMESTIC INSTITUTIONS.

Among the errors relating to slavery which have found their way into the public mind, — errors traceable directly to a class of politicians who are now in open rebellion, — the most important is, that *Congress has no right to interfere in any way with slavery.* Their assumption is, that the States in which slaves are held are alone competent to pass any law relating to an institution which belongs exclusively to the domestic affairs of the States, and in which Congress has no right to interfere in any way whatever.

From a preceding chapter, (see page 17,) it will be seen, that if slaves are *property*, property can be interfered with under the constitution; if slavery is a *domestic* institution, as *Mormonism* or *apprenticeship* is, each of them can lawfully be interfered with and annulled. But slavery has a double aspect. So long as it remains in truth "*domestic*," that is to say, according to Webster's Dictionary, "*pertaining to house or home*," so long government cannot be affected by it, and have no ground for interfering with it; when, on the contrary, it no longer pertains only to house and home, but enters into vital questions of war, aid and comfort to public enemies, or any of the national interests involved in a gigantic rebellion; when slavery, rising above its comparative insignificance as a household affair, becomes a vast, an overwhelming power which is used by traitors to overthrow the government, and may be used by government to overthrow traitors, it then ceases to be *merely* domestic; it becomes a *belligerent power*, acting against the "public welfare and common defence." No institution continues to be simply "domestic" after it has become the effective means of aiding and supporting a public enemy.

When an "institution" compels three millions of subjects to become belligerent traitors, because they are slaves of disloyal masters, slavery becomes an affair which is of the utmost public and national concern. But the constitution *not only empowers*, but, under certain contingencies, *requires* slavery in the States to be interfered with. No one who will refer to the sections of that instrument here cited, will probably venture to deny the power of Congress, in one mode or another, to *interfere* for or against the institution of slavery.

CONGRESS MAY PASS LAWS INTERFERING FOR THE PRESERVATION AND PROTECTION OF SLAVERY IN THE STATES.

Art. IV. Sect. 2, required that fugitive slaves should be *delivered up*, and the fugitive slave laws were passed to carry this clause into effect.

Art. I. Sect. 9, required that the foreign slave trade should not be interfered with prior to 1808, but allowed an importation tax to be levied on each slave, not exceeding ten dollars per head.

Art. V. provided that no amendment of the constitution should be made, prior to 1808, affecting the preceding clause.

Art. I. Sect. 2 provides that three fifths of all slaves shall be included in representative numbers.

CONGRESS MAY INTERFERE AGAINST SLAVERY IN THE STATES.

Art. I. Sect. 8. Congress has power to regulate commerce with foreign nations, and among the several States, and with the Indian tribes. Under this clause Congress can in effect prohibit the *inter-state slave trade*, and so pass laws diminishing or destroying the value of slaves in the border States, and practically *abolish slavery* in those States.

CONGRESS MAY INTERFERE WITH SLAVERY BY CALLING UPON THE SLAVES, AS SUBJECTS, TO ENTER MILITARY SERVICE.

Art. I. Sect. 8. Congress has the power to declare war and make rules for the government of land and naval forces, and under this power to decide who shall *constitute the militia of the United States*, and to enrol and compel into the service of the United States *all the slaves*, as well as their masters, and thus to interfere with slavery in the States.

CONGRESS MAY INTERFERE WITH SLAVERY IN THE STATES BY CUTTING OFF THE SUPPLY OF SLAVES TO SUCH STATES.

The law now prohibiting the importation of slaves, and making slave trading piracy, is an interference with slavery, by preventing their introduction into the slave States. So also is the treaty with England to suppress the slave trade, and to keep an armed naval force on the coast of Africa.

In case of servile insurrection against the laws and

authority of the United States, the government *are bound to interfere with slavery*, as much as in an insurrection of their masters, which may also require a similar interference. The President, with the advice and consent of the Senate, has the power to make treaties; and, under the treaty-making power, slavery can be and has been interfered with. In the last war with Great Britain, a treaty was made to evacuate all the forts and places in the United States without carrying away any of the slaves who had gone over to them in the States. Congress then interfered to *sustain* the institution of slavery, for it was only by *sustaining* slavery that this government could claim indemnity for slaves as *property*. The *treaty-making power* may abolish slavery in the whole country, as, by Art. VI., the constitution, the laws, and all treaties made or which shall be made under the authority of the United States, shall be the supreme law of the land. A clause in any treaty abolishing slavery would, *ipso facto*, become the supreme law of the land, and there is no power whatever that could interfere with or prevent its operation. By the treaty-making power, any part of the country burdened with slavery, and wrested from us by conquest, could be ceded to a foreign nation who do not tolerate slavery, and without claim of indemnity. The principle is well established that "the release of a territory from the dominion and sovereignty of the country, if that cession be the result of coercion or conquest, does not impose any obligation upon the government to indemnify those who may suffer loss of property by the cession."*

* 1 Kent Com. 178.

The State of New York had granted to her own citizens many titles to real estate lying in that part of her territory now called Vermont. Vermont separated itself from New York, and declared itself an independent State. It maintained its claims to such an extent, that New York, by act of July 14, 1789, was enforced to empower commissioners to assent to its independence; but refused to compensate persons claiming lands under grant from New York, though they were deprived of them by Vermont. The ground taken by the legislature was, that the government was not required to assume the burden of losses produced by conquest or by the violent dismemberment of the State.

Supposing England and France should, by armed intervention, compel the dismemberment of the United States, and the cession of the slave States to them as conquered territory; and that the laws of the conquerors allowed no slaveholding. Could any of the citizens of slave States, who might reside in the free States, having remained loyal, but having lost their slaves, make just legal claim for indemnity upon the government? Certainly not.

Other instances may be cited in which Congress has the power and duty of interference in the local and domestic concerns of States, other than those relating to slavery.* Chief Justice Taney says, —

"Moreover, the constitution of the United States, as far as it has provided for an emergency of this kind, and authorized the general government to interfere in the domestic concerns of a State, has treated the subject as political in its nature, and placed the power in the hands of that department. Art. IV. Sect. 4 of the constitution of the United States provides that the United States shall guarantee to

* *Luther* v. *Borden*, 7 How. 42.

every State in the Union a republican form of government, and shall protect each of them against invasion, and, on the application of the legislature, or of the executive when the legislature cannot be convened, against *domestic violence.* Under this article of the constitution it rests with Congress to decide what government is the established one in a State. For, as the United States guarantees to each State a republican government, Congress must necessarily decide what government is established, before it can determine whether it is republican or not. And when senators and representatives of a State are admitted into the councils of the Union, the authority of the government under which they are appointed, as well as its republican character, is recognized by the proper constitutional authority, and its decision is binding upon every other department of the government, and could not be questioned in a judicial tribunal. So, too, as relates to the clause in the above-mentioned article of the constitution, providing for cases of *domestic* violence. It rested with Congress, too, to determine the means proper to be adopted to fulfil this guaranty."

Suppose, then, that for the purpose of securing "*domestic tranquillity*" and to suppress *domestic violence,* Congress should determine that emancipation of the slaves was a necessary and proper means, it would be the duty of Congress to adopt those means, and thus to interfere with slavery.* If a civil war should arise in a single State between the citizens thereof, it is the duty of Congress to cause *immediate interference* in the domestic and local affairs of that State, and to put an end to the war; and this interference may be by force of arms and by force of laws; and the fact that the cause of quarrel is domestic and private, whether it be in relation to a proposed change in the form of government, as in Dorr's rebellion,* or a rebellion growing out of any other domestic matter, the constitution authorizes and requires interference by the general government. Hence it is obvious that if slaves be considered prop-

* See *Luther* v. *Borden,* 7 How.

erty, and if the regulation of slavery in the States be deemed in some aspects one of the domestic affairs of the States where it is tolerated, yet these facts constitute no reason why such property may not be interfered with, and slavery dealt with by government according to the emergencies of the time, whenever slavery assumes a new aspect, and rises from its private and domestic character to become a matter of national concern, and imperils the safety and preservation of the whole country. We are not to take our opinions as to the extent or limit of the powers contained in the constitution from partisans, or political parties, nor even from the dicta of political judges. We should examine that instrument in the light of history and of reason; but when the language is plain and clear, we need no historical researches to enable us to comprehend its meaning. When the interpretation depends upon technical law, then the contemporary law writers must be consulted. The question as to the meaning of the constitution depends upon what the people, the plain people who adopted it, intended and meant at the time of its adoption.

AUTHORITATIVE CONSTRUCTION OF THE MEANING OF THE CONSTITUTION.

The conclusive authority on its interpretation is the document itself. When questions have arisen under that instrument, upon which the Supreme Court have decided, and one which they had a right to decide, their opinion is, for the time being, the supreme authority, and remains so until their views are changed and new ones announced; and as often as the Supreme Court change their judgments, so often the authoritative interpretation of the constitution changes. The Supreme Court have the right to alter their opinions every time the same question is decided by them; and as new judges must take the place of those whose offices are vacated by death, resignation, or impeachment, it is not unlikely that opinions of the majority of the court may, upon constitutional as well as upon other questions, be sometimes on one side and sometimes on the other.

Upon political discussions, such as were involved in the Dred Scott case, the judges are usually at variance with each other; and the view of the majority will prevail until the majority is shifted. The judges are not legally bound to adhere to their own opinions, although litigants in their courts are. Whenever the majority of the court has reason to overrule a former decision, they not only have the right, but it is their duty, to do so.

The opinions of the framers of the constitution are not authority, but are resorted to for a more perfect understanding of the meaning they intended to convey by the words they used; but after all, the words should speak for themselves; for it was the language in which that instrument was worded that was before the people for discussion and adoption. We must therefore go back to that original source of our supreme law, and regard as of no considerable authority the platforms of political parties who have attempted to import into the constitution powers not authorized by fair interpretation of its meaning, or to deny the existence of those powers which are essential to the perpetuity of the government.

A political party may well waive a legal constitutional right, as matter of equity, comity, or public policy; and this waiver may take the form of a denial of the existence of the power thus waived. In this manner Mr. Douglas not merely waived, but denied, the power of Congress to interfere with slavery in the territories; and in the same way members of the Republican party have disclaimed the right, in time of peace, to interfere with slavery in the States; but such disclaimers, made for reasons of state policy, are not to be regarded as enlarging or diminishing the rights or duties devolved on the departments of government, by a fair and liberal interpretation of all the provisions of the constitution.

Rising above the political platforms, the claims and disclaimers of Federalists, Democrats, Whigs, Republicans, and all other parties, and looking upon the constitution as designed to give the government made by the people, for the people, the powers necessary to its own preservation, and to the enforcement of its laws, it is not possible justly to deny the right of government to interfere with slavery, Mormonism, or any other institution, condition, or social status into which the subjects of the United States can enter, whenever such interference becomes essential as a means of "public welfare or common defence in time of war." *

* In several preceding chapters other branches of this subject have been discussed.

APPENDIX.

Many of the leading doctrines contained in the foregoing work have received, since the publication of the fourth edition, the sanction of the Supreme Court of the United States, of whose authoritative and final decision in the prize cases, argued in the spring of 1863, the following is the substance: —

In the Supreme Court of the United States. — Claimant of schooners *Brilliant*, *Crenshaw*, barque *Hiawatha* and others, appellants, *vs.* United States.

These causes came up by appeal from decrees *in prize*, of the Circuit Courts for the Southern District of New York, and the District of Massachusetts, affirming respectively the sentences of condemnation passed upon the vessels and cargoes by the District Courts for said districts. The following opinion is confined to the general questions of law which were raised by *all* the cases. It does not discuss the *special facts* and circumstances of the respective cases.

March 9th, 1863. Opinion of the Court by Grier, J.

There are certain propositions of law which must necessarily affect the ultimate decision of these cases and many others, which it will be proper to discuss and decide before we notice the special facts peculiar to each. They are, —

First. Had the President a right to institute a blockade of ports in possession of persons in armed rebellion against the government, on the principles of international law, as known and acknowledged among civilized States?

Second. Was the property of persons domiciled or residing within those States a proper subject of capture on the sea as "*enemies' property*"?

I. Neutrals have a right to challenge the existence of a blockade *de facto*, and also the authority of the party exercising the right to institute it. They have a right to enter the ports of a friendly nation for the purposes of trade and commerce, but are bound to recognize the rights of a belligerent engaged in actual war, to use this mode of coercion for the purpose of subduing the enemy.

That a blockade *de facto* actually existed and was formally declared and notified by the President on the 27th and 30th of April, 1861, is an admitted fact in these cases. That the President, as the executive chief of the government, and commander-in-chief of the army and navy, was the proper person to make such notification, has not been, and cannot be, disputed.

The right of prize and capture has its origin in the *jus belli*, and is governed and adjudged under the law of nations. To legitimate the capture of a neutral vessel, or property on the high seas, a war must exist *de facto*, and the neutral must have a knowledge or notice of the intention of one of the parties belligerent to use this mode of coercion against a port, city, or territory in possession of the other.

Let us inquire whether, at the time this blockade was instituted, a state of *war* existed which would justify a resort to these means of subduing the hostile force.

War has been well defined to be "*that state in which a nation prosecutes its right by force.*" The parties belligerent in a public war are independent nations. But it is not necessary to constitute war, that both parties should be acknowledged as independent nations or sovereign States. A war may exist where one of the belligerents claims sovereign rights as against the other.

Insurrection against a government may or may not culminate in an organized rebellion; but a civil war always begins by insurrection against the lawful authority of the government. A civil war is never solemnly declared; it becomes such by its accidents — the number, power, and organization of the persons who originate and carry it on. When the party in rebellion occupies and holds in a hostile manner a certain portion of territory, have declared their independence, have cast off their allegiance, have organized armies, have commenced hostilities against their former sovereign, the world acknowledges them as belligerents, and the contest a *war*. *They* claim to be in arms to establish their liberty and independence, in order to become a sovereign State, while the sovereign party treats them as insurgents and rebels who owe allegiance, and who should be punished with death for their treason.

The laws of war, as established among nations, have their foundation in reason, and all tend to mitigate the cruelties and misery produced by the scourge of war. Hence the parties to a civil war usually concede to each other belligerent rights. They exchange prisoners, and adopt the other courtesies and rules common to public or national wars.

"A civil war," says Vattel, "breaks the bands of society and government, or, at least, suspends their force and effect; it produces in the nation two independent parties, who consider each other as enemies, and acknowledge no common judge. Those two parties, therefore, must necessarily be considered as constituting, at least for a time, two separate bodies — two distinct societies. Having no common superior to judge between them, they stand in precisely the same predicament as two nations who engage in a contest and have recourse to arms. This being the case, it is very evident that the common laws of war, those maxims of humanity, moderation, and honor, ought to be observed by both parties in every civil war. Should the sovereign conceive that he has a right to hang up his prisoners as rebels, the opposite party will make reprisals, &c., &c.: the war will be cruel, horrible, and every day more destructive to the nation."

As a civil war is never publicly proclaimed, *eo nomine*, against insurgents, its actual existence is a fact in our domestic history which the Court is bound to notice and to know.

The true test of its existence, as found in the writings of the sages of the common law, may be thus summarily stated: "When the regular course of justice is interrupted by revolt, rebellion, or insurrection, so that the courts of justice cannot be kept open, *civil war exists*, and hostilities may be prosecuted on the same footing as if those opposing the government were foreign enemies invading the land." By the constitution, Congress alone has the power to declare a national or foreign war. It cannot declare war against a State, or any number of States, by virtue of any clause in the constitution. The constitution confers on the President the whole executive power. He is bound to take care that the laws be faithfully executed. He is Commander-in-chief of the Army and Navy of the United States, and of the militia of the several States when called into the actual service of the United States. He has no power to initiate or declare a war, either against a foreign nation or a domestic State. But by the acts of Congress of February 28th, 1795, and 3d of March, 1807, he is authorized to call out the militia, and use the military and naval forces of the United States in case of invasion by foreign nations, and to suppress insurrection against the government of a State or of the United States.

If a war be made by invasion of a foreign nation, the President is not only authorized but bound to resist force by force. He does not initiate the war, but is bound to accept the challenge without waiting for any special legislative authority. And whether the hostile party be a foreign invader, or States organized in rebellion, it is none the less *a war*, although the declaration of it be "*unilateral*." Lord Stowell (1 Dodson, 247) observes, "It is not the less a war on *that account*, for war may exist without a declaration on either side. It is so laid down by the best writers on the law of nations. A declaration of war by one country only, is not a mere challenge, to be accepted or refused at pleasure by the other."

This greatest of civil wars was not gradually developed by popular commotion, tumultuous assemblies, or local unorganized insurrections. However long may have been its previous conception, it nevertheless sprung forth suddenly from the parent brain, a Minerva in the full panoply of war. The President was bound to meet it in the shape it presented itself, without waiting for Congress to baptize it with a name; and no name given to it by him or them could change the fact.

It is not the less a civil war, with belligerent parties in hostile array, because it may be called an "insurrection" by one side, and the insurgents be considered as rebels or traitors. It is not necessary that the independence of the revolted province or State be acknowledged, in order to constitute it a party belligerent in a war, according to the law of nations. Foreign nations acknowledge it as war by a declaration of neutrality. The condition of neutrality cannot exist unless there be two belligerent parties. In the case of *Santissima Trinidad*, 7 Wheaton, 337, this Court says, "The government of the United States has recognized the existence of a civil war between Spain and her colonies, and has avowed her determination to remain neutral between the parties. Each party is; therefore, deemed by us a belligerent nation, having, so far as concerns us, the sovereign rights of war." See also 3 Binn., 252.

As soon as the news of the attack on Fort Sumter, and the organization of a government by the seceding States, assuming to act as belligerents, could become known in Europe, to wit, on the 13th of May, 1861, the Queen of England issued her proclamation of neutrality, "recognizing hostilities as existing between the government of the United States of America and *certain States* styling themselves the Confederate States of America." This was immediately followed by similar declarations, or silent acquiescence, by other nations.

After such an official recognition by the sovereign, a citizen of a foreign State is estopped to deny the existence of a war, with all its consequences as regards neutrals. They cannot ask a Court to affect a technical ignorance of the existence of a war which all the world acknowledges to be the greatest civil war known in the history of the human race, and thus cripple the arm of the government and paralyze its powers by subtle definitions and ingenious sophisms.

The law of nations is also called the law of nature; it is founded on the common consent as well as the common sense of the world. It contains no such anomalous doctrine as that which this Court are now, for the first time, desired to pronounce, to wit: —

That insurgents who have risen in rebellion against their sovereign, expelled her Courts, established a revolutionary government, organized armies, and commenced hostilities, are not *enemies* because they are *traitors;* and a war levied on the government by traitors, in order to dismember and destroy it, is not *a war*, because it is an "insurrection."

Whether the President, in fulfilling his duties as commander-in-chief, in suppressing an insurrection, has met with such armed hostile resistance, and a civil war of such alarming proportions, as will compel him to accord to them the character of belligerents, is a question to be decided *by him;* and this Court must be governed by the decisions and acts of the political department of the government to which this power was intrusted. "He must determine what degree of force the crisis demands." The proclamation of blockade is itself official and conclusive evidence to the Court that a state of war existed which demanded and authorized a recourse to such a measure, under the circumstances, peculiar to the case. The correspondence of Lord Lyons with the Secretary of State admits the fact and concludes the question.

If it were necessary to the technical existence of a war that it should have a legislative sanction, we find it in almost every act passed at the extraordinary session of the Legislature of 1861, which was wholly employed in passing laws to enable the government to prosecute the war with vigor and efficiency. And finally, in 1861, we find Congress, "*ex majore cautela*," passing an act, approving, legalizing, and making valid all the acts, proclamations, and orders of the President, &c., "as if they had been *issued and done under the previous express authority* and direction of the Congress of the United States."

Without admitting that such an act was necessary under the circumstances, it is plain, if the President had in any manner assumed powers which it was necessary should have the authority or sanction of Congress, that the well-known principle of law, "*Omnis ratihabitio retrotrahitur et mandato equiparatur*," this ratification has operated to perfectly cure the defect.

In the case of Brown *vs.* United States, 8 Cranch, 131, 132, 133, Mr. Justice Story treats of this subject, and cites numerous authorities, to which we may refer, to prove this position, and concludes, "I am perfectly satisfied that no subject can commence hostilities or capture property of an enemy, when the sovereign has prohibited it. But suppose he did. I would ask if the sovereign may not ratify his proceedings; and then, by a retroactive operation, give validity to them."

Although Mr. Justice Story dissented from the majority of the Court on the whole case, the doctrine stated by him on this point is correct and fully substantiated by authority.

The objection made to this act of ratification, that it is *ex post facto*, and therefore unconstitutional and void, might possibly have some weight on the trial of an indictment in a criminal Court. But precedents from that source cannot be received as authoritative in a tribunal administering public and international law.

On this first question, therefore, we are of opinion that the President had a right *jure belli* to institute a blockade of ports in possession of the States in rebellion, which neutrals are bound to regard.

II. We come now to the consideration of the second question. What is included in the term "*enemies' property*"?

Is the property of all persons residing within the territory of the States now in rebellion, captured on the high seas, to be treated as "enemies' property," whether the owner be in arms against the government or not?

The right of one belligerent not only to coerce the other by direct force, but also to cripple his resources by the seizure or destruction of his property, is a necessary result of a state of war.

Money and wealth, the products of agriculture and commerce, are said to be the sinews of war, and as necessary in its conduct as numbers and physical force. Hence it is, that the laws of war recognize the right of a belligerent to cut these sinews of the power of the enemy, by capturing his property on the high seas.

The appellants contend that the term *enemies* is properly applicable to those only who are subjects or citizens of a foreign State at war with our own. They quote from the pages of the Common Law, which say, "that persons who wage war against the king may be of two kinds, subjects or citizens. The former are not proper enemies, but rebels and traitors; the latter are those that come properly under the name of enemies."

They insist, moreover, that the President himself, in his proclamation, admits that great numbers of the persons residing within the territories in possession of the insurgent government, are loyal in their feelings, and forced by compulsion and the violence of the rebellious and revolutionary party, and its "*de facto* government," to submit to their laws and assist in their scheme of revolution; that the acts of the usurping government cannot legally sever the bond of their allegiance; they have, therefore, a correlative right to claim the protection of the government for their persons and property, and to be treated as loyal citizens, till legally convicted of having renounced their allegiance, and made *war* against the government by treasonably resisting its laws.

They contend also that insurrection is the act of individuals, and not of a government or sovereignty; that the individuals engaged are subjects of law; that confiscation of their property can be effected only under municipal law; that, by the law of the land, such confiscation cannot take place without the conviction of the owner of some offence; and finally, that the secession ordinances are nullities, and ineffectual to release any citizen from his allegiance to the national government; consequently, the constitution and laws of the United States are still operative over persons in all the States for punishment as well as protection.

This argument rests on the assumption of two propositions, each of which is without foundation on the established law of nations.

It assumes that where a civil war exists, the party belligerent claiming to be sovereign cannot, for some unknown reason, exercise the rights of belligerents, although the revolutionary party may. Being sovereign, he can exercise only sovereign rights over the other party. The insurgent may be killed on the battle-field, or by the executioner; his property on land may be confiscated under the municipal law; but the commerce on the ocean, which supplies the rebels with means to support the war, cannot be made the subject of capture under the laws of war, because it is "*unconstitutional*"!!! Now, it is a proposition never doubted, that the belligerent party who claims to be sovereign, may exercise both belligerent and sovereign rights. (See 4 Cranch, 272.) Treating the other party as a belligerent, and using only the milder modes of coercion which the law of nations has introduced to mitigate the rigors of war, cannot be a subject of complaint by the party to whom it is accorded as a grace or granted as a necessity.

We have shown that a civil war, such as that now waged between the Northern and Southern States, is properly conducted, according to the humane regulations of public law, as regards capture on the ocean.

Under the very peculiar constitution of this government, although the citizens owe supreme allegiance to the Federal government, they owe also a qualified allegiance to the State in which they are domiciled; their persons and property are subject to its laws.

Hence, in organizing this rebellion, they have *acted as States*, claiming to be sovereign over all persons and property within their respective limits, and asserting a right to absolve their citizens from their allegiance to the

Federal government. Several of these States have combined to form a new confederacy, claiming to be acknowledged by the world as a sovereign State. Their right to do so is now being decided by wager of battle. The ports and territory of each of these States are held in hostility to the general government. It is no loose, unorganized insurrection, having no defined boundary or possession. It has a boundary, marked by lines of bayonets, and which can be crossed only by force. South of this line is enemy's territory, because it is claimed and held in possession by an organized, hostile, and belligerent power.

All persons residing within this territory, whose property may be used to increase the revenues of the hostile power, are in this contest liable to be treated as enemies, though not foreigners. They have cast off their allegiance, and made war on their government, and are none the less enemies because they are traitors.

But in defining the meaning of the term "enemies' property," we will be led into error if we refer to Fleta and Lord Coke for their definition of the word "enemy." It is a technical phrase peculiar to prize courts, and depends upon principles of public as distinguished from the common law.

Whether property be liable to capture as "enemies' property," does not in any manner depend on the personal allegiance of the owner. "It is the illegal traffic that stamps it as 'enemies' property.' It is of no consequence whether it belongs to an ally or a citizen." 8 Cranch, 384. "The owner *pro hac vice* is an enemy." 3 Wash. C. C. R. 183.

The produce of the soil of the hostile territory, as well as other property engaged in the commerce of the hostile power, as the source of its wealth and strength, is always regarded as legitimate prize, without regard to the domicile of the owner, and much more so if he reside and trade within its territory. (See Upton, chap. 3d, et cas. cit.)

The foregoing opinion of the highest judicial tribunal of the United States was delivered by Mr. Justice Grier, and was concurred in by Justices Wayne, Swayne, Miller, and Davis. An opinion was delivered by Mr. Justice Nelson, and concurred in by Chief Justice Taney, and Justices Clifford and Catron, who differed from the majority of the Court upon the question, "whether our *civil war* began *before July* 13, 1861?" the majority holding the affirmative, and the minority the negative.

Both opinions sanction many of the doctrines of international, constitutional, and belligerent law set forth in the treatise on the "*War Powers of the President, and the Legislative Power of Congress.*"

Mr. Justice NELSON, dissenting. The property in this case, vessel and cargo, was seized by a government vessel on the 20th of May, 1861, in Hampton Roads, for an alleged violation of the blockade of the ports of the State of Virginia. The Hiawatha was a British vessel, and the cargo belonged to British subjects. The vessel had entered the James River before the blockade, on her way to City Point, upwards of one hundred miles from the mouth, where she took in her cargo. She finished loading on the 15th of May, but was delayed from departing on her outward voyage till the 17th for want of a tug to tow her down the river. She arrived at Hampton Roads on the 20th, where, the blockade in the mean time having been established, she was met by one of the ships, and the boarding officer indorsed on her register, "Ordered not to enter any port in Virginia, or south of it." This occurred some three miles above the place where the flag ship was stationed, and the boarding officer directed the master to heave his ship to when he came abreast of the flag-ship, which was done, when she was taken in charge as prize.

On the 30th of April, flag-officer Pendergrast, U. S. ship Cumberland, off Fortress Monroe, in Hampton Roads, gave the following notice: "All vessels passing the capes of Virginia, coming from a distance and ignorant of the proclamation (the proclamation of the President of the 27th of April that a blockade would be established), will be warned off; and those passing Fortress Monroe will be required to anchor under the guns of the fort and subject themselves to an examination."

The Hiawatha, while engaged in putting on board her cargo at City Point, became the subject of correspondence between the British Minister and the Secretary of State, under date of the 8th and 9th of May, which drew from the Secretary of the Navy a letter of the 9th, in which, after referring to the above notice of the flag officer Pendergrast, and stating that it had been sent to the Baltimore and Norfolk papers, and by one or more published, advised the Minister that fifteen days had been fixed as a limit for neutrals to leave the ports after an actual blockade had commenced, with or without cargo. The inquiry of the British Minister had referred not only to the time that a vessel would be allowed to depart, but whether it might be ladened within the time. This vessel, according to the advice of the Secretary, would be entitled to the whole of the 15th of May to leave City Point, her port of lading. As we have seen, her cargo was on board within the time, but the vessel was delayed in her departure for want of a tug to tow her down the river.

We think it very clear, upon all the evidence, that there was no intention on the part of the master to break the blockade; that the seizure under the circumstances was not warranted, and upon the merits, that the ship and cargo should have been restored.

Another ground of objection to this seizure is, that the vessel was entitled to a warning indorsed on her papers by an officer of the blockading force, according to the terms of the proclamation of the President; and that she was not liable to capture except for the second attempt to leave the port.

The proclamation, after certain recitals, not material in this branch of the case, provides as follows: the President has "deemed it advisable to set on foot a blockade of the ports within the States aforesaid (the States referred to in the recitals), in pursuance of the laws of the United States and of the law of nations, in such case made and provided." "If, therefore, with a view to violate such blockade, a vessel shall approach, or shall attempt to leave either of said ports, she will be duly warned by the commander of one of the blockading vessels, who will indorse on her register the fact and date of such warning, and if the same vessel shall again attempt to enter or leave the blockaded port, she will be captured and sent to the nearest convenient port for such proceedings against her and her cargo, as prize, as may be deemed advisable."

The proclamation of the President of the 27th of April extended that of the 19th to the States of Virginia and North Carolina.

It will be observed that this warning applies to vessels attempting to enter or leave the port, and is therefore applicable to the Hiawatha.

We must confess that we have not heard any satisfactory answer to the objection founded upon the terms of this proclamation.

It has been said that the proclamation, among other grounds, as stated on its face, is founded on the "law of nations," and hence draws after it the law of blockade as found in that code, and that a warning is dispensed with in all cases where the vessel is chargeable with previous notice or knowledge that the port is blockaded. But the obvious answer to the suggestion is, that there is no necessary connection between the authority upon which the proclamation is issued and the terms prescribed as the condition of its penalties or enforcement, and, besides, if founded upon the law of nations, surely it was competent for the President to mitigate the rigors of that code, and apply to neutrals the more lenient and friendly principles of international law. We do not doubt but that considerations of this character influenced the President in prescribing these favorable terms in respect to neutrals; for, in his message a few months later to Congress (4th July), he observes, "a proclamation was issued for closing the ports of the insurrectionary districts" (not by blockade, but) "by proceedings *in the nature of a blockade.*"

This view of the proclamation seems to have been entertained by the Secretary of the Navy, under whose orders it was carried into execution. In his report to the President, 4th July, he observes, after referring to the necessity of interdicting commerce at those ports where the government were not permitted to collect the revenue, that "in the performance of this domestic municipal duty the property and interests of foreigners became, to some extent, involved in our home questions, and with a view of extending to them every comity that circumstances would justify, the rules of blockade were adopted, and, as far as practicable, made applicable to the cases that occurred under this embargo or non-intercourse of the insurgent States. The commanders, he observes, were directed to permit the vessels of foreigners to depart within fifteen days as in case of actual effective blockade, and their vessels were not to be seized unless they attempted, after having been once warned off, to enter an interdicted port in disregard of such warning."

The question is not a new one in this Court. The British government had notified the United States of the blockade of certain ports in the West Indies, but "not to consider blockades as existing, unless in respect to particular ports which may be actually invested, and, then, not to capture vessels bound to such ports, unless they shall have been previously warned not to enter them."

The question arose upon this blockade in *Mar. In. Co.* vs. *Woods* (6 Cranch, 29).

Chief Justice Marshall, in delivering the opinion of the court, observed, "The words of the order are not satisfied by any previous notice which the vessel may have obtained, otherwise than by her being warned off. This is a technical term which is well understood. It is not satisfied by notice received in any other manner. The effect of this order is, that a vessel cannot be placed in the situation of one having notice of the blockade until she is warned off. It gives her a right to inquire of the blockading squadron, if she shall not receive this warning from one capable of giving it, and, consequently, dispenses with her making that inquiry elsewhere. While this order was in force a neutral vessel might lawfully sail for a blockaded port, knowing it to be blockaded, and being found sailing towards such port, would not constitute an attempt to break the blockade until she should be warned off."

We are of opinion, therefore, that, according to the very terms of the proclamation, neutral ships were entitled to a warning by one of the blockading squadron, and could be lawfully seized only on the second attempt to enter or leave the port.

It is remarkable, also, that both the President and the Secretary, in referring to the blockade, treat the measure, not as a blockade under the law of nations, but as a restraint upon commerce at the interdicted ports under the municipal laws of the government.

Another objection taken to the seizure of this vessel and cargo is, that there was no existing war between the United States and the States in insurrection, within the meaning of the law of nations, which drew after it the consequences of a public or civil war. A contest by force between independent sovereign States is called a public war; and, when duly commenced, by proclamation or otherwise, it entitles both of the belligerent parties to all the rights of war against each other and as respects neutral nations. Chancellor Kent observes, "Though a solemn declaration, or previous notice to the enemy, be now laid aside, it is essential that some formal public act, proceeding directly from the competent source, should announce to the people at home their new relations and duties growing out of a state of war, and which should equally apprise neutral nations of the fact, to enable them to conform their conduct to the rights belonging to the new state of things." "Such an official act operates from its date to legalize all hostile acts, in like manner as a treaty of peace operates from its date to annul them." He further observes, "As a war cannot lawfully be commenced on the part of the United States without an act of Congress, such act is, of course, a formal notice to all the world, and equivalent to the most solemn declaration."

The legal consequences resulting from a state of war between two countries at this day are well understood, and will be found described in every approved work on the subject of international law. The people of the two countries become immediately the enemies of each other — all intercourse, commercial or otherwise, between them unlawful — all contracts existing at the commencement of the war suspended, and all made during its existence utterly void. The insurance of enemies' property, the drawing of bills of exchange or purchase on the enemies' country, the remission of bills or money to it, are illegal and void. Existing partnerships between citizens or subjects, of the two countries are dissolved, and, in fine, interdiction of trade and intercourse, direct or indirect, is absolute and complete by the mere force and effect of war itself. All the property of the people of the two countries on land or sea are subject to capture and confiscation by the adverse party as enemies' property, with certain qualifications as it respects property on land (*Brown* vs. *United States*, 8 Cranch, 110), all treaties between the belligerent parties are annulled. The ports of the respective countries may be blockaded, and letters of marque and reprisal geanted as rights of war, and the law of prizes, as defined by the law of nations, comes into full and complete operation, resulting from maritime captures, *jure belli*. War also effects a change in the mutual relations of all states or countries, not directly, as in the case of the belligerents, but immediately and indirectly, though they take no part in the contest, but remain neutral.

This great and pervading change in the existing condition of a country, and in the relations of all her citizens or subjects, external and internal, from a state of peace, is the immediate effect and result of a state of war: and hence the same code, which has annexed to the existence of a war all these disturbing consequences, has declared that the right of making war belongs exclusively to the supreme or sovereign power of the state.

This power, in all civilized nations, is regulated by the fundamental laws or municipal constitution of the country.

By our Constitution this power is lodged in Congress. Congress shall have power "to declare war, grant letters of marque and reprisal, and make rules concerning captures on land and water."

We have thus far been considering the status of the citizens or subjects of a country at the breaking out of a public war, when recognized or declared by the competent power.

In the case of a rebellion, or resistance of a portion of the people of a country against the established government, there is no doubt, if in its progress and enlargement the government thus sought to be overthrown sees fit, it may, by the competent power, recognize or declare the existence of a state of civil war, which will draw after it all the consequences and rights of war between the contending parties as in the case of a public war. Mr. Wheaton observes, speaking of civil war, "But the general usage of nations regards such a war as entitling both the contending parties to all the rights of war as against each other, and even as respects neutral nations." It is not to be denied, therefore, that if a civil war existed between that portion of the people in organized insurrection to overthrow this government at the time this vessel and cargo were seized, and if she was guilty of a violation of the blockade, she would be lawful prize of war. But before this insurrection against the established government can be dealt with on the footing of a civil war, within the meaning of the law of nations and the Constitution of the United States, and which will draw after it belligerent rights, it must be recognized or declared by the war-making power of the government. No power short of this can change the legal status of the government or the relations of its citizens from that of peace to a state of war, or bring into existence all those duties and obligations of neutral third parties growing out of a state of war. The war power of the government must be exercised before this changed condition of the government and people and of neutral third parties can be admitted. There is no difference in this respect between a civil or a public war.

We have been more particular upon this branch of the case than would seem to be required on account of any doubt or difficulties attending the subject, in view of the approved works upon the law of nations or from the adjudication of the courts, but, because some confusion existed on the argument as to the definition of a war that drew after it all the rights of prize of war. Indeed, a great portion of the argument proceeded upon the ground that these rights could be called into operation, enemies' property captured, blockades set on foot, and all the rights of war enforced in prize courts, by a species of war unknown to the law of nations and to the Constitution of the United States.

An idea seemed to be entertained that all that was necessary to constitute a war, was organized hostility in the district of country in a state of rebellion; that conflicts on land and on sea, the taking of towns and capture of fleets, in fine, the magnitude and dimensions of the resistance against the government, constituted war, with all the belligerent rights belonging to civil war. With a view to enforce this idea, we had, during the argument, an imposing historical detail of the several measures adopted by the Confederate States to enable them to resist the authority of the general government, and of many bold and daring acts of resistance and of conflict. It was said that war was to be ascertained by looking at the armies and navies or public force of the contending parties, and the battles lost and won; that in the language of one of the learned counsel, "Whenever the situation of opposing hostilities has assumed the proportions and pursued the methods of war, then peace is driven out, the ordinary authority and administration of law are suspended, and war in fact and by necessity is the *status* of the nation until peace is restored and the laws resumed their dominion."

Now, in one sense, no doubt this is war, and may be a war of the most extensive and threatening dimensions and effects, but it is a statement simply of its existence in a material sense, and has no relevancy or weight when the question is, what constitutes war, in a legal sense, in the sense of the law of nations, and of the Constitution of the United States? For it must be a war in this sense to attach to it all the consequences that belong to belligerent rights. Instead, therefore, of inquiring after armies and navies, and victories lost and won, or organized rebellion against the general government, the inquiry should be into the law of nations and into the municipal fundamental laws of the government. For we find there, that to constitute a civil war in the sense in which we are speaking, before it can exist, in contemplation of law, it must be recognized, or declared by the sovereign power of the state, and which sovereign powers by our Constitution is lodged in the Congress of the United States; — civil war, therefore, under our system of government, can exist only by an act of Congress, which requires the assent of two of the great departments of the government, the Executive and Legislative.

We have thus far been speaking of the war power under the Constitution of the United States, and as known and recognized by the law of nations. But we are asked, what would become of the peace and integrity of the Union in case of an insurrection at home or invasion from abroad if this power could not be exercised by the President in the recess of Congress, and until that body could be assembled?

The framers of the Constitution fully comprehended this question, and provided for the contingency. Indeed, it would have been surprising if they had not, as a rebellion had occurred in the State of Massachusetts while the Convention was in session, and which had become so general that it was quelled only by calling upon the military power of the State. The Constitution declares that Congress shall have power "to provide for calling forth the militia to execute the laws of the Union, suppress insurrections, and repel invasions." Another clause, "that the President shall be commander-in-chief of the army and navy of the United States, and of the militia of the several States when called into the actual service of the United States;" and, again, "he shall take care that the laws shall be faithfully executed." Congress passed laws on this subject in 1792 and 1795. 1 United States Laws, pp. 264, 424.

The last Act provided that whenever the United States shall be invaded, or be in imminent danger of invasion from a foreign nation, it shall be lawful for the President to call forth such number of militia most convenient to the place of danger, and in case of insurrection in any State against the government thereof, it shall be lawful for the President, on the application of the Legislature of such State, if in session, or if not, of the Executive of the State, to call forth such number of militia of any other State or States as he may judge sufficient to suppress such insurrection.

The 2d section provides, that when the laws of the United States shall be opposed, or the execution obstructed in any State by combinations too powerful to be suppressed by the course of judicial proceedings, it shall be lawful for the President to call forth the militia of such State, or of any other State or States as may be necessary to suppress such combinations and by the Act 3 March, 1807 (2 U. S. Laws, 443), it is provided tha in case of insurrection or obstruction of the laws, either in the United States or of any State or Territory, where it is lawful for the President to call forth the militia for the purpose of suppressing such insurrection, and causing the laws to be executed, it shall be lawful to employ for the same purpose such part of the land and naval forces of the United States as shall be judged necessary.

It will be seen, therefore, that ample provision has been made under the Constitution and laws against any sudden and unexpected disturbance of the public peace from insurrection at home or invasion from abroad. The whole military and naval power of the country is put under the control of the President to meet the emergency. He may call out a force in proportion to its necessities, one regiment or fifty, one ship of war, or any number at his discretion. If, like the insurrection in the State of Pennsylvania in 1793, the disturbance is confined to a small district of country, a few regiments of the militia may be sufficient to suppress it. If of the dimension of the present, when it first broke out, a much larger force would be required. But whatever its numbers, whether great or small, that may be required, ample provision is here made; and whether great or small, the nature of the power is the same. It is the exercise of a power under the municipal laws of the country and not under the law of nations; and, as we see, furnishes the most ample means of repelling attacks from abroad or suppressing disturbances at home until the assembling of Congress, who can, if it be deemed necessary, bring into operation the war power, and thus change the nature and character of the contest. Then, instead of being carried on under the municipal law of 1795, it would be under the law of nations, and the Acts of Congress as war measures, with all the rights of war.

It has been argued that the authority conferred on the President by the Act of 1795 invests him with the war power. But the obvious answer is, that it proceeds from a different clause in the Constitution, and which is given for different purposes and objects, namely, to execute the laws and preserve the public order and tranquillity of the country in a time of peace by preventing or suppressing any public disorder or disturbance by foreign or domestic enemies. Certainly, if there is any force in this argument, then we are in a state of war with all the rights of war, and all the penal consequences attending it every time this power is exercised by calling out a military force to execute the laws or to suppress insurrection or rebellion; for the nature of the power cannot depend upon the numbers called out. If so, what numbers will constitute war and what numbers will not? It has also been argued that this power of the President from necessity should be construed as vesting him with the war power, or the Republic might greatly suffer or be in danger from the attacks of the hostile party before the assembling of Congress. But we have seen that the whole military and naval force are in his hands under the municipal laws of the country. He can meet the adversary upon land and water with all the forces of the government. The truth is, this idea of the existence of any necessity for clothing the President with the war power, under the Act of 1795, is simply a monstrous exaggeration; for, besides having the command of the whole of the army and navy, Congress can be assembled within any thirty days, if the safety of the country requires that the war power shall be brought into operation.

The Acts of 1795 and 1807 did not, and could not under the Constitution, confer on the President the power of declaring war against a State of this Union, or of deciding that war existed, and upon that ground authorize the capture and confiscation of the property of every citizen of the State whenever it was found on the waters. The laws of war, whether the war be civil or *inter gentes*, as we have seen, convert every citizen of the hostile State into a public enemy, and treat him accordingly, whatever may have been his previous conduct. This great power over the business and property of the citizen is reserved to the legislative department by the express words of the Constitution. It cannot be delegated or surrendered to the Executive. Congress alone can determine whether war exists or should be declared; and until they have acted, no citizen of the State can be punished in his person or property, unless he has committed some offence against a law of Congress passed before the act was committed, which made it a crime, and defined the punishment. The penalty of confiscation for the acts of others with which he had no concern cannot lawfully be inflicted.

In the breaking out of a rebellion against the established government, the usage in all civilized countries, in its first stages, is to suppress it by confining the public forces and the operations of the government against those in rebellion, and at the same time extending encouragement and support to the loyal people with a view to their coöperation in putting down the insurgents. This course is not only the dictate of wisdom, but of justice. This was the practice of England in Monmouth's rebellion in the reign of James the Second, and in the rebellions of 1715 and 1745, by the Pretender and his son, and also in the beginning of the rebellion of the Thirteen Colonies of 1776. It is a personal war against the individuals engaged in resisting the authority of the government. This was the character of the war of our Revolution till the passage of the Act of the Parliament of Great Britain of the 16th of George Third, 1776. By that act all trade and commerce with the Thirteen Colonies was interdicted, and all ships and cargoes belonging to the inhabitants subjected to forfeiture, as if the same were the ships and effects of open enemies. From this time the war became a territorial civil war between the contending parties, with all the rights of war known to the law of nations. Down to this period the war was personal against the rebels, and encouragement and support constantly extended to the loyal subjects who adhered to their allegiance, and although the power to make war existed exclusively in the King, and of course this personal war carried on under his authority, and a partial exercise of the war power, no captures of the ships or cargo of the rebels as enemies' property on the sea, or confiscation in Prize Courts as rights of war, took place until after the passage of the Act of Parliament. Until the passage of the act the American subjects were not regarded as enemies in the sense of the law of nations. The distinction between the loyal and rebel subjects was constantly observed. That act provided for the capture and confiscation as prize of their property as if the same were the property "of open enemies." For the first time the distinction was obliterated.

So the war carried on by the President against the insurrectionary districts in the Southern States, as in the case of the King of Great Britain in the American Revolution, was a personal war against those in rebellion, and with encouragement and support of loyal citizens with a view to their coöperation and aid in suppressing the insurgents, with this difference, as the war-making power belonged to the King, he might have recognized or declared the war at the beginning to be a civil war, which would draw after it all the rights of a belligerent, but in the case of the President no such power existed; the war therefore from necessity was a personal war, until Congress assembled and acted upon this state of things.

Down to this period the only enemy recognized by the government was the persons engaged in the rebellion; all others were peaceful citizens, entitled to all the privileges of citizens under the Constitution. Certainly it cannot rightfully be said that the President has the power to convert a loyal citizen into a belligerent enemy, or confiscate his property as enemy's property.

Congress assembled on the call for an extra session the 4th of July, 1861, and among the first acts passed was one in which the President was authorized by proclamation to interdict all trade and intercourse between all the inhabitants of States in insurrection, and the rest of the United States, subjecting vessel and cargo to capture and condemnation as prize, and also to direct the capture of any ship or vessel belonging in whole or in part to any inhabitant of a State whose inhabitants are declared by the proclamation to be in a state of insurrection, found at sea or in any part of the rest of the United States. Act of Congress of 13th of July, 1861, secs. 5, 6. The 4th section also authorized the President to close any port in a Collection District obstructed so that the revenue could not be collected, and provided for the capture and condemnation of any vessel attempting to enter.

The President's Proclamation was issued on the 16th of August following, and embraced Georgia, North and South Carolina, part of Virginia, Tennessee, Alabama, Louisiana, Texas, Arkansas, Mississippi, and Florida.

This Act of Congress, we think, recognized a state of civil war between the government and the Confederate States, and made it territorial. The Act of Parliament of 1776, which converted the rebellion of the Colonies into a civil territorial war, resembles, in its leading features, the act to which we have referred. Government, in recognizing or declaring the existence of a civil war between itself and a portion of the people in insurrection, usually modifies its effects with a view, as far as practicable, to favor the innocent and loyal citizens or subjects involved in the war. It is only the urgent necessities of the government, arising from the magnitude of the resistance, that can excuse the conversion of the personal into a territorial war, and thus confound all distinction between guilt and innocence; hence the modification in the Act of Parliament declaring the territorial war.

It is found in the 44th section of the Act, which, for the encouragement of well affected persons, and to afford speedy protection to those desirous of returning to their allegiance, provided for declaring such inhabitants of any colony, county, town, port, or place, at peace with his majesty, and after such notice by proclamation there should be no further captures. The Act of 13th of July provides that the President may, in his discretion, permit commercial intercourse with any such part of a State or section, the inhabitants of which are declared to be in a state of insurrection (§ 5), obviously intending to favor loyal citizens, and encourage others to return to their loyalty. And the 8th section provides that the Secretary of the Treasury may mitigate or remit the forfeitures and penalties incurred under the act. The Act of 31st July is also one of a kindred character. That appropriates $2,000,000 to be expended under the authority of the President in supplying and delivering arms and munitions of war to loyal citizens residing in any of the States of which the inhabitants are in rebellion, or in which it may be threatened. We agree, therefore, that the Act 13th July, 1861, recognized a state of civil war between the government and the people of the States described in that proclamation.

The cases of the *United States* vs. *Palmer* (3 Wh. 610); *Divina Pastora*, and 4 Ibid, 52, and that class of cases to be found in the reports are referred to as furnishing authority for the exercise of the war power claimed for the President in the present case. These cases hold that when the government of the United States recognizes a state of civil war to exist between a foreign nation and her colonies, but remaining itself neutral, the courts are bound to consider as lawful all those acts which the new government may direct against the enemy; and we admit the President, who conducts the foreign relations of the government, may fitly recognize, or refuse to do so, the existence of civil war in the foreign nation under the circumstances stated.

But this is a very different question from the one before us, which is, whether the President can recognize or declare a civil war, under the Constitution, with all its belligerent rights, between his own government and a portion of its citizens in a state of insurrection. That power, as we have seen, belongs to Congress. We agree, when such a war is recognized or declared to exist by the war-making power, but not otherwise, it is the duty of the courts to follow the decision of the political power of the government.

The case of *Luther* vs. *Borden, et al.* (7 How., 45), which arose out of the attempt of an assumed new government in the State to overthrow the old and established government of Rhode Island by arms. The Legislature of the old government had established martial law, and the Chief Justice, in delivering the opinion of the court, observed, among other things, that "if the government of Rhode Island deemed the armed opposition so formidable and so ramified throughout the State as to require the use of its military force, and the declaration of martial law, we see no ground upon which this court can question its authority. It was a state of war, and the established government resorted to the rights and usages of war to maintain itself and overcome the unlawful opposition."

But it is only necessary to say, that the term "war" must necessarily have been used here by the Chief Justice in its popular sense, and not as known to the law of nations, as the State of Rhode Island confessedly possessed no power under the Federal Constitution to declare war.

Congress, on the 6th of August, 1862, passed an Act confirming all acts, proclamations, and orders of the President, after the 4th of March, 1861, respecting the army and navy, and legalizing them, so far as was competent for that body, and it has been suggested, but scarcely argued, that this legislation on the subject had the effect to bring into existence an *ex post facto* civil war, with all the rights of capture and confiscation, *jure belli*, from the date referred to. An *ex post facto* law is defined, when, after an action, indifferent in itself, or lawful, is committed, the Legislature then, for the first time, declares it to have been a crime, and inflicts punishment upon the person who committed it. The principle is sought to be applied in this case. Property of the citizen or foreign subject engaged in lawful trade at the time, and illegally captured, which must be taken as true if a confirmatory act be necessary, may be held and confiscated by subsequent legislation. In other words trade and commerce authorized at the time by acts of Congress and treaties, may, by *ex post facto* legislation, be changed into illicit trade and commerce with all its penalties and forfeitures annexed and enforced. The instance of the seizure of the Dutch ships in 1803 by Great Britain before the war, and confiscation after the declaration of war, which is well known, is referred to as an authority. But there the ships were seized by the war power, the orders of the government, the seizure being a partial exercise of that power, and which was soon after exercised in full.

The precedent is one which has not received the approbation of jurists, and is not to be followed. See W. B. Lawrence, 2d ed. Wheaton's Element of Int. Law, pt. 4, ch. 1, sec. 11, and note. But, admitting its full weight, it affords no authority in the present case. Here the captures were without any constitutional authority, and void; and, on principle, no subsequent ratification could make them valid.

Upon the whole, after the most careful consideration of this case which the pressure of other duties has admitted, I am compelled to the conclusion that no civil war existed between this government and the States in insurrection till recognized by the Act of Congress 13th of July, 1861; that the President does not possess the power under the Constitution to declare war or recognize its existence within the meaning of the law of nations, which carries with it belligerent rights, and thus change the country and all its citizens from a state of peace to a state of war; that this power belongs exclusively to the Congress of the United States, and, consequently, that the President had no power to set on foot a blockade under the law of nations, and that the capture of the vessel and cargo in this case, and in all cases before us in which the capture occurred before the 13th of July, 1861, for breach of blockade, or as enemies' property, are illegal and void, and that the decrees of condemnation should be reversed and the vessel and cargo restored.

Mr. Chief Justice TANEY, Mr. Justice CATRON, and Mr. Justice CLIFFORD, concurred in the Dissenting Opinion of Mr. Justice NELSON.

From the foregoing opinion of the judges who dissented from the opinion of the majority of the Court, it will be seen that the Court were *unanimous* on several great questions treated of in the preceding work. The judges all agree in considering *a civil war* (with all the *consequences* to *the residents of the seceding States* of a *public territorial war*) to have existed *since the act of July 13th*, 1861, and *still to exist*. The question on which the judges differed was, whether the rebellion was or was not a civil territorial war *prior to this Act of Congress*.

Among the points thus authoritatively settled by agreement of all the judges, are these : —

1. *Since* July 13th, 1861, there has existed between the United States and the Confederate States *a civil, territorial war*.

2. That the United States, since that time, have *full belligerent rights against all persons residing in the rebellious districts*.

3. That whether the inhabitants of the rebellious districts are guilty or innocent, loyal or disloyal, such persons are, in the eye of the law, *belligerent enemies*, and *they and their property are subject to the laws of war*. "The laws of war, whether the war be civil or *inter gentes*, converts *every citizen* of the hostile State into a *public enemy*, and treats him accordingly, whatever may have been his previous conduct."

4. All *the rights of war* now may be *lawfully* and *constitutionally* exercised against all the *inhabitants* of the seceded States.

The following extract from the same opinion shows what *some* of these *belligerent rights* are : —

"The legal consequences resulting from a state of war between two countries, at this day, are well understood, and will be found described in every approved work on the subject of international law. The people of the two countries immediately *become enemies* of each other ; *all intercourse, commercial or otherwise*, between them *unlawful* ; all contracts existing at the commencement of the war *suspended*, and all *made during its existence utterly void*. The insurance of enemies' property, the drawing of bills of exchange or purchase in the enemy's country, the remission of bills or money to it, are illegal and void. Existing partnerships between citizens or subjects of the two countries are dissolved, and in fine, *interdiction of trade and intercourse, direct or indirect*, is absolute *and complete* by the *mere force and effect of war itself*. *All the property of the people of the two countries, on land or sea, is subject to capture and confiscation by the adverse party*, as *enemies' property*, with certain qualifications as it respects property on land. (8 Cranch, 110, *Brown* vs. *United States*.) *All treaties between the belligerent parties are annulled*. The *ports* of the respective countaies may be blockaded, and *letters of marque* and reprisal granted as rights of war, and the *law of prize*, as defined by the law of nations, comes into full and complete operation, resulting from maritime captures *jure belli*. War also effects a change in the *mutual relations of all States or countries*, not directly, as in case of belligerents, but immediately and indirectly, though they take no part in the contest, but remain neutral.

"The great and pervading change in the condition of a country, *and in the relations of all her citizens and subjects, external and internal*, from a state of peace, is the immediate effect and result of a state of war."

MILITARY ARRESTS

IN

TIME OF WAR.

PREFACE TO MILITARY ARRESTS.

In November, 1862, when the author was first requested by the Government to act as Solicitor and special counsel of the War Department, civil suits and criminal prosecutions were pending against military officers and other persons who, acting under orders of the War Department, had arrested and detained in custody citizens of the United States, and aliens. It was a part of the duty assigned to him to instruct counsel employed in different parts of the country for the defence of those who had been wrongfully subjected to such proceedings by reason of their obedience to orders. As time advanced, suits and prosecutions multiplied, involving men in high position. Treason reared its head in many shapes and in many places in the Northern States. Attempts were constantly made to bring the judicial power of individual States into collision with the military forces of the Union.

In all such cases, it was essential to preserve the power and dignity of the General Government unimpaired, and at the same time to avoid open rupture with the courts; hence it was desirable to meet and foil the secret enemies of their country by the use of *judicial* weapons. The stern demands of military necessity were to be reconciled with the maintenance of civil liberty, and with the preservation of local self-government. It became necessary to show that when, in time of war, the life of the body politic was in danger, the surgeon's knife was the only instrument by which that life could be saved.

The judicial mind was then far from comprehending either the perilous condition of public affairs, the change wrought by civil war in the rights, powers, and duties of the bench, or the danger of destroying the government itself by collision between its Political and Judicial Departments. The powers of war, the rights of war, and the courts of war, seemed equally strange and alarming; and it is a gratifying proof of the learning and wisdom of the bench, of the bar, and of Congress, that recognition and sanction of doctrines of constitutional law, which two years ago were confined to a few individuals, have now become so general among our most eminent judges, lawyers, and legislators.

The following pages on Military Arrests were written in the winter and spring of 1862–3, in order to express, in a form convenient for transmission to counsel acting under his instructions, the views of the author on the general legal principles on which military arrests are justifiable and defensible. They contain in more extended form the same doctrines of constitutional law expressed in the WAR POWERS, page 83; and were originally published and distributed by order of the Secretary of War.

W. W.

WAR DEPARTMENT,
WASHINGTON, June 30, 1864.

MILITARY ARRESTS.

The people of America, educated to make their own laws, and to respect and abide by them, having made great sacrifices in olden times to acquire and maintain civil liberty under the law, and holding the rights of every citizen, however humble, as sacred as the rights of a sovereign, accustomed to an almost uninterrupted tranquillity, and to the full enjoyment of the rights guaranteed by our Constitution and laws to citizens in time of peace, have been suddenly thrown into a new and startling position. The same Constitution which has guarded their rights in peace is unexpectedly wheeled round for their protection against their former associates, who have now become public enemies. A safeguard to its friends, it is an engine of destruction to its foes. Can it be wondered at that the sudden transition from their accustomed personal liberty to the stern restrictions imperatively required by the necessities of public safety, in time of civil war, should have found many intelligent and patriotic men, unprepared for this great change, alarmed by its consequences, and fearful that civil liberty itself might go down by military usurpation?

ARRESTS IN LOYAL STATES REGARDED WITH ALARM.

The arrest by military authority of enemies who are still left in the loyal States, and who are actually committing, or who entertain the will and intention to commit, hostile acts tending to obstruct, impede, or destroy the military operations of the army or navy, and the detention of such persons for the purpose of preventing hostilities, have been looked upon with alarm.

RIGHT OF FREEDOM FROM ARREST CLAIMED BY PUBLIC ENEMIES.

And it has happened that loyal and peaceful citizens have in some instances made the mistake of setting up unjustifiable claims in behalf of public enemies, and of asserting for them the privilege of freedom from military arrest or of discharge from imprisonment. Citizens, meaning to be loyal, have thus aided the public enemy by striving to prevent the military power of the government from temporarily restraining persons who were acting in open hostility to the country in time of war.

CIVIL WAR CHANGES OUR LIBERTIES

In time of civil war every citizen must needs be curtailed of some of his accustomed privileges.

The soldier and sailor give up most of their personal liberty to the will and order of their commanding officers.

The person capable of bearing arms may be enrolled in the forces of the United States, and is liable to be made a soldier.

Our property is liable to be diminished by unusual taxes, or wholly appropriated to public use, or to be destroyed on the approach of an enemy.

Trade, intercourse, the uses to which it is usually lawful to put property of all kinds, are changed by war.

No civil, municipal, constitutional or international right is unchanged by the intervention of war.

Shall the person who is disloyal or hostile to the government and country complain that his privileges are also modified in order to protect the country from his own misconduct?

GENERAL WAR POWERS OF THE PRESIDENT.

Some remarks on the *general* war powers of the President being essential to an explanation of the subject of *military arrests*, it has been found most convenient to reprint from a former treatise the following extracts on that subject:

"It is not intended (in this chapter*) to explain the *general* war powers of the President. They are principally contained in the Constitution, Art. II, Sect. 1, Cl. 1 and 7; Sect. 2, Cl. 1; Sect. 3, Cl. 1; and in Sect. 1, Cl. 1, and by necessary implication in Art. I, Sect. 9, Cl. 2. By Art. II, Sect. 2, the President is made commander-in-chief of the army and navy of the United States, and of the militia of the several States when called into the service of the United States. This clause gives ample powers of war to the President, when the army and navy are lawfully in "actual service." His military authority is supreme, under the Constitution, while governing and regulating the land and naval forces, and treating captures on land and water in accordance with such rules as Congress may have passed in pursuance of Art. I, Sect. 8, Cl. 11, 14. Congress may effectually control the military power, by refusing to vote supplies, or to raise troops, and by impeachment of the President; but for the military move-

*Chapter III "War Powers of the President, &c.," pages 82, 83, seventh edition.

ments, and measures essential to overcome the enemy—for the general conduct of the war—the President is responsible to, and controlled, by no other department of government. His duty is to uphold the Constitution and enforce the laws, and to respect whatever rights loyal citizens are entitled to enjoy in time of civil war, to the fullest extent that may be consistent with the performance of the military duty imposed on him.*

"What is the extent of the military power of the President over the persons and property of citizens at a distance from the seat of war—whether he or the War Department may lawfully order the arrest of citizens in loyal States on reasonable proof that they are either enemies or aiding the enemy; or that they are spies or emissaries of rebels sent to gain information for their use, or to discourage enlistments; whether martial law may be extended over such places as the commander deems it necessary to guard, even though distant from any battle-field, in order to enable him to prosecute the war effectually; whether the writ of *habeas corpus* may be suspended, as to persons under military arrest, by the President, or only by Congress, (on which point judges of the United States courts disagree;) whether, in time of war, all citizens are liable to military arrest, on reasonable proof of their aiding or abetting the enemy, or whether they are entitled to practice treason until indicted by some grand jury; thus, for example, whether Jefferson Davis, or General Lee, if found in Boston, could be arrested by military authority and sent to Fort Warren? Whether, in the midst of wide-spread and terrific war, those persons

---

* The effect of a state of war, in changing or modifying civil rights, is explained in the "War Powers of the President," &c.

who violate the laws of war and the laws of peace, traitors, spies, emissaries, brigands, bushwhackers, guerillas, persons in the free States supplying arms and ammunition to the enemy, must all be proceeded against by civil tribunals only, under due forms and precedents of law, by the tardy and ineffectual machinery of arrests by *marshals*, (who can rarely have means of apprehending them,) and of grand *juries*, (who meet twice a year, and could seldom if ever seasonably secure the evidence on which to indict them?) Whether government is not entitled by military power to PREVENT the traitors and spies, by arrest and imprisonment, from doing the intended mischief, as well as to punish them after it is done? Whether war can be carried on successfully, without the power to save the army and navy from being betrayed and destroyed, by *depriving* any citizen temporarily of the power of acting as an enemy, whenever there is reasonable cause to suspect him of being one? Whether these and similar proceedings are, or are not, in violation of any civil rights of citizens under the Constitution, are questions to which the answers depend on the construction given to the war powers of the Executive. Whatever any commander-in-chief, in accordance with the usual practice of carrying on war among civilized nations, may order his army and navy to do, is within the *power* of the President to order and to execute, because the Constitution, in express terms, gives him the supreme command of both. If he makes war upon a foreign nation, he should be governed by the law of nations; if lawfully engaged in civil war, he may treat his enemies as subjects and as belligerents.

"The Constitution provides that the government and

regulation of the land and naval forces, and the treatment of captures, should be according to law; but it imposes, in express terms, no other qualification of the war power of the President. It does not prescribe any territorial limits, within the United States, to which his military operations shall be restricted; nor to which the picket guards or military officers (sometimes called *provost marshals*) shall be confined. It does not exempt any person making war upon the country, or aiding and comforting the enemy, from being *captured*, or arrested, wherever he may be found, whether within or out of the lines of any division of the army. It does not provide that public enemies, or their abettors, shall find safe asylum in any part of the United States where military power can reach them. It requires the President, as an executive magistrate, in time of peace, to see that the laws existing in time of peace are faithfully executed; and as commander-in-chief, in time of war, to see that the laws of war are executed. In doing both duties he is strictly obeying the Constitution."

MARTIAL LAW IS THE LAW OF WAR.

It consists of a code of rules and principles regulating the rights, liabilities, and duties, the social, municipal, and international relations in time of war of all persons, whether neutral or belligerent. These rules are liable to modification in the United States by statutes, usually termed "military law," or "articles of war," and the "rules and regulations made in pursuance thereof."

FOUNDATION OF MARTIAL LAW.

Municipal law is founded upon the necessities of social organization. Martial law is founded upon the necessities of war. Whatever compels a resort to war, compels the enforcement of the laws of war.

THE EXTENT OF THE MEANS OF WAR AS SHOWN BY THE NECESSITIES OF WAR, AND ITS OBJECTS.

The objects and purposes for which war is inaugurated required the use of the instrumentalities of war.

When the law of force is appealed to, force must be sufficiently untrammelled to be *effectual.* Military power must not be restrained from reaching the public enemy in all localities, under all disguises. In war there should be no asylum for treason. The ægis of law should not cover a traitor.

A public enemy, wherever he may be found, may, if he resists, be killed, or captured, and if captured he may be detained as a prisoner.

The purposes for which war is carried on may and must be accomplished. If it is justifiable to commence and continue war, then it is justifiable to extend the operations of war until they shall have completely attained the end for which it was commenced, by the use of all means employed in accordance with the rules of civilized warfare.

And among those means none are more familiar or more essential than that of capturing, or arresting, and confining the enemy. Necessity arbitrates the rights and the methods of war. Whatever hostile military act is essential to public safety in civil war is lawful.

POWERS AND RESPONSIBILITIES OF MILITARY COMMANDERS.

"The law of nature and of nations gives to belligerents the right to employ such force as may be necessary in order to obtain the object for which the war was undertaken." Beyond this the use of force is unlawful. This necessity forms the limit of hostile operations.

We have the same rights of war against the allies or associates of an enemy as against the principal belligerent.

When military forces are called into service for the purpose of securing the public safety, they may lawfully obey military orders made by their superior officers. The commander-in-chief is responsible for the mode of carrying on war: He determines the persons or people against whom his forces shall be used. He alone is constituted the judge of the nature of the exigency, of the appropriate means to meet it, and of the hostile character or purposes of individuals whose conduct gives him cause to believe them public enemies. His right to seize, capture, detain, and imprison such persons is as unquestionable as his right to carry on war. The extent of the danger he is to provide against must be determined by him; he is responsible, if he neglects to use the means of meeting or avoiding it.

The nature of the difficulty to be met and the object to be accomplished afford the true measure and limit of the use of military powers. The military commander must judge *who* the public enemy are, where they are, what degree of force shall be used against them, and what warlike measures are best suited to conquer the enemy or restrain him from future mischief. If the enemy be in small force, they may be captured by another small force; if the enemy be a single individual, he may be captured by a provost guard or marshal. If an officer in the honest exercise of his duty makes a mistake in arresting a friend instead of an enemy, or in detaining a suspicious person, who may be finally liberated, he is not for such error responsible in criminal or civil courts.

Any other rule would render war impracticable, and by exposing soldiers to the hazard of ruinous litigation, by reason of liability to civil tribunals, would render obedience to orders dangerous, and thus would break down the discipline of armies.

ARRESTS ON SUSPICION.

Arrests or captures of persons whose conduct gives reasonable cause of suspicion that they contemplate acts of hostility, are required and justified by military and martial law. Such arrests are precautionary. The detention of such suspected persons by military authority is, for the same reason, necessary and justifiable.*

Nothing in the Constitution or laws can define the possible extent of any military danger. Nothing therefore in either of them can fix or define the extent of power necessary to meet the emergency, to control the military movements of the army, or of any detachments from it, or of any single officer, provost marshal, or private.

Hence it is worse than idle to attempt to lay down rules of law defining the territorial limits of military operations, or of martial law, or of captures and arrests.

Wherever danger arises, there should go the military means of defence or safeguard against it. Wherever a single enemy makes his appearance, there he should be arrested and restrained.

---

* Luther *vs.* Borden, 7 Howard's Supreme Court Reports, p. 1.

ABUSE OF POWER OF ARREST.

The power of arrest and imprisonment is doubtless liable to abuse. But the liability to abuse does not prove that the power does not exist. "There is no power, says the Supreme Court, that is not susceptible of abuse The remedy for this as well as for all other official misconduct, if it should occur, is to be found in the Constitution itself. In a free government the danger must be remote, since in addition to the high qualities which the Executive must be presumed to possess of public virtue, and honest devotion to the public interests, the frequency of elections, and the watchfulness of the representatives of the nation, carry with them all the checks which can be useful to guard against usurpation or wanton tyranny."*

SAFEGUARDS.

Our safeguard against the misuse of power is not, by denying its existence, to deprive ourselves of its protection in time of war, but to rely on the civil responsibility of the officer.

The right of impeachment of the commander-in-chief, the frequent change of public officers, the control of the army and navy by the legislative power of Congress, the power of Congress over supplies, the power of Congress to make laws regulating and controlling the use of military power wherever it is liable to abuse, the fact that the Commander-in-chief is also President and chief executive officer of government, and the great intelligence and high character of our soldiers, are all safe-

* 12 Wheaton's Reports, page 32.

guards against arbitrary power or the abuse of legal authority.

EFFECT OF WAR UPON THE COURTS AND OF COURTS UPON THE WAR.

Justice should rule over the deadly encounters of the battle-field; but courts and constables are there quite out of place. Far from the centres of active hostilities, judicial tribunals may still administer municipal law, so long as their proceedings do not interfere with military operations. But if the members of a court should impede, oppose, or interfere with military operations in the field, whether acting as magistrates or as individuals, they, like all other public enemies, are liable to capture and imprisonment by martial law. They have then become a belligerent enemy.

The character of their actions is to be determined by the military commander; not by the parchment which contains their commissions. A judge may be a public enemy as effectually as any other citizen. The rebellious districts show many examples of such characters. Is a judge sitting in a northern court, and endeavoring to commit acts of hostility under the guise of administering law, any less a public enemy than if he were holding court in South Carolina, and pretending to confiscate the property of loyal men? Are the black gown and wig to be the protection of traitors?

General Jackson arrested a judge in the war of 1812, kept him in prison in order to prevent his acts of judicial hostility, and liberated him when he had repulsed the enemy. The illegal fine imposed on him by that judge was repaid to the general after many years under a vote of Congress. Why should a judge be protected from the consequences of his act of hostility more than the clergyman, the lawyer, or the governor of a State ?

The public safety must not be hazarded by enemies whatever position they may hold in public or private life. The more eminent their position, the more dangerous their disloyalty.

Among acts of hostility which constitute judges, public enemies, and subject them to arrest, are these:

1. When a State judge is judicially apprised that a party is in custody under the authority of the United States, he can proceed no further, under a *habeas corpus* or other process, to discharge the prisoner.

If he orders the prisoner to be discharged, it is the duty of the officer holding the prisoner to resist that order, and the laws of the United States will sustain him in doing so, and in arresting and imprisoning the judge, if necessary.*

2. So long as the courts do not interfere with military operations ordered by the commander-in-chief, litigation may proceed as usual; but if that litigation entangles and harasses the soldiers or the officers so as to disable them from doing their military duty, the judges and the actors being hostile, and using legal processes for the purpose and design of impeding and obstructing the necessary military operations in time of war, the courts and lawyers are liable to precautionary arrest and confinement, whether they have committed a crime known to the statute law or not. Military restraint is to be used for the prevention of hostilities, and public safety in time of civil war will not permit courts or constables, colleges

* Ableman *vs.* Booth, 21 How. 524–5.

or slave-pens, to be used as instruments of hostility to the country.

When a traitor is seized in the act of committing hostility against the country, it makes no difference whether he is captured in a swamp or in a court-house, or whether he has in his pocket the commission of a judge or a colonel.

Commanders in the field are under no obligations to take the opinions of judges as to the character or extent of their military operations, nor as to the question who are and who are not public enemies, nor who have and who have not given reasonable cause to believe that acts of hostility are intended. These questions are, by the paramount laws of war, to be settled by the officer in command.

MILITARY ARRESTS ARE NOT FORBIDDEN BY THE CONSTITUTION.

The framers of the Constitution having given to the commander-in-chief the full control of the army when in active service, subject only to the articles of war, have therefore given him the full powers of capture and arrest of enemies, and have placed upon him the corresponding obligation to use any and all such powers as may be proper to insure the the success of our arms. To carry on war without the power of capturing or arresting enemies would be impossible. We should not, therefore, expect to find in the Constitution any provision which would deprive the country of any means of self-defence in time of unusual public danger.

We look in vain in the Constitution for a clause which in any way limits the methods of using war powers when war exists.

Some persons have turned attention to certain passages in the amendments relating, as was supposed, to this subject. Let us examine them:

ARTICLE IV. "The right of the people to be secure in their persons, houses, papers, and effects against *unreasonable* searches and seizures shall not be violated."

This amendment merely declares that the right of being secure against UNREASONABLE seizures or arrests shall not be violated. It does not declare that NO ARRESTS shall be made. Will any one deny that it is *reasonable* to arrest or capture the person of a public enemy?

If all arrests, reasonable or unreasonable, were prohibited, public safety would be disregarded in favor of the rights of individuals.

Not only may military, but even civil, arrests be made when *reasonable*.

ARRESTS WITHOUT WARRANT.

It is objected that military arrests are made without warrant. The military order is the warrant authorizing arrest, issuing from a commander, in like manner as the judicial order is the warrant authorizing arrest, issuing from a court. But even civil arrests at common law may be made without warrant by constables, or by private persons.—(1 Chitty, C. L., 15 to 22.) There is a liability to fine and imprisonment if an offender is voluntarily permitted to escape by a person present at the commission of a felony or the infliction of a dangerous wound.

Whenever there is probable ground of suspicion that a felony has been committed, a private person may without warrant arrest the felon, and probable cause will protect the captor from civil liability.

"When a felony has been committed, a constable may arrest a supposed offender on information without a positive charge, and without a positive knowledge of the circumstances." And Chitty says, page 217, "A constable may justify an imprisonment, without warrant, on a reasonable charge of felony made to him, although he afterwards discharge the prisoner without taking him before a magistrate, although it turns out that no felony was committed by any one."

In Wakely *vs.* Hart, 6 Binney, 318, Chief Justice Tilghman says of the constitution of Pennsylvania, which is nearly in the same words on this subject as the Constitution of the United States:

"The plaintiffs insist that by the constitution of this State no arrest is lawful without warrant issued on probable cause, supported by oath. Whether this be the true construction of the constitution is the main point in the case. It is declared in the 9th article, section 7, 'that the people shall be secure in their persons, houses, papers, and possessions, from unreasonable arrests and that no warrant to search any place, or seize any person or thing, shall issue without describing them as nearly as may be, nor without probable cause, supported by oath or affirmation.'

"The provisions of this section, so far as concern warrants, only guard against their abuse by issuing them without good cause, and in so general and vague a form as may put it in the power of officers who execute them to harass innocent persons under pretence of suspicion; for, if general warrants were allowed, it must be left to the discretion of the officer on what persons or things they are to be executed. But *it is nowhere said* that there shall be *no arrest without warrant.* To have said so would have endangered the safety of society. The felon who is seen to commit murder or robbery must be arrested on the spot, or suffered to escape. So, although if not seen, yet if known to have committed a felony, and pursued with or without warrant, he may be arrested by any person.

"And even where there is only probable cause of suspicion, a *private person* may, without warrant, at his peril, make the arrest. I say at his peril, for nothing short of proving the felony will justify the arrest;" (that is, by a private person on suspicion.) "These principles of common law are essential to the welfare of society, and not intended to be altered or impaired by the constitution."

The right, summarily, to arrest persons in the act of committing heinous crimes has thus been sanctioned from ancient times by the laws of England and America. No warrant is required to justify arrests of persons committing felonies. The right to make such arrests is essential to the preservation of the existence of society, though its exercise ought to be carefully guarded. The great problem is to reconcile the necessities of government with the security of personal liberty.

If, in time of peace, civil arrests for felonies may be made by private citizens without warrant, *a fortiori*, military arrests in time of war for acts of hostility, either executed or contemplated, may be made under the warrant of a military command. And the provision that *unreasonable* seizures or arrests are prohibited has no application to military arrests in time of war.

OBJECTION THAT ARRESTS ARE MADE WITHOUT INDICTMENT.

The 5th article of the amendments of the Constition provides that—

"No person shall be held to answer for a capital, or otherwise infamous crime, unless on a presentment or indictment of a grand jury, except in cases arising in the land or naval forces, or in the militia when in actual service in time of war or public danger; nor shall any person be subject for the same offence to be twice put in jeopardy of life or limb; nor shall be compelled in any criminal case to be a witness against himself, nor be deprived of life, liberty, or property, without due process of law; nor shall private property be taken for public use without just compensation."

This article has no reference to the rights of citizens under the exigencies of war, but relates only to their rights in time of peace. It is provided that no person shall be subject for the same offence to be twice put in jeopardy of life or limb. If rebellion or treason be one of the offences here alluded to, and a rebel has been once *under fire*, and thus been put in jeopardy of life or limb, (in one sense of that phrase,) he could not be fired at a second time without violating the Constitution, because a second shot would put him twice in jeopardy for the same offence.

"Nor shall he be deprived of life, liberty, or property without due process of law." If this provision relates to the rights of citizens *in time of war*, it is obvious that no property can be captured, no rebel killed in battle or imprisoned by martial law.

The claim that "no person shall be held to answer for a capital or otherwise infamous crime, unless upon a presentment or indictment of a grand jury, except in cases," &c., in like manner applies only to the rights of citizens in time of peace.

What are "cases arising in the land or naval forces, or in the militia, when in actual service in time of war or public danger?"

Suppose the Union forces arrest a spy from the enemy's camp, or catch a band of guerillas, neither the spy nor the guerillas belong to OUR land forces or navy. The enemy are no part of *our* forces or of *our* militia; and while this provision covers offences therein specified, if committed by *our* troops, and allows them to be dealt with by martial law, it would (if it is applicable in time of war) prevent our executing martial law against such enemies captured in war. We should, under such a construction, be required to indict and prosecute our enemy for capital crimes, instead of capturing and treating them as prisoners of war, or punishing them according to the laws of war.

The absurdity of such a construction is obvious. The language is inapplicable to a case of military arrest in war time. No soldier is held to answer for a crime; he is captured as a prisoner of war, to be released, paroled, or exchanged. He is never expected to answer to any indictment; prisoners of war are not indicted.

Nor can any prisoner be held to answer for any crime unless upon a charge of such crime made before some tribunal. No such charge is made against prisoners of war, nor are they charged with any crime, infamous or otherwise, and therefore they are not held to answer any.

Hence that clause in the Constitution which provides for trial by jury, the right to be informed of the nature and cause of the accusation, &c., relates in express terms only to criminal prosecutions, and has nothing to do with military arrests or the procedures of martial law.

Therefore it is obvious that while criminal proceedings against persons not in the naval or military service are guarded in time of peace, and the outposts of justice are secured by freedom from unreasonable arrests, and in requiring indictment to be found by grand jurors, speedy and public trial by an impartial jury, information of the nature of the charges, open examination of witnesses, and aid of counsel, &c., all these high privileges are not accorded to our public enemy in time of war, nor to those citizens who commit military offences, which, not being against any statute or municipal law, cannot be the foundation of any indictment, punishment, or trial by jury, and do not constitute any capital or otherwise infamous crime, or to persons who commit acts which impede, embarrass, and tend to thwart the military measures of the government.

The safeguards of criminal procedures in courts of justice in time of peace are not to be construed into protection of public enemies in time of war.

THE CONSTITUTION SANCTIONS MILITARY ARRESTS.

The Constitution itself authorizes courts-martial. These courts punish for offences different from those provided for by any criminal statute. Therefore it follows that crimes not against statute laws may be punished by law according to the Constitution, and also that arrests necessary to bring the offenders before that tribunal are lawful.

In *Dynes* vs. *Hoover*,* the evidence was that an attempt had been made to hold a marshal liable for executing the order of the President of the United States in committing Dynes to the penitentiary for an offence of which he had been adjudged guilty by a naval court martial.

This case shows that the crimes to be punished, and the modes of procedure by courts-martial are different from those of ordinary civil tribunals; that the jurisdiction of these classes of tribunals is distinct, and that the judicial power and the military power of courts-martial are independent of each other, and both authorized by the same Constitution, and courts-martial may punish offences other than those provided for by criminal statutes. And if they may do so, it follows that persons

---

* 20 Howard's Supreme Court Reports, page 65.

may be arrested for such offences. The law is laid down by the court as follows:

"The demurrer admits that the court-martial was legally organized, and the crime charged was one forbidden by law; that the court had jurisdiction of the charge as it was made; that a trial took place before the court upon the charge, and the defendant's plea of not guilty; and that, upon the evidence in the case, the court found Dynes guilty of an attempt to desert, and sentenced him to be punished as has been already stated; that the sentence of the court was approved by the Secretary, and by his direction Dynes was brought to Washington; and that the defendant was marshal for the District of Columbia, and that in receiving Dynes and committing him to the keeper of the penitentiary, he obeyed the orders of the President of the United States in execution of the sentence. Among the powers conferred upon Congress by the 8th section of the 1st article of the Constitution are the following: 'To provide and maintain a navy;' 'to make rules for the government of the land and naval forces.' And the eighth amendment, which requires a presentment of a grand jury in cases of capital or otherwise infamous crime, expressly excepts from its operation 'cases arising in the land or naval forces.' And by the 2d section of the 2d article of the Constitution, it is declared that 'the President shall be commander-in-chief of the army and navy of the United States, and of the militia of the several States when called into the actual service of the United States.'

"These provisions show that Congress has the power to provide for *the trial and punishment of military and naval offences in the manner then and now practiced by civilized nations*, and that the power to do so is given without any connexion between it and the 3d article of the Constitution, defining the judicial power of the United States; *indeed, that the two powers are entirely independent of each other*."

The fact that the power exists of suspending the writ of *habeas corpus* in time of rebellion, when the public safety requires it, shows that the framers of the Constitution expected that arrests would be made for crimes not against municipal law, and that the administration of the ordinary rules of law on *habeas corpus* would require discharge of prisoners, and that such discharge might endanger public safety. It was to protect public safety in time of rebellion that the right to suspend the *habeas corpus* was left in the power of government.

MILITARY POWERS MAY BE DELEGATED.

In the course of the preceding remarks the commander-in-chief has been the only military authority spoken of as authorized to order arrests and seizures His powers may be delegated to officers, and may be exercised by them under his command. So also the Secretaries of War and State are public officers through whom the President acts in making orders for arrests, and their acts are in law the acts of the President. It is necessary to the proper conduct of war that many if not most of the powers of the President or commander should be exercised by his Secretaries and his generals, and that many of their powers should be executed by officers under them; and although it not seldom happens that subalterns use the powers of arrest and detention yet the inconvenience resulting from this fact is one of the inevitable misfortunes of war.

OBEDIENCE OF ORDERS IS JUSTIFICATION.

Whatever military man obeys the order of his superior officer, is justified by law in doing so. Obedience to orders is a part of the law of the land; a violation of that law subjects the soldier to disgraceful punishment. Acts done in obedience to military orders will not subject the agent to civil or criminal liability in courts of law. But, on the other hand, any abuse of military authority subjects the offender to civil liability for such abuse, and he who authorized the wrong is responsible for it.

OFFICERS MAKING ARRESTS NOT LIABLE TO CIVIL SUIT OR CRIMINAL PROSECUTION.

That military arrests are deemed necessary for public safety by Congress is shown by the act of March 3, 1863, ch. 81, wherein it is provided that no person arrested by authority of the President of the United States shall be discharged from imprisonment so long as the war lasts, and the President shall see fit to suspend the privilege of the writ of *habeas corpus*.

The 4th section of the same act provides "that any order of the President, or under his authority, made at any time during the existence of this present rebellion, shall be a defence in all courts to any action or prosecution, civil or criminal, pending or to be commenced for any search, seizure, arrest, or imprisonment, made, done, or committed, or acts omitted to be done under and by virtue of such order, or under color of any law of Congress, and such defence may be made by special plea, or under the general issue."

The same act further provides that actions against officers and others for torts in arrests commenced in State courts may be removed to circuit courts, and thence to the Supreme Court. The jurisdiction of State courts thereupon ceases, and the rights of the defendant may be protected by the laws of the United States administered by the Supreme Court. By these provisions there are secured protection for the past and security in the future performance of military and civil duties under orders of the President in time of war; and the statute contains an implied admission of the necessity to public welfare of arrests for crimes not against statutes, but endangering public safety, and of imprisonments for offences not known to the municipal laws, but yet equally dangerous to the country in civil war.

ARBITRARY POWER NOT CONSISTENT WITH CONSTITUTIONAL OR FREE GOVERNMENTS.

The exercise of irresponsible powers is incompatible with constitutional government. Unbridled will, the offspring of selfishness and of arrogance, regards no rights, and listens to no claims of reason, justice, policy, or honor. Its imperious mandate being its only law, arbitrary power sucks out the heart's blood of civil liberty. Vindicated by our fathers on many a hard-fought battle-field, and made holy by the sacrifice of their noblest sons, that liberty must not be wounded or destroyed; and in time of peace, in a free country, its power should shelter loyal citizens from arbitrary arrests and unreasonable seizures of their persons or property.

TRUE MEANING OF "ARBITRARY" AS DISTINGUISHED FROM "DISCRETIONARY."

What arrests are "arbitrary?"

Among the acts of war which have been severely censured is that class of military captures reproachfully styled "arbitrary" arrests.

What is the true meaning of the word "arbitrary?" When used to characterize military arrests it means such as are made at the mere will and pleasure of the officer, without right, and without lawful authority. But powers are not arbitrary because they may be discretionary. The authority of judges is often discretionary; and even if discretion be governed by rules, the judge makes his own rules; yet no one can justly claim that such judicial authority is arbitrary.

The existence of an authority may be undeniable, while the mode of using it may be discretionary. A power is arbitrary only when it is founded upon no rightful authority, civil or military. It may be within the discretion of a commander to make a military order; to dictate its terms; to act upon facts and reasons known only to himself; it may suddenly and violently affect the property, liberty, or life of soldiers or of citizens; yet such an order, being the lawful use of a discretionary authority, is not the exercise of arbitrary power. When such orders are issued on the field, or in the midst of active operations, no objection is made to them on the pretence that they are lawless or unauthorized, nor for the reason that they must be instantly and absolutely obeyed.

The difference is plain between the exercise of arbitrary power and the arbitrary exercise of power. The former is against law; the latter, however, ungraciously or inconsiderately used, is lawful.

MILITARY ARRESTS LAWFUL.

The laws of war, military and martial, written and unwritten, founded on the necessities of government, are sanctioned by the Constitution and laws, and recognized as valid by the Supreme Court of the United States.

Arrests made under the laws of war are neither arbitrary nor without legal justification.

In *Cross* vs. *Harrison*, *Judge Wayne*, delivering the opinion, (16 Howard, 189, 190,) says:

"Early in 1847 the President, as constitutional commander-in-chief of the army and navy, authorized the military and naval commanders of our forces in California to exercise the belligerent rights of a conqueror, and to form a civil government for the conquered country, and to impose duties on imports and tonnage as military contributions for the support of the government and of the army, which had the conquest in possession. No one can doubt that these orders of the President and the action of our army and navy commanders in California, in conformity with them, were according to the law of arms," &c.

So, in *Fleming* vs. *Paige*, (9 Howard, 615,) Chief Justice Taney says:

"The person who acted in the character of collector in this instance, acted as such under the authority of the military commander and in obedience to his orders; and the regulations he adopted were not those prescribed by law, but by the President in his character as commander-in-chief."

It is established by these opinions that military orders, in accordance with martial law or the laws of war, though they may be contrary to municipal laws; and the use of the usual means of enforcing such orders by military power, including capture, arrest, imprisonment, or the destruction of life and property, are authorized and sustained upon the firm basis of martial law, which is, in time of war, constitutional law.

A military arrest being one of the recognized necessities of warfare, is as legal and constitutional a procedure, under the laws of war, as an arrest by civil authority by the sheriff, after the criminal has been indicted by a grand jury for a statute offence.

In time of peace the interference of military force is offensive to a free people. Its decrees seem overbearing, and its procedures violent. It has few safeguards and no restraints. The genius of republican government revolts against permanent military rule. Hence the suspicions of the people are easily aroused upon any appearance of usurpation. It is for this reason that some opponents of the government have endeavored to cripple the war power of the President by exciting a natural, but unfounded apprehension that military arrests, a familiar weapon of warfare, can be employed only at the hazard of civil liberty.

ON WHAT GROUND FORCE IS JUSTIFIABLE.

When the administration of laws is resisted by an armed public enemy; when government is assaulted or overthrown; when magistrate and ruler are alike powerless, the nation must assert and maintain its rights by force of arms. Government must fight or perish. Self-preservation requires the nation to defend its rights by military power. The right to use military power rests on the universal law of self-defence.

MARTIAL LAW.

When war is waged, it ought not to degenerate into unbridled brutality, but it should conform to the dictates of justice and of humanity. Its objects, means, and methods should be justifiable in the forum of civilized and Christian nations. The laws or rules which usually govern this use of force are called military and martial law, or the laws of war.

Principles deducible from a consideration of the nature, objects, and means of war will, if understood, remove from the mind the apprehension of danger to civil liberty from military arrests and other employment of force. When war exists, whatever is done in accordance with the laws of war is not arbitrary, and is not in derogation of the civil rights of citizens, but is *lawful*, justifiable, and indispensable to public safety.

WAR POWER HAS LIMITS.

Although the empire of the war power is vast, yet it has definite boundaries, wherein it is supreme. It overrides municipal laws and all domestic institutions or relations which impede or interfere with its complete sway. It reigns uncontrollable until its legitimate work is executed; but then it lays down its dripping sword at the feet of Justice whose wrongs it has avenged.

It is not now proposed to define the limits and restrictions imposed by the laws of warfare upon the general proceedings of belligerents. It is to one only of the usual methods of war that attention is now directed, namely, to the capture and detention of public enemies.

ARRESTS NECESSARY.

Effectual hostilities could not be prosecuted without exercising the right to capture and imprison hostile persons. Barbarous nations only would justify the killing of those who might fall into their power. It is now too late to question the authority of martial law which sanctions the arrest and detention of those who engage in foreign or civil war. The imprisonment of such persons is much more important to the public safety in civil than in international warfare.

MILITARY CRIMES.

Military crimes, or crimes of war, include all acts of hostility to the country, to the government, or to any department or officer thereof; to the army or navy, or to any person employed therein: *provided* that such acts of hostility have the effect of opposing, embarrassing, defeating, or even of interfering with our military or naval operations in carrying on the war, or of aiding, encouraging, or supporting the enemy.

According to the laws of war, military arrests may be made for the punishment or prevention of military crimes.

DOUBLE LIABILITY.

Such crimes may or may not be offences against statutes. The fact that an act of hostility is against municipal as well as martial law, even though it may subject the offender to indictment in civil tribunals, does not relieve him from responsibility to military power.

To make civil war against the United States is to commit treason. Such act of treason renders the traitor liable to indictment and condemnation in the courts, and to capture, arrest, or death on the field of battle. But because a traitor may be hung as a criminal by the sheriff, it does not follow that he may not be captured, arrested, or shot as a public enemy by the soldiers.

An act of hostility may thus subject the offender to twofold liability: first to civil, and then to military tribunals. Whoever denies the right to make military arrests for crimes which are punishable by civil tribunals, would necessarily withhold one of the usual and most effective and essential means of carrying on war. Whoever restricts the right to cases where crimes have been committed in violation of some special statute, would destroy one of the chief safeguards of public security and defence.

ACTS MADE CRIMINAL BY A STATE OF WAR.

The quality of an act depends on the time, place, and circumstances under which it is performed.

Acts which would have been harmless and innocent in time of peace, become dangerous, injurious, and guilty in time of war. The rules and regulations of "the service" contain many illustrations of this fact. For a soldier to speak contemptuously of a superior officer might, as between two civilians, be a harmless or beneficial use of "free speech;" but as in time of war such "free speech" might destroy discipline, encourage disobedience of orders, or even break up the confidence of the soldiers in their commanders, such speaking is strictly forbidden, and becomes a crime.

Most of the regulations which require obedience to orders are such that disregard of them would, in time of peace, by civilians, be no breach of law or of morals, yet a breach of them by soldiers becomes a moral and a military crime.

In like manner, a citizen may commit acts to which he is accustomed in ordinary times, but which become grave offences in time of war, although not embraced in the civil penal code.

Actions not constituting any offence against the municipal code of a country, having become highly injurious and embarrassing to military operations, may and must be *prevented* if not *punished.* Such actions, being crimes against military or martial law or the laws of war, can be prevented only by arrest and confinement or destruction of the offender. If an act which interferes with military operations is not against municipal law, the greater is the reason for preventing it by martial law. And if such an action cannot be punished or prevented by civil or criminal law, this fact makes stronger the necessity for preventing evil consequences by arresting the offender.

Absence of penal law imperatively demands application of military preventive process—*i. e.*, ARREST.

ARREST OF INNOCENT PERSONS.

Innocent persons are, under certain circumstances, liable to military arrest in time of civil war. Suppose an army retreating from an unsuccessful battle, and desirous of concealing from the enemy the number, position, and directions taken by the forces; and if, in order to prevent these facts from becoming known to their pursuers, the persons who are met on the retreat are captured and carried away, can any one doubt the right of making such arrests? However loyal or friendly those persons may be, yet, if seized by a pursuing enemy, they might be compelled to disclose facts by which the retreating army could be destroyed. *Hence*, when war *exists*, and the arrest and detention of even innocent persons are essential to the *success* of military operations, such arrest and detention are lawful and justifiable.

Suppose a loyal judge holding a court in a loyal State, and a witness on the stand who knows the details of a proposed military expedition which it would be highly injurious to the military operations of the army or navy to have disclosed or made public, would any one doubt the right of the military commander to *stop the trial* on the instant, and, if necessary, to imprison the judge or the witness, to prevent betrayal of our military plans and expeditions, so that they might come to the knowledge of our enemy?

The innocence of the person who may through ignorance, or weakness, or folly, endanger the success of military expeditions, does not deprive the military commander of the power to guard against hazard and prevent mischief.

The true principle is this: the military commander has the power, in time of war, to arrest and detain all persons who, being at large he has reasonable cause to believe will impede or endanger the military operations of the country.

The true test of liability to arrest is, therefore, not alone the guilt or innocence of the party; not alone the neighborhood or distance from the places where battles are impending; not alone whether he is engaged in active hostilities: but whether his being at large will actually tend to *impede*, embarrass, or hinder the *bona fide* military operations in creating, organizing, maintaining, and most effectually using the military forces of the country.

No other motive or object for making military arrests, except for military crimes, is to be tolerated; no arrests, made under pretence of military power for other objects, are *lawful* or justifiable. The dividing line between *civil liberty* and military power is precisely here: civil liberty secures the right to freedom from arrests except by civil process in time of peace; or by military power when war exists, and the exigencies of the case are such that the arrest is required in order to prevent embarrassment or injury to the *bona fide* military operations of the army or navy.

It is not enough to justify an arrest to say that *war exists*, or that it is a *time* of war, (unless martial law is declared.) Nor is it necessary to justify arrests that active hostilities should be going on at the *place* of the arrest. It is, however, enough to justify arrests in any locality, however far removed from the battle-fields of contending armies, that it is *a time* of war, and the *arrest* is required to punish a military crime, to *prevent* an act of hostility, or even to avoid the danger that military operations of any description may be impeded, embarrased, or prevented.

In considering the subject of arrests, it must be borne

in mind that "a person taken and held by the military forces, whether before, or in, or after a battle, or without any battle at all, is virtually *a prisoner of war*. No matter what his alleged offence, whether he is a rebel, a traitor, a spy, or an enemy in arms, he is to be held and punished according to *the laws of war*, for these have been substituted for the laws of peace."

CAUSE OF ARREST CANNOT BE SAFELY DISCLOSED.

It cannot be expected, when government finds it necessary to make arrests for causes which exist during civil war, that the reasons for making such arrests should be at once made public; otherwise the purpose for which the arrest is made might be defeated. Thus, if a conspiracy has been formed to commit hostilities, and one conspirator is arrested, publishing the facts might enable other conspirators to escape, and take advantage of their information. It may be necessary to make arrests on grounds justifying suspicion of hostile intentions, when it might be an act of injustice to the party suspected, if innocent, to publish the facts on which such suspicions were entertained; and if guilty, it might prevent the government from obtaining proof against him, or preventing the hostile act. Under these circumstances the safety of civil liberty must rest in the honesty, integrity, and responsibility of those who have been for the time clothed with the high powers of administering the government.

ARRESTS TO PREVENT HOSTILITIES.

The best use of armies and of navies is not to punish criminals for offences against laws, but to prevent public enemies from committing future hostilities. Victory and conquest are not for revenge of wrongs, but for security of rights. Arch traitors and consummate villains are not those on whom the avenging sword is most apt to fall, but the dupes and victims of their crimes are those who oftenest bear the sharp catastrophy of battles.

We arrest and hold an enemy not to punish, but to restrain him from acts of hostility; we hang a spy not only to deter others from committing a similar offence but chiefly to prevent his betraying us to the enemy.

We capture and destroy the property even of friends, if exposed in an enemy's country, not to injure those who wish us well, but to withdraw their property from liability to be used by our opponents.

In a defensive civil war, many, if not most, military operations have for their legitimate object the prevention of acts of hostility.

In case of foreign war, an act of Congress provides that to prevent hostilities by aliens they may be arrested.

In case of "Declared war between the United States and any foreign nation, or of any invasion or predatory incursion being *attempted* or *threatened* against any territory of the United States by any foreign government, and the President shall make public proclamation of the event, all natives, citizens, denizens, or subjects of the hostile nation or government, being males of the age of fourteen years and upwards, who shall be within the United States and not actually naturalized, shall be liable to be *apprehended, restrained, secured,* and *removed as alien enemies.*"

"Power over this subject is given to the President, having due regard to treaty stipulations by the act of the 6th of July, 1798; and by this act the President was authorized to direct the *confinement* of *aliens*, although such confinement was not for the purpose of removing them from the United States, and means were conferred on him to enforce his orders, and it was not necessary that any judicial means should be called in to enforce the regulations of the President."*

Thus express power is given by statute to the President to make military arrests of innocent foreign-born persons under the circumstances above stated, for the purpose of preventing them from taking part in the contest.

While this ample authority is given to the commander-in-chief to arrest the persons of aliens residing here, as a precautionary measure, a *far greater power over the persons of our own citizens* is, for the same reason, given to the President in case of *public danger.*

RESTRAINT OF LIBERTY BY COMPULSORY MILITARY DUTY EXCEEDS TEMPORARY RESTRAINT BY ARREST.

To *prevent* hostilities in case of *threatened danger*, the President may call into service the army and navy of the United States and the militia, and thereby *subject* vast numbers of citizens to *military duty* under all the severity of martial law, whereby they are required to act under restraints more severe, and to incur dangers more formidable than any mere *arrest* and detention in a safe place for a limited time.

The law of Congress (1795) provides that the army may be called into actual service not only in cases of actual *invasion*, but when there is *danger* of *invasion*. Such is the power of the President under the Constitu-

* Lochington *vs.* Smith, Peters C. C. Rep. 466.

tion, as interpreted by the Supreme Court of the United States in the case of Martin *vs.* Mott, 12 *Wheaton R.* 28.

The President of the United States is the sole arbiter of the question whether such danger exists, and he alone can call into action the proper force to meet the danger.

He alone is the judge as to *where* the danger is, and he has a right to place his troops *there*, in whatever State or Territory that danger is apprehended. He may issue orders to his army to take such military measures as may, in his judgment, be necessary for public safety; whether these measures require the destruction of public or private property, *the arrest or capture of persons*, or other speedy and effectual military operations, sanctioned by the laws of war.

Such are the principles settled in Martin *vs.* Mott,* and reaffirmed in Luther *vs.* Borden,† where, in a civil war *in a State*, the *apprehension of danger*, and the right to use military power to *prevent* it, and to restrain the public enemy, are held to justify the violation of rights of person and property, invariably held sacred and inviolable in time of peace.

MILITARY ARRESTS MADE BY ALL GOVERNMENTS IN CIVIL WAR.

Capture of prisoners, seizures of property, are, all over the world, among the familiar proceedings of belligerents. No existing government has ever hesitated, while civil war was raging, to make military arrests. Nor could warlike operations be successfully conducted without a frequent use of the power to take and restrain hostile persons. Such is the lesson taught by the history of

* 12 Wheaton's Reports, page 28.

† 8 Howard's Reports, page 1.

England and France. While the laws of war place in the hands of military commanders the power to capture, arrest, and imprison the army of the enemy, it would be unreasonable not to authorize them to capture a hostile individual, when his going at large would endanger the success of military operations. To carry on war with no right to seize and hold prisoners would be as impracticable as to carry on the administration of criminal law with no right to arrest and imprison culprits.

PECULIAR NECESSITIES OF CIVIL WAR.

In foreign wars, where the belligerents are separated by territorial boundaries, or by difference of language, there is little difficulty in distinguishing friend from foe. But in civil war, those who are now antagonists but yesterday walked in the same paths, gathered around the same fireside, worshipped at the same altar; there is no means of separating friend from foe, except by the single test of loyalty, or hostility to the government.

MARKS OF HOSTILITY.

It is a sentiment of hostility which in time of war seeks to overthrow the government, to cripple its powers of self-defence, to destroy or depreciate its resources, to undermine confidence in its capacity or its integrity, to diminish, demoralize, or destroy its armies, to break down confidence in those who are intrusted with its military operations in the field.

He is a public enemy who seeks falsely to exalt the motives, character, and capacity of armed traitors, to magnify their resources, to encourage their efforts by sowing dissensions at home, and inviting intervention of foreign powers in our affairs, by overrating the success, increasing the confidence, and strengthening the hopes of our adversary, and by underrating, diminishing, and weakening our own, seeking false causes of complaint against our government and its officers, sowing seeds of dissension and party spirit among ourselves, and by many other ways giving aid and comfort to the enemy—aid more valuable to them than many regiments of soldiers or many millions of dollars.

All these ways and means of aiding a public enemy ought to be prevented or punished. But the connexions between citizens residing in different sections of the country are so intimate, the divisions of opinion on political or military questions are so numerous, the balance of affection, of interest, and of loyalty is so nice in many instances that civil war, like that which darkens the United States, is fraught with peculiar dangers, requires unusual precautions, and warrants and demands the most thorough and unhesitating measures for preventing acts of hostility, and for the security of public safety.

WHO OUGHT AND WHO OUGHT NOT TO BE ARRESTED.

All persons who *act* as public enemies, and all who by word or deed give reasonable cause to believe that they *intend* to act as such, may lawfully be arrested and detained by military authority for the purpose of preventing the consequences of their acts.

No person in loyal States can rightfully be captured or detained unless he has engaged, or there is reasonable cause to believe he intends to engage, in acts of hostility to the United States—that is to say, in acts which may tend to impede or embarrass the United States in such military proceedings as the commander-in-chief may see fit to institute.

INSTANCES OF ACTS OF HOSTILITY.

Among hostile proceedings, in addition to those already suggested, and which justify military arrests, may be mentioned contraband trade with hostile districts or commercial intercourse with them, forbidden by statutes or by military orders;* aiding the enemy by furnishing them with information which may be useful to them; correspondence with foreign authorities with a view to impede or unfavorably affect the negotiations or interests of the government;† enticing soldiers or sailors to desertion; prevention of enlistments; obstruction to officers whose duty it is to ascertain the names of persons liable to do military duty, and to enrol them; resistance to the draft, to the organization or to the movements of soldiers; aiding or assisting persons to escape from their military duty, by concealing them in the country or transporting them away from it.

NECESSITY OF POWER TO ARREST THOSE WHO RESIST DRAFT.

The creation and organization of an army are the foundation of all power to suppress rebellion or repel invasion, to execute the laws, and to support the Constitution, when they are assailed.

Without the power to capture or arrest those who oppose the draft no army can be raised. The necessity of such arrests is recognized by Congress in the 75th chapter of the act of March 3, 1863, for "*enrolling the forces of the United States, and for other purposes,*" which pro-

* See acts June 13, 1861; May 20, 1862, and March 12, 1863.

† See act February 12, 1863, ch. 60.

vides for the *arrest* and punishment of those who oppose the draft. This provision is an essential part of the general system for raising an army embodied in that statute.

Those citizens who are secretly hostile to the Union may attempt to prevent the board of enrolment from proceeding with the draft, or may refuse, when drafted, to enter the service.

Military power is called on to aid the proceedings by which the army is created. If the judiciary only is relied on, then raising the army must depend at last on the physical force which the judiciary can bring forward to enforce its mandates; and so, if the *posse comitatus* is not able to overpower those opposed to draft, the draft cannot be made according to law. If the draft is generally resisted in any locality, as it may be, no draft can be made, no law enforced, except mob law and lynch law, unless military power is lawfully applied to arrest the criminals.

If the power to raise an army be denied, the government will be broken down; and because we are too anxious to secure the supposed rights of certain individuals, all our rights will be trampled under foot.

TERRITORIAL EXTENT OF MARTIAL AND MILITARY LAW.

It is said that martial law must be confined to the immediate field of action of the contending armies, while in other and remote districts the martial law is not in force. Let us see the difficulty of this view.

Is martial law to be enforced only where the movements of our enemy may carry it?

Do we lose our military control of a district when the enemy have passed through and beyond it?

Is there no martial law between the base of operations of our army and the enemy's lines, even though it be a thousand miles from one to the other?

Must there be two armies close to each other to introduce martial law?

Is it not enough that there is one army in a locality to enforce the law?

If a regiment is encamped, is there not within its lines martial law?

If a single file of soldiers is present under a commanding officer, is it not the same?

Where must the enemy be to authorize martial law?

Suppose the enemy is an army, a regiment, or a single man; yet, be the number of persons more or less, it is still the enemy.

Who is the enemy? Whoever makes war.

Who makes war? Whoever aids and comforts the enemy. He commits treason. He makes war.

A raid into a northern State with arms is no more an act of hostility than a conspiracy to aid the enemy in the northern States by northern men.

All drafts of soldiers are made in places remote from the field of conflict. If no arrest can be made there, then the formation of the army can be prevented.

Can a spy be arrested by martial law? Formerly there was no law of the United States against spies outside of camps. There was nothing but martial law against them. A spy from the rebel army no one could doubt should be arrested. Why should not a spy from the northern States be arrested?

Thus it is obvious that the President, if deprived of the power to seize or capture the enemy, wherever they may be found, whether remote from the field of hostilities or near to it, cannot effectually suppress the rebellion.

Where is the limit to which the military power of the commander of the army must be confined in making war against the enemy? Wherever military operations are actually extended, there is martial law.

Whenever a person is helping the enemy, then he may be taken as an enemy; whenever a capture is made, there war is going on, there martial law is inaugurated, so far as that capture is concerned.

Stonewall Jackson, it is said, visited Baltimore a few months since in disguise. While there, it is not known that he committed any breach of the laws of Maryland or of the United States. Could he not have been captured, if he had been caught, by the order of the President? If captured, could the State court of Maryland have ordered him to be surrendered to its judge, and so turned loose again?

HABEAS CORPUS.

The military or executive power to prevent prisoners of war from being subject to discharge by civil tribunals, or, in other words, the power to suspend as to these prisoners the privilege of *habeas corpus*, is an essential means of suppressing the rebellion and providing for the public safety, and is therefore, by necessary implication, conferred by the Constitution on that department of government to which belongs the duty of suppressing rebellion by force of arms in time of war. In times of civil war or rebellion it is the duty of the President to call out the army and navy to suppress it. To use the army effectually for that purpose it is essential that the commanders should have the power of retaining in their control all persons captured and held in prison.

It must be presumed that the powers necessary to execute the duties of the President are conferred on him by the Constitution. Hence he must have the power to hold whatever persons he has a right to capture without interference of courts during the war, and he has the right to capture all persons who he has reasonable cause to believe are hostile to the Union, and are engaged in hostile acts. The power is to be exercised in emergencies. It is to be used suddenly. The facts on which public safety in time of civil war depends can be known only to the military men, and not to the legislatures in any special case. To pass a law as to each prisoner's case, whenever public safety required the privilege of the writ to be suspended, would be impracticable.

Shall there be no power to suspend the writ as to any single person in all the northern States unless Congress pass a law depriving all persons of that privilege?

Oftentimes the exposure of the facts and circumstances requiring the suspension in one case would be injurious to the public service by betraying our secrets to the enemy. Few acts of hostility are more dangerous to public safety, none require a more severe treatment, either to prevent or to punish than an attempt to interfere with the formation of the army by preventing enlistments, by procuring desertions, or by aiding and assisting persons liable to do military duty in escaping from the performance of it. Military arrest and confinement in prison during the war are but a light punishment for a crime which, if successful, would place the country in the power of its enemies, and sacrifice the lives of soldiers now in the field for want of support.

Whoever breaks up the fountain head of the army strikes at the heart of the country.

All those proceedings which tend to break down the army when in the field, or to prevent or impede any step necessary to be taken to collect and organize it, are acts of hostility to the country, and tend directly to impede the military operations on which the preservation of the government now in time of war depends. All persons who commit such acts of hostility are liable to military arrest and detention; and if they are at the same time liable to be proceeded against for violation of municipal laws, that liability cannot shelter them from responsibility to be treated as public enemies arrested and detained so as to prevent them from perpetrating any act of hostility.

In determining the character of acts in the free States committed by persons known to be opposed to the war, it must be borne in mind that those who in the loyal States aid and comfort the enemy are partakers in the crime of rebellion as essentially as if present with rebel armies. They are in law *participes criminis.* Though their overt acts, taken alone and without connection with the rebellion might not amount to treason, or to any crime, yet under the circumstances, many of these acts, otherwise innocent, become dangerous, injurious and criminal.

A person who by his mere presence lends support and gives confidence to a murderer while perpetrating his foul crime, is sharer in that crime, whether he is at the time of the murder in actual presence of his victim, or stands off at a distance, and is ready to warn the cut-throat of the approach of danger. Such was the rule administered in the trial of Knapp for murdering a citizen of Massachusetts. This is familiar law. What difference does it make whether the conspirator is near or far away from his associates; whether he is in a slave or a free State? The real question is whether the person accused has given or means to give aid or comfort to the enemy of his country, whether near by or far off; if so, then he is an enemy, and may be captured on the door steps of a court-house, or even on the bench itself.

CONSTITUTIONALITY OF THE ENROLMENT ACT OF MARCH 3, 1863

No power to arrest or detain prisoners can be conferred upon the President or his provost marshals by an act of Congress which is void for being unconstitutional. No person can be civilly or criminally liable to imprisonment for violation of a void statute. Hence the question may arise whether the enrolment act is a legitimate exercise by Congress of powers conferred upon it by the Constitution.

That Congress has full power to pass the enrolment act is beyond reasonable doubt, as will be apparent from the following references:*

The Constitution, article 1, section 8, clause 12, gives to Congress the power "to raise and support armies."

It must be observed that the *Constitution* recognizes a clear distinction between the "*army of the United States*" and the "*militia*" of the several States, even when called into actual service. Thus, by article 2, section 2, clause 1, "The President shall be commander-in-chief of the *army* and navy of the United States, *and of the militia* of the several States, when called into actual service of the United States."

By article 1, section 8, clause 15, "Congress shall

* So decided in several cases, since the publication of the first edition.

have power to provide for calling forth the militia to execute the laws of the Union, suppress insurrections, and repel invasions."

By article 1, section 8, clause 16, Congress shall have power "to provide for organizing, arming, and disciplining the militia, and for governing such part of them as may be employed in the service of the United States, reserving to the States respectively the appointment of the officers, and the authority of training the militia according to the discipline prescribed by Congress."

In addition to these powers of Congress to call into the service of the Union the militia of the States by requisitions upon the respective governors thereof, the Constitution confers upon Congress another distinct, independent power, by article 1, section 8, clause 12, which provides "That Congress shall *have power to raise and support armies;* but no appropriation for that use shall be for a longer term than two years."

By article 1, section 8, clause 14, Congress shall have power to make rules for the government and regulation of the land and naval forces.

The statutes of 1795, and other recent acts of 1861 and 1862, authorizing the enlistment of volunteers, were mainly founded on the power to receive militia of the States into the service of the Union, and troops were raised principally through the agency of governors of States.

But the enrolment act of 1863 is an exercise of power conferred upon Congress, to "raise and support armies," and not of the power to call out the militia of the States. Neither the governors nor other State authorities have any official functions to perform in relation to this act, nor any right to interfere with it. It is an act of the

United States, to be administered by United States officers, applicable to citizens of the United States in the same way as all other national laws.

The confounding of these separate powers of Congress and the rights and proceedings derived from them has been a prolific source of error and misapprehension.

Article 1, section 8, clause 13, gives Congress power "to make rules for the government and regulation of the land and naval forces."

Article 1, section 8, clause 18, gives Congress power "to pass all laws which shall be necessary and proper for carrying into effect the foregoing powers and all other powers vested by this Constitution in the government or in any *department* or *officer thereof*."

RULES OF INTERPRETATION AND THEIR APPLICATION TO THIS ACT.

The Constitution provides that Congress shall have power to pass "all laws necessary and proper" for carrying into execution all the powers granted to the government of the United States, or any department or officer thereof. The word "necessary," as used, is not limited by the additional word "proper," but enlarged thereby.

"If the word *necessary* were used in the strict, rigorous sense, it would be an extraordinary departure from the usual course of the human mind, as exhibited in solemn instruments, to add another word, the only possible effect of which is to qualify that strict and rigorous meaning, and to present clearly the idea of a choice of means in the course of legislation. If no means are to be resorted to but such as are *indispensably* necessary, there can be neither sense nor utility in adding the word '*proper*,' for the *indispensable necessity* would shut out from view all consideration of the *propriety* of the means."

Alexander Hamilton says—

"The authorities essential to the care of the common defence are these: To raise armies; to build and equip fleets; to prescribe rules for the government of both; to direct their operations; to provide for their support. These powers ought to exist WITHOUT LIMITATION because it is impossible to foresee or to define the extent and variety of national exigencies, and the correspondent extent and variety of the means necessary to satisfy them. The circumstances which endanger the safety of nations are infinite, and for this reason no constitutional shackles can wisely be imposed on the power to which the care of it is committed. * * * This power ought to be under the direction of the same councils which are appointed to preside over the *common defence*. * * * It must be admitted, as a necessary consequence, that there can be no limitation of that authority which is to provide for the defence and protection of the community in any matter essential to its efficacy—that is, in any matter essential to the *formation*, *direction*, or *support* of the NATIONAL FORCES."

This statement, Hamilton says—

"Rests upon two axioms, simple as they are universal: the *means* ought to be proportioned to the *end*; the persons from whose agency the attainment of the *end* is expected ought to possess the *means* by which it is to be attained."

The doctrine of the Supreme Court of the United States, announced by Chief Justice Marshall, and approved by Daniel Webster, Chancellor Kent, and Judge Story, is thus stated:

"The government of the United States is one of enumerated powers, and it can exercise only the powers granted to it; but though limited in its powers, it is supreme within its sphere of action. It is the government of the people of the United States, and emanated from them. Its powers were delegated by all, and it represents all, and acts for all.

"There is nothing in the Constitution which excludes *incidental* or *implied* powers. The articles of confederation gave nothing to the United States but what was expressly granted; but the new Constitution dropped the word *expressly*, and left the question whether a particular power was granted to depend on a fair construction of the whole instrument. No constitution can contain an accurate detail of all the subdivisions of its powers, and all the *means* by which they might be carried into execution. It would render it too prolix. Its nature requires that only the great outlines should be marked, and its important objects designated, and all the minor ingredients left to be deduced from the nature of those objects. The sword and the purse all the external relations, and no inconsiderable portion of the industry of the nation, were intrusted to the general government; and a government intrusted with such ample powers, on the due execution of which the happiness and prosperity of the people vitally depended, must also be intrusted with *ample means of their execution.* Unless the words imperiously require it, we ought not to adopt a construction which would impute to the framers of the Constitution, when granting great powers for the public good, the intention of impeding their exercise by withholding a *choice of means.* The powers given to the government imply the ordinary means of execution; and the government, in all sound reason and fair interpretation, must have the choice of the means which it deems the most convenient and appropriate to the execution of the power. The Constitution has not left the right of Congress to employ the necessary means for the execution of its powers to general reasoning. Art. 1, sect. 8, of the Constitution expressly confers on Congress the power 'to make all laws that may be necessary and proper to carry into execution the foregoing powers.'

"Congress may employ such means and pass such laws as it may deem necessary to carry into execution great powers granted by the Constitution; and *necessary* means, in the sense of the Constitution, does not import an absolute physical necessity so strong that one thing cannot exist without the other. It stands for any means calculated to produce the end. The word *necessary* admits of all degrees of comparison. A thing may be necessary, or very necessary, or absolutely or indispensably necessary. The word is used in various senses, and in its construction the subject, the context, the intention, are all to be taken into view. The powers of the government were given for the welfare of the nation. They were intended to endure for ages to come, and to be adapted to the various *crises* in human affairs. To prescribe the specific means by which government should in all future time execute its power, and to confine the choice of means to such narrow limits as should not leave it in the power of Congress to adopt any which might be appropriate and conducive to the end, would be most unwise and pernicious, because it would be an attempt to provide, by immutable rules, for exigencies which, if foreseen at all, must have been foreseen dimly, and would deprive the legislature of the capacity to avail itself of experience, or to exercise its reason, and accommodate its legislation to circumstances. If the end be legitimate, and within the scope of the Constitution, all means which are appropriate, and plainly adapted to this end, and which are not prohibited by the Constitution, are lawful."*

Under the power of Congress to pass all laws necessary and proper to raise and support armies the only question is, whether the act of Congress is "plainly adapted to the end proposed," namely, "*to raise an army.*" If it is a usual mode of raising an army to enrol and draft citizens, or, if unusual, it is *one appropriate mode* by which the end may be accomplished, it is within the power of Congress to pass the law. Congress, having the power to raise an army, has an unlimited choice of "means" appropriate for carrying that power into execution.

In a republic, the country has a right to the military service of every citizen and subject. The government is a government of tho people, and for the safety of the people. No man who enjoys its protection can lawfully escape his share of public burdens and duties. *Public safety* and *welfare* in time of war depend wholly upon the success of *military* operations. Whatever stands in the way of military success must be sacrificed, else all is lost. The triumph of arms is the *tabula in naufragio*, the last plank in the shipwreck, on which alone our chance of national life depends. *Hence*, in the struggle of a great people for *existence*, private rights, though not to be disregarded, become comparatively insignificant, and are held subject to the paramount rights of the community. The life of the nation must be preserved at all hazards, and the Constitution must not, without im-

* On the interpretation of constitutional power, see 1 Kent's Com., 351, 352, *McCulloch* v. *The State of Maryland*, 4 Wheat. R., 413—420.

perative necessity, be so construed as to deprive the people of the amplest means of self-defence.

Every attempt to fetter the power of Congress in calling into the field the military forces of the country in time of war is only a denial of the people's right to fight *in their own defence.*

If a foreign enemy were now to invade the country, who would dare to cavil at the forms of statutes whereby the people sought to organize the army to repel the invader? It must not be forgotten that Congress has the same power to-day to raise and organize armies to suppress rebellion that would belong to it if the Union were called upon to meet the world in arms.

INDEMNITY TO PERSONS ARRESTED.

Persons who reside in a country engaged in active hostilities, and who so conduct themselves as to give reasonable cause to believe that they are aiding and comforting a public enemy, or that they are participating in any of those proceedings which tend to embarrass military operations, may be arrested; and if such persons shall be *arrested* and imprisoned for the purpose of punishing or preventing such acts of hostility, they are not entitled to claim indemnity for the injury to themselves or to their property, suffered by reason of such arrest and imprisonment.

If the persons so arrested be subjects of a foreign government, they cannot lawfully claim indemnity, because their own hostile conduct, while it has deprived them of the shelter of "neutrality," has subjected them to penalties for having violated the laws of war.

If a foreigner join the rebels, he exposes himself to the treatment of rebels. He can claim of this government no indemnity for wounds received in battle, or for loss of time or suffering by being captured and imprisoned. It can make no difference whether his acts of hostility to the United States are committed in open contest under a rebel flag, or in the loyal States, where his enmity is most dangerous. If it be said that he has violated no municipal law, and therefore ought not to be deprived of liberty without indemnity, it must be remembered that if he has violated any of the laws of war he may have thereby committed an offence more dangerous to the country and more destructive in its consequences than any crime defined in statutes.

If a person, detained in custody in consequence of having violated the laws of war and for the purpose of *preventing* hostilities, be liberated from confinement without having been *indicted* by a grand jury, it does not follow therefrom that he has committed no *crime*. He may have been guilty of grave offences, while the government may not have deemed it necessary to prosecute him. Clemency and forbearance are not a just foundation for a claim of indemnity. An offender may not have been indicted, because the crime committed, being purely a military crime, or crime against martial law; may not have come within the jurisdiction of civil tribunals.

In such a case the arrest and imprisonment, founded on martial law, justified by military necessity, cannot be adjudicated by civil tribunals.

If the person so arrested is the subject of a foreign power, and claims exemption from arrest and custody for that reason, he can have no right to indemnity under any circumstances, by reason of being an alien, until such fact of alienage is made known to the government. His claim to indemnity thereafter will depend on a just application of the principles already stated.

APPENDIX.

INSTRUCTIONS OF THE WAR DEPARTMENT TO OFFICERS HAVING CHARGE OF DESERTERS.

WAR DEPARTMENT,
PROVOST MARSHAL GENERAL'S OFFICE,
Washington, D. C., July 1, 1863.

[CIRCULAR No. 36.]

The following opinion of Hon. William Whiting, Solicitor of the War Department, is published for the information and guidance of all officers of this Bureau:

ARREST OF DESERTERS—HABEAS CORPUS.

Opinion.

It is enacted in the 7th section of the act approved March 3, 1863, entitled "An act for enrolling and calling out the national forces, and for other purposes," that it shall be the duty of the Provost Marshals appointed under this act "to arrest *all deserters, whether regulars, volunteers, militia men, or persons called into the service under this or any other act of Congress,* wherever they may be found, and to send them to the nearest military commander, or military post."

If a writ of *habeas corpus* shall be issued by a State court, and served upon the Provost Marshal while he holds under arrest a deserter, before he has had opportunity "to send him to the nearest military commander, or military post," the Provost Marshal is not at liberty to disregard that process. "It is the duty of the Marshal, or other person having custody of the prisoner, to make known to the judge or court, by a proper return, the authority by which he holds him in custody. But after this return is made, and the State judge or court judicially apprised that the party is in custody under the authority of the United States, they can proceed no further.

"They then know that the prisoner is within the dominion and jurisdiction of another government, and that neither the writ of *habeas corpus*, nor any other process issued under State authority, can pass over the line of division between the two sovereignties. He is then within the dominion and exclusive jurisdiction of the United States. If he has committed an offence against their laws, their tribunals alone can punish him. If he is wrongfully imprisoned, their judicial tribunals can release him and afford him redress. And although, as we have said, it is the duty of the Marshal, or other person holding him, to make known, by a proper return, the authority under which he retains him, it is, at the same time, imperatively his duty to obey the process of the United States, to hold the prisoner in custody under it, and to refuse obedience to the mandate or process of any other government. And, consequently, it is his duty not to take the prisoner, nor suffer him to be taken, before a State judge or court, upon a *habeas corpus* issued under State authority. No State judge or court, after they are judicially informed that the party is imprisoned under the authority of the United States, has any right to interfere with him, or require him to be brought before them. And if the authority of a State, in the form of judicial process or otherwise, should attempt to control the Marshal, or other authorized officer or agent of the United States, in any respect, in the custody of his prisoner, it would be his duty to resist it, and to call to his aid any force that might be necessary to maintain the authority of law against illegal interference. 'No judicial process, whatever form it may assume, can have any lawful authority outside the limits of the jurisdiction of the court or judge by whom it is issued; and an attempt to enforce it beyond these boundaries is nothing less than lawless violence.'"

The language above cited is that of Chief Justice Taney in the decision of the Supreme Court of the United States in the case of Ableman *vs.* Booth.—(21 Howard's Reports, 506.)

If a writ of *habeas corpus* shall have been sued out from a State court, and served upon the Provost Marshal while he holds the deserter under arrest, and before he has had time or opportunity to "send him to the nearest military commander, or military post," it is the duty of the Marshal to make to the court a respectful statement, in writing, as a return upon the writ, setting forth:

1st. That the respondent is Provost Marshal, duly appointed by the President of the United States, in accordance with the provisions of the act aforesaid.

2d. That the person held was arrested by said Marshal as a

deserter, in accordance with the provision of the 7th section of the act aforesaid. That it is the legal duty of the respondent to deliver over said deserter "to the nearest military commander, or military post," and that the respondent intends to perform such duty as soon as possible.

3d. That the production of said deserter in court would be inconsistent with, and in violation of the duty of the respondent as Provost Marshal, and that the said deserter is now held under authority of the United States. For these reasons, and without intending any disrespect to the honorable judge who issued process, he declines to produce said deserter, or to subject him to the process of the court.

To the foregoing all other material facts may be added.

Such return having been made, the jurisdiction of the State court over that case ceases. If the State court shall proceed with the case and make any formal judgment in it, except that of dismissal, one of two courses must be taken. (1) The case may be carried up, by appeal or otherwise, to the highest court of the State, and removed therefrom by writ of error to the Supreme Court; or, (2) the judge may be personally dealt with in accordance with law, and with such instructions as may hereafter be issued in each case.

WILLIAM WHITING,
Solicitor of the War Department.

NOTE A. — For those who desire to examine the practice and authorities on the question, whether a government has the right to treat its subjects, in civil war, as belligerents or as subjects, reference may be had to the following, viz: (Stephen's) Blackstone's Com., Vol. 4, p. 286. Marten's Essai concernant les Armateurs, ch. 2, sect. 11. See 17 Geo. III. ch. 9 (1777). Pickering's Statutes, Vol. 31, p. 312. See President's Proclamation, April 19, 1861. U. S. Stat. at Large, 1861, App. p. ii. See charge of *Nelson*, J., on the trial of the officers, &c., of the *Savannah*, p. 371.

In this case the rebel privateer put in as a defence his commission to cruise under the confederate flag; and the same defence was made in Philadelphia by other persons indicted for piracy. It was held in both of these tribunals, that they must *follow the decision of the executive and legislative departments* in determining the political status of the Confederate States; and, that the *exercise of belligerent* rights by the Federal Government *did not imply any waiver or renunciation of its sovereign or municipal rights, or rights to hold as subjects the belligerent inhabitants of the seceded States.* See also Smith's Trial, page 96.

The pirates tried in New York were not convicted. Those who were convicted in Philadelphia were not sentenced, but, by order of the Secretary of State (Jan. 31, 1862), were sent to a military prison, to be exchanged as prisoners of war, — this being done to avoid threatened retaliation.

See also authorities cited in "War Powers," p. 44.

It has been decided, since this edition was in type, that citizens of States in rebellion are considered as *public enemies, and are not entitled to sue in the Courts of the United States*, by Nelson, J., U. S. C. C., of Minnesota. *Nash* v. *Dayton*, also by the Court of Appeals in Kentucky; and this decision is approved by Governor Bramlette (see his Message to Ho. of Rep., Feb. 13, 1864).

The following case has been decided in Ohio since the seventh edition of the "War Powers" went to press:—

FROM THE CINCINNATI COMMERCIAL.

THE CASE OF KEES VS. TOD.

John W. Kees *vs.* David Tod and others, Pickaway County Common Pleas; civil action. On petition to remove the case, for trial, to the United States Circuit Court.

The defendants, under the Act of Congress of March 3, 1863, present a sworn petition, stating the facts, clearly within the Act, and tendering surety as provided by the Act.

Section 4 of the Act provides, "That any order of the President, or under his authority, made at any time during the existence of the present rebellion, shall be a defence in all courts to any action or prosecution, civil or criminal, pending, or to be commenced, for any search or seizure, arrest or imprisonment, made, done, or committed, or acts omitted to be done, under and by virtue of such order, or under color of any law of Congress, and such defence may be made by special plea, or under the general issue."

Section 5 provides, "That if any suit or prosecution, civil or criminal, has been or shall be commenced in any State court against any officer civil or military, or against any other person, for any arrest or imprisonment made, or other trespasses or wrongs done or committed, or any act omitted to be done, at any time during the present rebellion, by virtue or under color of any authority derived from or exercised by or under the President of the United States, or any Act of Congress, and the defendant shall, at the time of entering his appearance in such court, or, if such appearance shall have been entered before the passage of this Act, then at the next session of the court in which such suit or prosecution is pending, file a petition, stating the facts, and verified by affidavit, for the removal of the cause for trial at the next Circuit Court of the United States, to be holden in the district where the suit is pending, and offer good and sufficient surety for his filing in such court, on the first day of its session, copies of such process or proceedings against him, and also for his appearing in such court, and entering special bail in the cause, if special bail was originally required therein, it shall be the duty of the State court to accept the surety, and proceed no further in the cause or prosecution, and the bail that shall have been originally taken shall be discharged, and such copies being filed, as aforesaid, in such court of the United States, the cause shall proceed therein in the same manner as if it had been brought in said court by original process, whatever may be the amount in dispute or the damages claimed, or whatever the citizenship of the parties, any former law to the contrary notwithstanding.

OPINION OF JUDGE DICKEY.

The plaintiff brought his action in this court to recover damages for an alleged trespass and false imprisonment by the defendants, and filed his petition on the 14th of September, 1863, and caused summons to be issued and served, &c. In his petition he alleges that the defendants, on the 29th day of June, 1862, at the county of Pickaway, unlawfully and maliciously assaulted the plaintiff, and that the defendants, Bliss, Goodell, and Dougherty, at the instance and by the procurement of the defendants, Tod and Gregg, seized and laid hold of the plaintiff, and then and there unlawfully and maliciously, and without any reasonable and probable cause, arrested and imprisoned said plaintiff, with intention of having him carried out of the State of Ohio contrary to the laws thereof, and that defendants Scott and Goodell, then and there, at the instance and by the procurement of the said Tod, Dougherty, and Gregg, forced and compelled the said plaintiff to go from and out of his house, situate and being in said county of Pickaway, into the public street, and so on; charging that they compelled him to go out of the State of Ohio, to the military prison, called the "Old Capitol Prison," in Washington City, and there the defendants caused him to be unlawfully and maliciously, and against his will, without reasonable or probable cause, imprisoned for seventeen days, &c., to his damage, $30,000.

On the 27th of October, 1863, defendants Tod, Gregg, and Dougherty, the only defendants served with process, filed their petitions against the plaintiff Kees, stating, in substance, that the plaintiff Kees, on the 12th of September, 1863, filed his petition in the court, and commenced a civil action for the wrongs, injuries, &c., as stated in plaintiff's petition, making reference to it for particulars, and then going on to set forth that having been summoned, they come and enter their appearance to the plaintiff's action, and state, that, so far as the arrest, imprisonment, wrongs, &c., were committed, as alleged in plaintiff's petition, the same was done during the present rebellion, about the 29th day of June, 1862, and prior to the 3d day of March, 1863, by virtue and under color of authority derived from and exercised by the President of the United States, and by virtue of and under an order issued from the War Department of the United States (a copy of which order is given).

The defendants then, after a full statement of the facts as they claim them, relating to the authority, &c., further state, that they, desiring to have the case removed to the next Circuit Court of the United States, to be holden at Cincinnati, &c., come and offer good and sufficient surety, &c., and then pray this court to accept the surety and proceed no further in the case, and to make such further order as may be necessary for the removal of the case to the Circuit Court of the United States.

The following is the order of the War Department referred to:

War Department, Washington, D. C.,
June 27, 1862.

Sir: Proceed, with one assistant, by first train, to Circleville, in the State of Ohio, arrest there, or wherever else he may be found, John W. Kees, editor and publisher of the "Circleville Watchman," and deliver him to the commandant at Camp Chase, permitting no communication with him except by yourself, and your subordinates charged with his safe keeping, and, if you think fit, by his family in your presence. Examine all papers, private or otherwise, found at the office of the paper, the residence of Kees, or on his person, and bring with you to the department all that may be found of a treasonable or suspicious nature, as well as a copy of each issue of the "Watchman" during the last four months. Close the office, locking up the presses, type, paper, and other material found therein, and place it in charge of a discreet and trustworthy person, who will see that it is safely kept. If you think any further aid will be necessary, call on Governor Tod, at Columbus, who will be requested to give you such information and aid as you may think needful in enabling you to fulfil your duty.

Let this order be executed promptly, discreetly, and quietly; and, when executed, make full report of your doings hereunder to this department.

By order of the Secretary of War.

(Signed) C. P. WOLCOTT,
Assistant Secretary of War.

It was set forth in defendant's petition that this order was addressed to Wm. H. Scott, Washington, D. C., and delivered to him, and that he proceeded to its execution, and called at the Executive office, in Columbus, was given information in regard to Kees, his paper, and persons, to call on at Circleville, &c., by one of the Governor's staff; and that Scott did proceed to Circleville, and arrest Kees under and by virtue of the command of the order referred to, &c. And the petition of the defendant, David Tod, further states, that about the 6th of June, 1862, prior to the issuing of the order, the Circleville Watchman of that date, edited and published by Kees, was mailed to him as Governor, containing marked editorial articles, highly libellous, inflammatory, and treasonable in their character, well calculated and intended to prevent enlistments, weaken the military power of the government, and produce opposition to it in its efforts to crush the rebellion, and excite further rebellion—copies of which articles, and others of like character issued prior to the order, are shown with the petition.

The defendant Tod further states that he enclosed the Watchman containing the marked articles by mail to the Secretary of War, with a letter, calling the Secretary's attention to the marked articles, and hoping that the Secretary would at once put its editor, John W. Kees, with his secession rebel friends, in Camp Chase prison, where it would be his (the Governor's) pleasure to see that he (Kees) would be safely kept.

He further states that he has set forth his only connection with the alleged arrest, &c., and that he did nothing more; and all he did was in his capacity as Governor of Ohio, and in performance of his duty to the national government.

The case has been argued and heard upon the defendant's petitions for the removal of it to the Circuit Court of the United States.

It nowhere appears in the petition of the plaintiff, that the defendants, in the commission of the trespasses and wrongs against the person of the plaintiff, as alleged, were acting under any authority, or color of authority, from any source whatever. And so far as appears from the petition of the plaintiff, this Court has complete jurisdiction of the case.

But, the defendants having filed their petitions for the removal of the case under the fifth section of the act of Congress, approved March 3, 1863, "relating to *habeas corpus* and regulating judicial proceedings in certain cases," which, if applicable, and not clearly invalid, so far as applicable, would require that the prayer of the defendants should be granted, no objection to the manner and form in which the application has been made having been raised by the plaintiff.

[Here follows the sections of the law, as quoted above.]

The mere reading of this fifth section, of itself, shows its applicability to the case before us; indeed, I believe that is not denied by the council for the plaintiff.

But it is claimed that the law is invalid, because not authorized by the Constitution of the United States, and because, when applied to the case in hand, is *ex post facto*, the right of action having accrued prior to the passage of the law. Whatever may be said of the attempt in the fourth section to create a defence, or provide an indemnity against trespasses committed prior to its passage, cannot be urged successfully against the fifth section, which only affects the remedy, and does not, in any manner, touch either the subject-matter of the action or of the defence.

These sections of the act are so far distinct and separable, that the fifth may be sustained independent of the fourth.

The object of the fourth section seems to be, to declare what is, or to provide what shall be, a defence in certain cases, to wit: "any order of the President, or under his authority." This applies only to cases where there *is an order*, and constitutes *such order* a defence in all courts where it shall be pleaded, whether in State or Federal Courts. The object of the fifth section is to provide a mode for the transfer of certain cases from the State to the Federal Courts, to wit: "all suits or prosecutions for act done or committed by virtue or under color of any authority derived from the President, or any act of Congress." This section applies to cases not included in the fourth section; it applies to all such cases as stated, whether there be any order or not.

In order to secure the benefit of it, its provisions must be strictly followed.

Thus it will be seen that either of these sections may be invoked without the other, and that the fifth is applicable to cases to which the fourth is not; and while the object of the fourth is to provide or declare rights, the object of the fifth is to regulate the practice in those and certain other cases. For these reasons, the two sections are so far separable and independent of each other, that the fifth may be held constitutional and the fourth unconstitutional. And, as it is not claimed that the fifth section is of itself unconstitutional, but only becomes so by reason of its inseparable connection with the fourth, I conclude that, as there is no such connection between them, the argument fails, and the Court may be justified in holding the fifth valid, without determining the validity of the fourth.

It will not be denied but that the Legislature of Ohio might, even after the right of an action of trespass in favor of a party had accrued against a Constable or Sheriff, pass a law providing that where such Constable or Sheriff had been sued in trespass, before a Justice of the Peace, as an individual, that if such officer desired to justify under a writ, and should make that known to the Justice, then it should be his duty to certify the case to a Court of Record having cognizance of the official acts of such defendant. Neither the subject-matter of the right of action nor the defence would be in the least interfered with; the mode of proceeding and the remedy are changed; that is all.

A more appropriate tribunal is provided; and so here this fifth section provides another tribunal — one having cognizance of United States officers, their official acts, and of the Constitution and laws of the United States, under which they act: no new defence is created, nor the right of action any way impaired. This section, therefore, is not invalid on the ground of its being retroactive.

It is, however, claimed that the facts set forth in the petition of defendant can constitute no defence, as the order under which the arrest was made was issued without authority under the Constitution of the United States, or the laws thereof, and that the fourth section of the act cannot support the defence, although in terms it may include it — for two reasons: first, because *that* section attempts to create a defence to a valid cause of action after it arose, and is, therefore, retroactive; and, second, because Congress can confer no power on the President to issue, or cause to be issued, such orders, either in time of war or peace, by virtue of any grant in the Constitution, by inference or otherwise; and that the *attempt*, therefore, to make such defence, is a nullity, and being so, the defence and the application to remove must fall together.

As to the first reason, suffice it to say, "sufficient unto the day is the evil thereof." When the defence provided by the fourth section is set up upon the trial of the cause upon its merits, either in this court or in the court to which it may be removed, it will be time enough to decide the question. To do so now would be to prejudge the case without a full hearing on the merits, and, if decided for the defendants, there would be no need for a removal, and if for the plaintiff, the only matter left would be an inquiry into damages; it would be equivalent to the decision of a demurrer to defendant's answer, on this preliminary application, and would be taking from the tribunal whose jurisdiction is sought, one of the questions upon which it should pass.

Again, granting that this fourth section is, so far as the case at bar is concerned, *ex post facto* in terms, and should be so held when the case is tried upon its merits, we are brought to consider the second reason given for its invalidity. Suppose the power to issue the order in question existed in the President, independent of section fourth, would its enactment annul that power, or only declare it? The act in question does not attempt to confer the power on the President to issue, or cause to be issued, such order; it merely declares that such orders, when issued shall be a good defence, proceeding upon the hypothesis, as we suppose, that he always possessed the power; so that in this view the fourth section partakes more of the nature of an act declaratory, than of the enactment of a new law conferring power. Enough, perhaps, has already been said to justify this court in granting the prayer of the defendants' petitions, and leave the question as to the authority of the War Department to issue the order set forth, for decision in the Circuit Court as the appropriate tribunal. But, inasmuch as it is claimed by the plaintiff, that no such authority, or color of authority exists, and that therefore there is no foundation for the jurisdiction sought by the defendants, I will proceed to offer reasons and authority, to show that it is at least a question of serious doubt, and, therefore, proper for the United States Court, as the doubt should be resolved in favor of the law.

Then, let us inquire into the power of the President, under the constitution, as commander-in chief of the army and navy, in time of a fearful rebellion like the present, to issue, or cause to be issued, such orders of arrest, &c. We all know the history of the sad times that have fallen upon us. The fact of a most violent, bloody, and terrific war, threatening our entire destruction as a nation — the imminent and immediate danger which threatens us in all we have and are in life — and of this contemporaneous history, of course the court should and will take notice.

In view of this, then, let us turn to the petition of the defendant David Tod, and ascertain, if we can, something of the cause of the arrest. It appears in the petition that the defendant, prior to the issuing of the order, wrote a letter to the War Department, enclosing certain marked editorials of the Watchman, of which Kees was editor and publisher, calling the attention of the Secretary of War thereto, and expressing a hope that the Secretary would at once put Kees, with his secession rebel friends, in Camp Chase Prison, &c. Copies of the editorials are referred to in, and filed with, the petition. In the article of June 6, 1862, this passage occurs: "We advised all Democrats to stay at home, and let the authors and provokers of this war, the Abolition Republicans, fight out their own war themselves; this is what ought to have been done. If such had been the policy of the Democracy, we would not to-day have a devastated country, drenched in fraternal blood." Again, in an editorial article of the Watchman, June 13, 1862, is this question, (after speaking of Ben. Butler in exceedingly harsh terms,) "Why don't the men of New Orleans shoot the infamous wretch like they would a reptile or a dog." These, with many kindred extracts, are filed with the petition, and are characterized in the petition of Governor Tod as highly libellous, inflammatory and treasonable in character, well calculated and intended to prevent enlistments, weaken the military power of the government, and produce opposition to it in its efforts to crush the rebellion, and excite further rebellion. This is all the information we have as to the cause of the arrest of Kees; whether the War Department had other and further foundation we know not — the presumption is, so far as this motion is concerned, that the information it had, whether under oath or otherwise, was deemed sufficient by it, for his arrest; sufficient to establish the fact, that the danger from Kees to the public service, while left at liberty, was immediate and impending, and that the urgent necessity for the public service demanded his arrest. Whether this was so or not, I do not undertake to say, nor is it necessary to decide, in disposing of this motion.

Article 3d, Section 2d, of the Federal Constitution provides that "The judicial power (of the United States) shall extend to all *cases* in law and equity *arising under this Constitution* and the laws of the United States," &c.

The President is commander in-chief of the army and navy, by express provision of the Constitution. Now, if the power to issue this order of arrest is incident to his office as Commander-in-chief, then, by necessary implication, the power is derived from the Constitution, without the aid of the fourth section referred to, and, if Kees was arrested by virtue of such order, then the case arose under the constitution, and the United States courts have jurisdiction, and, as we have seen, it may be transferred in the manner pointed out by the fifth section of that act, independent of the fourth.

And, if such power belongs to the President, as an incident to his office of Commander-in-chief, no question but he may transfer it to his subordinates, for all the war power vested in him may be, and is, distributed to the vast army of war officers who act under him as his agents. Upon this question there is, and has been, a great conflict of opinion, both legal and political. The order by which Mr. Vallandigham was arrested, was from the same source of power. Judge Leavitt passed upon the question and upheld the power, and Mr. Vallandigham was tried and sentenced under it.

It is claimed that the power in question is exercised under what is called martial law, or the right of war, and not under military law, which, it is said, is defined by the articles of war and the decisions under them, and is for the government of the army, &c. And it is claimed that this martial authority belongs, as a necessary incident, to the commander-in-chief, and that when that office is conferred, the necessary incident, in time of war, is conferred with it, and is as much a part of the office as any other.

Now, if this be so, it follows, of course, that when the office of commander-in-chief is conferred by the Constitution upon the President, this martial power is also conferred and secured, as clearly as the right of trial by jury, the liberty of the person, the freedom of speech and of the press, is secured to the citizen in time of peace.

The question here is, not whether the power was exercised under proper restraint, but whether it exists all, and it is not necessary to its exercise that martial law shall first have been declared. Cases are numerous, both in America and in Europe, where the authority, of the nature of the power in question has been exercised in time of war, by the commander-in-chief and his subordinates, in the absence of the declaration of martial law, and afterwards sustained by the civil courts. In the case of Mitchell *vs.* Harmony, reported in 13 Howard, 115, which was an action brought by the plaintiff against the defendant, to recover damages for the seizure of property, as a commander in the Mexican war, under the pretext of military necessity, Chief Justice Taney, in delivering the opinion of the court in that case, said, "It is impossible to define the particular circumstances of danger or necessity in which the power may be lawfully exercised. Every case must depend on its own circumstances. It is the emergency that gives the right. In deciding upon this necessity, however, the state of facts, as they appeared to the officer at the time he acted, must govern the decision, for he must necessarily act upon the information of others as well as his own observation. And if, with such information as he had a right to rely on, there is reasonable ground for believing that the peril is immediate and menacing, or the necessity urgent, he is justified in acting upon it, and the discovery afterwards, that it was false and erroneous, will not make him a trespasser." Now, it is urged that the power exercised by the defendants in the case named, was a partial exercise of martial law, and did not depend upon time or place, but upon the *emergency*, and that it was the *emergency* that gave the right to exercise it.

Chancellor Kent lays down the doctrine that martial law is quite a distinct thing from military law; that it exists only in time of war, and originates only in military necessity. It derives no authority from the civil law, no assistance from the civil tribunals, for it overrules, suspends, and replaces them. See Cushing's Opinions of Attorney Generals of the United States, vol. 8, page 365, &c., and the authorities there cited. See also the case of Luther *vs.* Borden, *et. al.*, 7 Howard, page 1.

It is also claimed that Washington's army exercised the power in question, during the whiskey insurrection of 1794 and 1795, and that General Wilkinson, under the authority of Jefferson, exercised it during the Burr conspiracy, in 1806; and that General Jackson called it into requisition at New Orleans, in 1814.

In the case of the application of Nicholas Kemp, for a writ of *habeas corpus*, the Supreme Court of Wisconsin recently decided against the power it gave the President to suspend the writ, but recognized the war right, or martial law, under certain limitations.

See also the case of Brown *vs.* the United States, book 8, Cranch, page 153, where Chief Justice Marshall, in delivering the opinion of the court, holds that "as a consequence of the power of declaring war and making treaties, &c., when the legislative authority has declared war, the Executive, to whom its execution is confided, is bound to carry it into effect; he has a *discretion* vested in him as to the *manner* and *extent*: but he cannot, morally, transcend the rules of warfare established among civilized nations."

See Vattel, pages 5 and 6, where the rule is laid down, that "a nation has a right to every thing that can help to ward off imminent dangers, and keep at a distance whatever is capable of causing its ruin, and that from the very same reasons that establish its rights to the things necessary for its preservation." He also lays down the rule, that the same rules of war apply to civil as to foreign wars.

It is not controverted but that the commander of an army may exercise, in proper cases, the power in question, over both property and person, within the territory and its vicinity under the control of the army, although martial law has not been declared, nor the civil law entirely suspended. What is it, then, but a partial exercise of martial law? And what gives the right but a military necessity, or emergency? And from what source does the power come, if not from the President, as commander-in-chief? Now, what good reason can there be for confining the power to and within the lines of the army, provided a like urgent necessity and emergency arises or exists at any other point outside of the lines of the army, and within the territory of the government or nation? What is the theatre of the present war in this country? Is it only that portion of the country included within the lines of the armies, which extend from the Chesapeake Bay to the spurs of the Rocky Mountains? or is it not rather the whole nation, the loyal States upon the one side, and the disloyal upon the other? and are not *all* within the vicinity of the lines of the armies, as far as that vicinity is to be considered as affecting the exercise of the authority in dispute?

The right to impress private property, either for the use of the government, or to prevent it from falling into the hands of the enemy, arising from urgent necessity, or from immediate impending danger, any where within the territory of the country, although outside the lines of the army, has never, that I am aware of, been disputed; but whether the emergency existed, or the impressment was properly made, may be disputed, and is a question of fact. There are numerous instances where this power has been exercised outside of the lines of the army, and no one has doubted its legitimacy. Railroads and telegraphs, with their machinery and employès, are frequently seized and impressed into the service of the government, and controlled per force, and the emergency relied upon to justify the act, the whole country acquiescing therein. In such cases the commander must be the judge of the urgent necessity, and if he decides that the necessity exists, and issues the order for the impressment, his subordinates are bound to obey. And it would seem from a well-settled principle of the common law that such subordinates would be justified, although their commander may have had but slight foundation for the exercise of the authority, and this upon the principle that, if the power existed at all, the commander, and not the soldier, is to judge of the limitations under which it is to be exercised. If the order is wanton, the party injured has his remedy against the commander. If it is said that the recognition of such a doctrine is dangerous to the liberties and rights of the people, and tends to subvert free government and establish despotism, the answer is, that the *abuse* of any power tends to the same end, and that it is the abuse, and not the legitimate exercise of it, which makes it dangerous. The limitations are well defined, and if he who undertakes to exercise it oversteps the bounds, he may be called to an account; and if the President corruptly and wantonly exercises it, he may be impeached, and at the end of his term the people will correct the error. But it is claimed, that although the authority may be exercised over property as stated, yet it cannot be so exercised over persons, although the same danger and urgent necessity may exist; for the reason that, in the case of the impressment of property, a compensation is made by the government to the owner, while in the case of the arrest of the person no such compensation can be made. Now, does the fact of compensation give the right to impress? It is not so laid down by any authority which has come under my notice. Compensation is not the test of the right, but one of the results of the act. The right arises from a far higher source, to wit, the right of a nation to do any act which will ward off a dangerous blow aimed at its existence, and which tends to preserve its life in time of war.

This test, it is claimed with great force, applies as well to the arrest of a person as to the impressment of his property, under proper restraints and in a proper case.

But, again, it is claimed that the recognition of this doctrine subverts the guarantees of the Constitution, of the right of trial by jury, and against unreasonable search, seizure &c. While, on the other hand, it is argued that the power is incident to the office of commander-in-chief of the armies in time of war, and necessarily implied. And, I ask, is this not true when the case arises within the limits of the army, where its exercise is uncontroverted? And if the guarantees of the Constitution are inapplicable in the one case, are they not equally so in the other? and if the immediate danger and urgent necessity is the foundation of the right, and that may be exercised outside as well as inside the lines, where is the line of distinction to be drawn?

Again, was the order of arrest in question issued upon the charge of the commission of any crime, or only because there was supposed to be imminent and impending danger that an irreparable injury would be committed, and in this view may not the government act upon the same principle that civil courts act in cases of peace warrants? Where a citizen has been arrested and brought before the court on a peace warrant, and tried, without a jury, and the court find that the complainant has just cause to fear, and does fear, that the accused will kill him, the court will require bail to keep the peace, and, in default of bail, will imprison the defendant, not for any crime that he has committed, but for fear that he will commit an irreparable injury. Now, shall the government be denied a remedy in a like case, where an irreparable injury to it in time of war is threatened and impending, and where the commander-in-chief, or his subordinates, are convinced that a citizen, inimical to the government, is about to commit some act against the government and in favor of the enemy, which, if committed, will be irreparable, and that there is imminent and immediate danger that the act will be committed? May not the authorities, in order to prevent it, take steps to avert it, and, if necessity requires, to restrain such citizen per force — even by imprisonment — until the danger is past, although no crime has actually been committed, and this be justified under the usages of war, or a partial exercise of martial law, it matters not by what name it is called?

I do not intend to decide, nor do I wish to be understood as deciding, whether the Secretary of War was justifiable in issuing the order in question, or whether the defendants can justify under it, for that, I consider, should be left for the trial on the merits of the case.

I have made these suggestions, and cited authorities to show, that it would look like an unwarranted usurpation in this court, more dangerous, perhaps, than the military power objected to, to pass upon and nullify the fifth section of the act of Congress, under which the defendants' petitions are filed, in this summary and preliminary proceeding, and thus wrench from the defendants, who stand in a United States relation to the case, the right to have it heard and determined by a United States court.

The plaintiff has all the guarantees for a fair and impartial hearing and trial in that court that he has in the State courts; and, besides, one principal reason why such cases should be tried in the Federal courts, is, to secure uniformity in the rules governing such cases. If it were left to the State courts — as these cases concerning United States laws, Constitution, and officers arise in every State — there might be as great a variety of contradictory decisions as there are State courts. The consequence would be, that no man would or could know the law governing United States officers, and the affairs of the nation would run into utter confusion, and the officer would be constantly liable to be harassed in each State, and subject to a different law or rule every time he crossed a State line. The prayer of the defendants' petitions is granted.

RETURN

OF

REBELLIOUS STATES

TO THE UNION.

THE

RETURN OF REBELLIOUS STATES

TO THE UNION.*

TWOFOLD WAR.

However brilliant the success of our military operations has been, the country is encompassed by dangers. Two wars are still waged between the citizens of the United States — a war of Arms and a war of Ideas. Achievements in the field cannot much outstrip our moral victories. While we fix our attention upon the checkered fortunes of our heroic soldiers, and trace their marches over hills and valleys made memorable through all time by their disasters or their triumphs; while we are agitated by hope and fear, by exultation and disappointment; while our brothers and sons rush

* During the spring and summer of 1863 efforts were made by certain citizens of Florida, Louisiana, Arkansas, and Eastern Virginia to obtain the assent of the President to the formation of local state governments, and to the recognition thereof by the Executive and Legislative departments. The views on this subject contained in the following pages, having been communicated verbally to the President, were subsequently embodied in a letter to the Union League of Philadelphia, published July 28, 1863.

joyfully to the post of danger and of honor, although the mourning weeds of the mother and sister record in the family the tearful glory of the fallen brave; while the movements of our vast armies, in all the "pride, pomp, and circumstance of glorious war," are watched with intense solicitude, let us not forget that there is another war, waged by men not less brave, for victories not less renowned than those which are won on battle-fields.

The deadliest struggle is between Civilization and Barbarism, Freedom and Slavery, Republicanism and Aristocracy, Loyalty and Treason.

The true patriot will watch with profound interest the fortunes of this intellectual and moral conflict, because the issue involves the country's safety, prosperity, and honor. If victory shall crown the efforts of those brave men who believe and trust in God, then shall all this bloody sacrifice be consecrated, and years of suffering shall exalt us among the nations; if we fail, no triumph of brute force can compensate the world for our unfathomable degradation.

Let us then endeavor to appreciate the difficulties of our present position.

BREAKERS AHEAD.

Of several subjects, to which, were it now in my power, I would ask your earnest attention, I can speak of one only.

As the success of the Union cause shall become more certain and apparent to the enemy in various localities, they will lay down arms and cease fighting.

Their bitter and deep-rooted hatred of the Government, and of all Northern men who are not traitors, and of all Southern men who are loyal, will still remain interwoven in every fibre of their hearts, and will be made, if possible, more intense by the humiliation of conquest and subjection. The foot of the conqueror planted upon their proud necks will not sweeten their tempers, and their defiant and treacherous nature will seek to revenge itself in murders, assassinations, and all underhand methods of venting a spite which they dare not manifest by open war, and in driving out of their borders all loyal men. To suppose that a Union sentiment will remain in any considerable number of men, among a people who have strained every nerve and made every sacrifice to destroy the Union, indicates dishonesty, insanity, or feebleness of intellect.

The slaveholding inhabitants of the conquered districts will begin by claiming the right to exercise the powers of government, and, under their construction of State rights, to get control of the lands, personal property, slaves, free blacks, and poor whites, and a legalized power, through the instrumentality of State laws, made to answer their own purposes, to oppose and prevent the execution of the constitution and laws of the United States, within the districts of country inhabited by them.

Thus, for instance, when South Carolina shall have ceased fighting, she will say to the President, "We have now laid down our arms; we submit to the authority of the United States government. You may restore your custom-houses, your courts of justice, and, if we hold any public property, we give it up; we now have chosen senators and representatives to Congress, and demand their admission, and the full establishment of all our State rights and our restoration to all our former privileges and immunities as citizens of the United States."

This demand is made by men who are traitors in heart; men who hate and despise the Union; men who never had a patriotic sentiment; men who, if they could, would hang every friend of the government. But, for the sake of getting power into their own hands by our concession, which they could not obtain by fighting, and, for the sake of avoiding the penalty of their national crimes, they will demand restoration to the Union under the guise of claiming State rights.

CONSEQUENCES OF BEING OUTWITTED BY REBELS.

What will be the consequence of yielding to this demand?

Our public enemy will gain the right of managing their affairs according to their will and pleasure, and not according to the will and pleasure of the people of the United States.

They will be enabled, by the intervention of their State laws and State courts, to put and maintain themselves in effectual and perpetual opposition to the laws and constitution of the United States, as they have done for thirty-five years past. They will have the power to pass such local laws as will effectually exclude from the slave States all northern men, all soldiers, all free blacks, and all persons and things which shall be inconsistent with the theory of making slavery the corner-stone of their local government; and they may make slavery perpetual, in violation of the laws of the United States and proclamations of the President.

They may continue the enforcement of those classes of laws against free speech and freedom of the press, which will forever exclude popular education, and all other means of moral, social, and political advancement. They may send back to Congress the same traitors and conspirators who have once betrayed the country into civil war, and who will thwart and embarrass all measures tending to restore the Union by harmonizing the interests and the institutions of the people, and so, being introduced into camp, as the wooden horse into Troy, they will gain by fraud and treason that which they could not achieve by feats of arms. The insanity of State rights doctrines will be nourished and strengthened by admitting back a conquered people as our equals, and its baleful influences cannot be estimated!

To satisfy *them*, the solemn pledge of freedom offered to colored citizens by Congress and by the Proclamation, must be broken, and the country and the government must be covered with unspeakable infamy, so that even foreign nations might then justly consider us guilty of treachery to the cause of civilization and of humanity.

Suppose, to-day, the rebellion quelled, and the question put, Will you give to your enemy the power of making your laws?

Eastern Virginia, Florida, and Louisiana are now knocking at the door of Congress for admission into the Union. Men come to Washington, chosen to office by a handful of associates; elevated, by revolution, to unaccustomed dignity; representing themselves as Union men, and earnest to have State rights bestowed on their constituents.

If their constituents are clothed with the power

to constitute a State, into whose hands will that power fall?

Beware of committing yourselves to the fatal doctrine of recognizing the existence in the Union, of States which have been declared by the President's Proclamation to be in rebellion. For, by this new device of the enemy, this new version of the poisonous State rights doctrine, the secessionists will be able to get back by fraud what they failed to get by fighting. Do not permit them, without proper safe-guards, to resume in your counsels in the Senate and in the House the power which their treason has stripped from them.

Do not allow old States, with their constitutions still unaltered, to resume State powers.

Be true to the Union men of the south, not to the designing politicians of the border States. The rebellious States contain ten times as many traitors as loyal men. The traitors will have a vast majority of the votes. Clothed with State rights under our constitution, they will crush every Union man by the irresistible power of their legislation. If you would be true to the Union men of the south, you must not bind them hand and foot, and deliver them over to their bitterest enemies.

STATE RIGHTS IN CIVIL WAR.

Beware of entangling yourselves with the technical doctrine of forfeitures of State rights, as such doctrines admit, by necessary implication, the operation of a code of laws, and of corresponding civil rights, the existence of which you deny.

To preserve the Union, requires the enforcement

against public enemies of our belligerent rights of civil war.

ATTITUDE OF THE GOVERNMENT IN THE BEGINNING OF THE WAR TOWARDS THE REBELS, AND TOWARDS LOYAL MEN IN REBEL DISTRICTS.

When the insurrection commenced by illegal acts of secession, and by certain exhibitions of force against the government, in distant parts of the country, it was supposed that the insurgents might be quelled, and peace might be restored, without requiring a large military force, and without involving those who did not actively participate in overt acts of treason.

Hence the government, relying upon the patriotism of the people, and confident in its strength, exhibited a generous forbearance towards the insurrection.

When, at last, 75,000 of the militia were called out, the President, still relying upon the Union sentiment of the South, announced his intention not to interfere with loyal men, but, on the contrary, to regard their rights as still under the protection of the constitution. The action of Congress was in accordance with this policy. The war waged by this government was then a personal war, a war against rebels; a war prosecuted in the hope and belief that the body of the people were still friendly to the Union, who, temporarily overborne, would soon right themselves by the aid of the army. Hence Congress declared, and the President proclaimed, that it was not their object to injure loyal men, or to interfere with their rights or their domestic institutions.

THE PROGRESS OF EVENTS CHANGED THE CHARACTER OF THE WAR, AND REQUIRED THE USE OF MORE EFFECTIVE WAR POWERS.

This position of the government towards the rebellious States was forbearing, magnanimous, and just while the citizens thereof were generally loyal. But the revolution swept onward. The entire circle of the southern States abandoned the Union, and carried with them all the border States within their influence or control.

Having set up a new government for themselves; having declared war against us; having sought foreign aid; having passed acts of non-intercourse; having seized public property, and made attempts to invade States which refused to serve their cause; having raised and maintained large armies and an incipient navy; assuming, in all respects, to act as an independent, hostile nation, at war with the United States — claiming belligerent rights as an independent people alone could claim them, and offering to enter into treaties of alliance with foreign countries and treaties of peace with ours — under these circumstances they were no longer merely insurgents and rebels, but became a belligerent public enemy. The war was no longer against "certain persons" in the rebellious States. It became a territorial war; that is to say, a war by all persons situated in the belligerent territory against the United States.

CONSEQUENCES RESULTING FROM CIVIL TERRITORIAL WAR.

If we were in a war with England, every Englishman would become a public enemy, irrespective of his personal feelings towards us. However friendly he might be towards America, his ships on the sea would be liable to capture, himself would be liable to be killed in battle, or his property, situated in this country, would be subject to confiscation.

By a similar rule of the law of nations, whenever

two nations are at war, every subject of one belligerent nation is a public enemy of the other.

An individual may be a personal friend, and at the same time a public enemy, to the United States. The law of war defines international relations.

When the civil war in America became a territorial war, every citizen residing in the belligerent districts became a public enemy, irrespective of his private sentiments, whether loyal or disloyal, friendly or hostile, Unionist or secessionist, guilty or innocent.

As public enemies, the belligerents have claimed to be exchanged as prisoners of war, instead of admitting our right to hang them as murderers and pirates. As public enemies, they claim the right to make war upon us, in plain violation of many of the obligations they would have admitted if they acknowledged the obligations or claimed the protection of our constitution.

If they had claimed any State rights, under our constitution, they would not have violated every one of the provisions thereof limiting the powers of States. Asserting no such rights, they claim immunity from all obligations as States, or as a people, to this government or to the United States.

WHEN DID THE REBELLION BECOME A TERRITORIAL WAR?

This question has been settled by the Supreme Court of the United States, in the case of the Hiawatha, decided on the 9th of March, 1863. In that case, which should be read and studied by every citizen of the Union, the members of the court differed in opinion as to the time when the war became territorial. The majority decided that, when the fact of general hostilities existed, the war was territorial, and the Supreme Court was bound to take judicial cognizance thereof. The minority argued that, as Congress alone had power to declare war, so Congress alone has power to recognize the existence of war; and they contended that it was not until the Act of Congress of July 13, 1861, commonly called the Non-intercourse Act, that a state of civil, territorial war was legitimately recognized. All the judges agree in the position "that since July 13, 1861, there has existed between the United States and the Confederate States, civil, territorial war."

WHAT ARE THE RIGHTS OF THE PUBLIC ENEMY SINCE THE REBELLION BECAME A TERRITORIAL CIVIL WAR.

The Supreme Court have decided, in the case above named, in effect:* "That since that time the United

* If this decision be restricted to its most technical and narrow limits, the only point actually decided was, that the captured vessels and cargoes were lawful prize. The parties before the court are alone bound by the judgment. Viewed in like manner, the only point decided in the case of Dred Scott was, that the court had no jurisdiction of the matter. Nevertheless, learned judges have taken occasion to express opinions upon legal or political questions. Their opinions are of great importance, not because they are or are not *technical decisions* of points in issue, but because they record the deliberate judgment of those to whom the same questions will be referred for final determination. The judge who has pronounced an extra-judicial opinion, and has placed it upon the records of the court, is not, it may be said, *bound* to follow it; but it is equally true, that the court is never bound to follow its previous most solemn "*decisions.*" These decisions may be, and often have been, modified, overruled, or disregarded by the same court which pronounced them. If the members of a judicial tribunal, though differing upon minor questions, agree upon certain fundamental propositions, it is worse than useless to deny that these propositions, even though not "*technically decided,*" *have the authoritative sanction of the court.* The unanimous agreement of all the members of a judicial court to certain principles, affords to the community as satisfactory evidence of their views of the law as could be derived from a decision in which these principles were technically the points in controversy. It is for these reasons that it has been stated in

States have full belligerent rights against all persons residing in the districts declared by the President's Proclamation to be in rebellion."

That the laws of war, "whether that war be civil or *inter*

qualified language "that the Supreme Court have *decided in effect*" the propositions as stated.

To show wherein all the judges agree, the following extracts are collected from the Decision and from the Dissenting Opinion.

EXTRACTS FROM THE OPINION OF THE COURT.

No declaration of war is necessary in case of civil war.

Test of its existence.

"As a civil war is never publicly proclaimed *eo nomine*, against insurgents, its *actual existence* is a fact in our domestic history, which the court is bound to notice and to know. The true test of its existence, as found in the writings of the sages of the common law, may be thus summarily stated: 'When the course of justice is interrupted by revolt, rebellion, or insurrection, so that the courts of justice cannot be kept open, CIVIL WAR EXISTS, *and hostilities may be prosecuted on the same footing as if those opposing the government were foreign enemies invading the land.*' See 2 Black R. 667, 668.

Rebels to be treated as foreign invaders.

"They (foreign nations) cannot ask a court to affect a technical ignorance of the existence of a war, which all the world acknowledges to be the greatest civil war known in the history of the human race, and thus cripple the arm of the government, and paralyze its powers by *subtle* definitions and ingenious sophisms. The law of nations is also called the law of nature. It is founded on the common sense as well as the common consent of the world. It *contains no such anomalous doctrine*, as that which this court is now, for the first time, desired to pronounce, to wit, 'that insurgents, who have risen in rebellion against their sovereign, expelled her courts, established a revolutionary government, organized armies, and commenced hostilities, are not *enemies*, because they are TRAITORS; and a war levied on the government by traitors, in order to dismember and destroy it, is not a *war* because it is an "insurrection."

President must decide whether the enemy shall be deemed belligerents.

Whether the President, in fulfilling his duties as commander-in-chief in suppressing an insurrection, has met with such armed hostile resistance, and a civil war of such alarming proportions, as will compel him to *accord to them the character gentes, converts every citizen of the hostile State into a public enemy, and treats him accordingly, whatever may have been his previous conduct."*

That all the rights derived from the laws of war

Court must follow the decision of the President.

of belligerents, is a question to be decided by him, *and this court must be governed* by the decision and acts of the *political department* of the government to which this power was intrusted. *He* must determine what degree of force the crisis demands." The proclamation of blockade is of itself official and conclusive evidence to the court that a *state of war* existed which demanded and authorized a recourse to such a measure, under the circumstances peculiar to the case.

Belligerent right to seizure and destruction of enemy's property of all kinds, on land or sea.

"*The right of one belligerent, not only to coerce the other by direct force, but also to cripple his resources by the seizure or destruction of his property, is a necessary result of a state of war. Money and wealth, the products of agriculture and commerce, are said to be the sinews of war, and as necessary in its conduct as numbers and physical force. Hence* it is, that the laws of war recognize the right of a belligerent to cut these sinews of the power of the enemy by capturing his property on the high seas." Page 671.

CONFISCATION.

All persons residing in belligerent districts are *public enemies*, and their property liable to be captured.

"*All persons* residing within this territory (seceded States) whose property may be used to increase the revenues of the hostile power, are, in this contest, *liable to be treated as enemies*, though not foreigners. *They have cast off their allegiance, and made war on their government, and are none* the less *enemies because they are traitors.*" Opinion, page 674.

EXTRACTS FROM THE DISSENTING OPINION.

Public war entitles both parties to *the rights of war* against each other.

"A contest by force, between independent sovereign States, is called a *public* war; and when duly commenced, by proclamation or otherwise, *it entitles both of the belligerent parties to all the rights of war against each other*, and as respects neutral nations." Page 686, 687.

Legal consequences of war, shown by international law.

"*The legal consequences* resulting from a *state of war* between two countries, at this day, are well understood, and will be found described in every approved work on the subject of international law."

may now, since 1861, be lawfully and constitutionally exercised against all the citizens of the districts in rebellion.

People of the two countries become, in law, enemies.

All enemies' property on land and sea is subject to capture and confiscation.

"The *people of the two countries immediately become the enemies of each other, &c. . . . All the property* of the people of the two countries, *on land or sea,* are subject to *capture and confiscation* by the adverse party as enemies' property, with certain qualifications as it respects property on land. (Brown *vs.* U. S., 8 Cranch, 110.) All treaties between the belligerent parties are annulled." Page 677.

"This great and pervading change in the existing condition of a country, and in the relation of all her citizens or subjects, external and internal, is the immediate effect and result of a state of war." Page 688.

The government may recognize civil war.

Civil war draws after it all the rights of war, the same as in a foreign war.

"In the case of a *rebellion,* or resistance of a portion of the people of a country, against the established government, there is *no doubt,* if, in its progress and enlargement, the *government thus sought to be* overthrown, *sees fit,* it may, by the competent power, recognize or declare the existence of a *state of civil war, which will draw after it all the consequences and rights of war, between the contending parties, as in the case of a public war,* Mr. Wheaton observes, speaking of civil war: "But the general usage of nations regards such a war as entitling both the contending parties to *all the rights of war,* as against each other, and even as respects neutral nations." Page 688.

Civil war must be recognized by Congress before it can draw after it full belligerent rights.

"Before this insurrection against the established government can be dealt with on the footing *of a civil war,* within the meaning of the law of nations and the Constitution of the United States, and *which will draw after it belligerent rights,* it must be *recognized* or declared by the war-making power of the government. No power short of this can change the legal status of the government, or the relations of its citizens from that of peace to a state of war, or bring into existence all those duties and obligations of neutral third parties, growing out of a state of war. The war power of the government must be exercised before this changed condition of the government and people, and of neutral third parties, can be admitted. *There is no difference in this respect between a civil or a public war.*" Page 689.

RIGHTS OF REBELS AS PERSONS, AS CITIZENS OF STATES, AND AS SUBJECTS OF THE UNITED STATES, ARE, ACCORDING TO THE CONSTITUTION, TO BE SETTLED BY THE LAWS OF WAR.

Such being the law of the land, as declared by the Supreme Court, in order to ascertain what are the legal or constitutional rights of public enemies, we have only

Civil war attaches to it all the consequences of belligerent rights, when once recognized by Congress.

"It must be a war in a legal sense (in the sense of the law of nations, and of the Constitution of the United States) *to attach to it all the consequences that belong to belligerent rights.* Instead, therefore, of inquiring after armies and navies, and victories lost and won, or organized rebellion against the general government, the inquiry should be into the law of nations, and into the municipal and fundamental laws of the government. For we find there, that to constitute a civil war, in the sense in which we are speaking, before it can exist in contemplation of law, *it must be recognized* or declared by the sovereign power of the state; and which sovereign power, by our Constitution, is lodged in the Congress of the United States. Civil war, therefore, under our system of government, can exist *only by an act of Congress,* which requires the assent of two of the great departments of the government, the executive and the legislative." Page 690.

Civil war converts every citizen of the hostile state into a *public enemy.*

"The laws of war, *whether the war be civil* or *inter gentes,* as we have seen, convert every citizen of the hostile state into a public enemy, and treats him accordingly, whatever may have been his previous conduct."

Innocent persons cannot lawfully be punished, or their lands confiscated as enemies, until Congress has recognized a state of civil war.

"Congress alone can determine whether war exists or should be declared. *And until they have so acted,* no citizen of the state can be punished in his person or property unless he has committed some offence against a law of Congress, passed before the act was committed, which made it a crime and defined the punishment. Until then, the penalty of confiscation for the acts of others with which he had no concern, cannot lawfully be inflicted."

"By the Act of 16 Geo. III., 1776, all trade between the colonies and Great Britain was interdicted."

Congress did recognize civil war by Act of July 13, 1861.

"From this time the war (of the revolution) became a *territorial, civil war* between the contending parties, *with all the rights of war known to the law of nations.*"

"The Act of Congress of July 13, 1861, we think *recog-*

to refer to the settled principles of the belligerent law of nations or the laws of war.

Some of the laws of war are stated in both the Opinions in the case above mentioned. A state of foreign war instantly annuls the most solemn treaties between nations. It terminates all obligations in the nature of

nized a state of civil war between the government and the Confederate States, and made it territorial." Page 695.

"We agree, therefore, that the Act of the 13th of July, 1861, recognized a state of civil war between the government and the people of the States described in that Proclamation (of August 16, 1861). Page 696.

"But this (the right of the President to recognize a state of civil war as existing between a foreign government and its colonies) is a very different question from *the one before us, which is,* whether the President can recognize or declare a civil war, *under the Constitution, with all its belligerent rights,* between his own government and a portion of its citizens in a state of insurrection. *That power,* as we have seen, *belongs to Congress. We agree* when *such a war is recognized,* or declared to exist by the war-making power, but not otherwise, it is the *duty of courts to follow the decision* of the *political* power of the government." Page 697.

Courts must follow the decision of the *political* powers.

"No civil war existed between this government and the States in insurrection till recognized by the Act of Congress of July 13, 1861. The President does not possess the power, under the Constitution, to declare war, or *recognize* its *existence* within *the meaning of the law of nations, which carries with it belligerent rights, and thus change the country and all its citizens* from a state of peace to a state of war. This power belongs exclusively to the Congress of the United States, and consequently the President had no power to set on foot a blockade under the law of nations, and the capture of the vessel and cargo in all the cases before, *in which the capture occurred before the 13th of July,* 1861, for breach of blockade, or as enemy's property, is illegal and void." Page 699.

Civil war did not exist until July 13, 1861, so as to carry with it all belligerent rights.

Mr. Chief Justice TANEY and Messrs. Justices CATRON and CLIFFORD concurred with Mr. Justice NELSON in the Dissenting Opinion.

compacts or contracts, at the option of the party obligated thereby. It destroys all claims of one belligerent upon the other, except those which may be sanctioned by a treaty of peace. A civil territorial war has the same effect, excepting only that the sovereign may treat the rebels as subjects as well as belligerents. Hence civil war, in which the belligerents have become territorial enemies, instantly annuls all rights or claims of public enemies against the United States, under the constitution or laws, whether that constitution be called a compact, a treaty, or a covenant, and whether the parties to it were States, in their sovereign capacity, or the people of the United States, as individuals. Any other result would be as incomprehensible as it would be mischievous. A public enemy cannot lawfully claim the right of entering Congress and voting down the measures taken to subdue him.

Why not? Because he is a public enemy; because, by becoming a public enemy, he has annulled and lost his rights in the government, and can never regain them excepting by our consent.

STATE RIGHTS TO BE REGAINED ONLY BY OUR CONSENT.

If the inhabitants of a large part of the Union have, by becoming public enemies, surrendered and annulled their former rights, the question arises, Can they recover them? Such rights cannot be regained by reason of their having ceased to fight. The character of a public enemy having once been stamped upon them by the laws of war, remains fixed until it shall have been, by our consent, removed. To stop fighting does not make them cease to be public enemies, because they may have laid down their arms for want of powder not for want of will. Peace does not restore the noble dead who have fallen a sacrifice to treason. Nor does it revive the rights once extinguished by civil, territorial war. The land of the Union belongs to the people of the United States, subject to the rights of individual ownership. Each person inhabiting those sections of the country declared by the President's Proclamation to be in rebellion, has the right to what belongs to a public enemy, and no more. He can have no right to take any part in our government. That right does not belong to an enemy of the country while he is waging war, or after he has been subdued. A public enemy has a right to participate in, or to assume the government of the United States, only when he has conquered the United States. We find in this well-settled doctrine of belligerent law the solution of all questions in relation to State rights. After the inhabitants of a district have become public enemies they have no rights, either State or National, as against the United States. They are belligerents only, and have left to them only belligerent rights.

STATE RIGHTS ARE NOT APPURTENANT TO LAND.

Suppose that all the inhabitants living in South Carolina should be swept off, so that solitude should reign throughout its borders, unbroken by any living thing; would the State rights of South Carolina still exist as attached to the land itself? Can there be a sovereignty without a people, or a State without inhabitants? State rights, so far as they concern the Union, are the rights of persons, as members of a State, in relation to the general government; and when the person has become a public enemy, then he loses all rights except the rights of war. And when *all* the inhabitants have (by engaging in civil, territorial war) become public enemies, it is the same, in legal effect, as though the inhabitants had been annihilated. So far as this government is concerned, civil, territorial war obliterates from districts in rebellion all lines of States or counties; the only lines recognized by war are the lines which separate us from a public enemy.

FORFEITURE NOT CLAIMED—THE RIGHT OF SECESSION NOT ADMITTED, SINCE CITIZENS MAY BE DEEMED BELLIGERENTS AND SUBJECTS.

I do not place reliance upon the common law doctrine of forfeitures of franchises as applicable to this revolution, for forfeiture can be founded only upon an admission of the validity of the act on which forfeiture is founded. Nor does the belligerent law of civil, territorial war, whereby a public enemy loses his rights as a citizen, admit the right of secession. It is not any vote or law of secession that makes an individual a public enemy. A person may commit heinous offences against municipal law, and commit acts of hostility against the government, without being a public enemy. To be a personal enemy, is not to be a public enemy to the country, in the eye of belligerent or international law. Whosoever engages in an insurrection is a personal enemy, but it is not until that insurrection has swelled into territorial war that he becomes a public enemy. It must also be remembered that the right of secession is not conceded by enforcement of belligerent law, since in civil war a nation has the right to treat its citizens either as subjects or belligerents, or as both. Hence, while belligerent law destroys all claims of subjects engaged in civil war, as against the parent government, it does not release the subject from his duties to that government. By war, the subject loses his rights, but does not escape his obligations. The inhabitants of the conquered districts will thus lose their right to govern us, but will not escape their obligations to obey us. Whatever rights are left to them besides the rights of war, will be such as we choose to allow them. It is for us to dictate to them, not for them to dictate to us, what privileges they shall enjoy.

THE PLEDGE OF THE COUNTRY TO ITS SOLDIERS, ITS CITIZENS, AND ITS SUBJECTS, MUST BE KEPT INVIOLATE.

Among the war measures sanctioned by the President, to which he has, more than once, pledged his sacred honor, and which Congress has enforced by solemn laws, is the liberation of slaves. The government has invited them to share the dangers, the honor, and the advantages of sustaining the Union, and has pledged itself to the world for their freedom. Whatever disasters may befall our arms, whatever humiliation may be in store for us, it is earnestly hoped that we may be saved the unfathomable infamy of breaking the nation's faith with Europe, and with colored citizens and slaves in the Union.

If the rebellious States shall attempt to return to the Union with constitutions guaranteeing the perpetuity of slavery, if the laws of these States shall be again revived and put in force against free blacks and slaves, we shall at once have reinstated in the Union, in all its force and wickedness, that very curse which has brought on the war and all its terrible train of sufferings. The war is fought by slaveholders for the perpetuity of slavery. Shall we hand over to them, at the end of the war, just what they have been fighting for? Shall all our blood and treasure be spilled uselessly upon the ground? Shall the country not protect itself against the evil which has caused all our woes? Will you breathe new life into the strangled serpent, when, without your aid, he will perish?

If you concede State rights to your enemies, what security can you have that traitors will not pass State laws which will render the position of the blacks intolerable, *or reduce them all to slavery?*

Would it be honorable on the part of the United States to free these men, and then hand them over to the tender mercy of slave laws?

Will it be possible that State slave laws should exist and be enforced by slave States without overriding the rights guaranteed by the United States law to men, irrespective of color, in the slave States?

Will you run the risk of these angry collisions of State and National laws while you have the remedy and antidote in your own hands?

PLAN OF RECONSTRUCTION RECOMMENDED.

One of two things should be done in order to keep faith with the country and save us from obvious peril. Allow the inhabitants of conquered territory to form themselves into States, only by adopting constitutions such as will forever remove all cause of collision with the United States, by excluding slavery therefrom, or continue military government over the conquered district, until there shall appear therein a sufficient number of loyal inhabitants to form a republican government, which, by guaranteeing freedom to all, shall be in accordance with the true spirit of the constitution of the United States. These safeguards of freedom are requisite to render permanent the domestic tranquillity of the country which the constitution itself was formed to secure, and which it is the legitimate object of this war to maintain.

EXTRACT FROM THE PRESIDENT'S MESSAGE.

EMANCIPATION AND ITS RESULTS.

When Congress assembled a year ago, the war had already lasted nearly twenty months, and there had been many conflicts on both land and sea, with varying results.

The rebellion had been pressed back into reduced limits, yet the tone of public feeling at home and abroad was not satisfactory. With other signs, the popular election, then just past, indicated uneasiness among ourselves, which, amid much that was cold and menacing, the kindest words coming from Europe were uttered in accents of pity that we were too blind to surrender a hopeless cause.

Our commerce was suffering greatly by a few armed vessels, built upon and furnished from foreign shores, and were threatened with such additions from the same quarter as would sweep our trade from the sea and raise our blockade. We had failed to elicit from European governments any thing hopeful on this subject.

The preliminary Emancipation Proclamation, issued in September, was running its assigned period to the beginning of the new year. A month later the final proclamation came, including the announcement that colored men, of suitable condition, would be received in the war service.

The policy of emancipation and of employing black soldiers give to the future a new aspect, about which hope, and fear, and doubt contended in uncertain conflict.

According to our political system, as a matter of civil administration, the general government had no lawful power to effect emancipation in any State, and for a long time it had been hoped that the rebellion could be suppressed without resorting to it as a military measure.

It was all the while deemed possible that the necessity for it might come, and that if it should, the crisis of the contest would then be presented. It came; and, as was anticipated, it was followed by dark and doubtful days.

Eleven months having now passed, we are permitted to take another review. The rebel borders are pressed still further back, and by the complete opening of the Mississippi, the country dominated by the rebellion is divided into distinct parts, with no practical communication between them. Tennessee and Arkansas have been cleared of insurgents, and influential citizens in each, owners of slaves, and advocates of slavery at the beginning of the rebellion, now declare openly for emancipation in their respective States; and of those States not included in the emancipation proclamation, Maryland and Missouri, neither of which, three years ago, would tolerate restraint upon the extension of slavery into territory, only dispute now as to the best mode of removing it within their own limits.

Of those who were slaves at the beginning of the rebellion, full one hundred thousand are now in the United States military service, about one half of which number actually bear arms in the ranks, thus giving the double advantage of taking so much labor from the insurgent cause, and supplying the places which otherwise must be filled with so many white men. So far as tested, it is difficult to say that they are not as good soldiers as any.

No servile insurrection or tendency to violence or cruelty has marked the measures of emancipation and arming the blacks.

These measures have been much discussed in foreign countries, and contemporary with such discussion the tone of public sentiment there is much improved. At home the same measures have been fully discussed, supported, criticised, and denounced, and the annual elections following are highly encouraging to those whose official duty it is to bear the country through this great trial. Thus we have the new reckoning. The crisis which threatened to divide the friends of the Union is past.

RECONSTRUCTION.

Looking now to the present and future, and with reference to a resumption of the national authority with the States wherein that authority has been suspended, I have thought fit to issue a Proclamation, a copy of which is herewith transmitted. On examination of this proclamation it will appear, as is believed, that nothing is attempted beyond what is amply justified by the Constitution; true, the form of an oath is given, but no man is coerced to take it. The man is only promised a pardon in case he voluntarily takes the oath.

The Constitution authorizes the executive to grant or withhold the pardon at his own absolute discretion, and this includes the power to grant on terms, as is fully established by judicial and other authorities; *it is also proposed that if in any of the States named a State government shall be, in the mode prescribed, set up, such governments shall be recognized and guaranteed by the United States, and that under it the State shall, on the constitutional conditions, be protected against invasion and domestic violence.*

The constitutional obligation of the United States to guarantee to every State in the Union a republican form of government, and to protect the State in the cases stated, is explicit and full.

But why tender the benefits of this provision only to a State government set up in this particular way? This section of the Constitution contemplates a case wherein the element within a State favorable to republican government in the Union may be too feeble for an opposite and hostile element external to or even within the State, and such are precisely the cases with which we are now dealing.

An attempt to guarantee and protect a revived State government, constructed in whole or in preponderating part from the very element against whose hostility and violence it is to be protected, is simply absurd.

There must be a test by which to separate the opposing elements so as to build only from the sound, and that test is a sufficiently liberal one which accepts as sound whoever will make a sworn recantation of his former unsoundness; but if it be proper to require as a test of admission to the political body an oath of allegiance to the Constitution of the United States and to the Union under it, *why not also to the laws and proclamations in regard to slavery?*

These laws and proclamations were enacted and put forth for the purpose of aiding in the suppression of the rebellion. To give them their fullest effect, there had to be a pledge for their maintenance. In my judgment, they have aided, and will further aid, the cause for which they were intended.

To now abandon them, would be not only to relinquish a lever of power, *but would also be a cruel and astounding breach of faith.* I may add at this point, that while I remain in my present position, *I shall not attempt to retract or modify* the *emancipation proclamation,* nor shall I return to *slavery any person who is free by the terms of that proclamation, or by any of the acts of Congress.*

For these and other reasons it is thought best that support of these measures shall be included in the oath, and it is believed that the Executive may lawfully claim it in return for pardon and restoration of forfeited rights, which he has clear constitutional power to withhold altogether, or grant upon the terms he shall deem wisest for the public interest.

It should be observed, also, that this part of the oath is subject to the modifying and abrogatory power of legislation and *Supreme Judicial decisions.**

The proposed acquiescence of the National Executive in any reasonable temporary State arrangement for the freed people, is made with the view of possibly modifying the confusion and destitution which must, at best, attend all classes by a total revolution of labor throughout whole States.

It is hoped that the already deeply afflicted people in those States may be somewhat more ready to give up the cause of their affliction, if to this extent this vital matter be left to themselves, while no power of the national executive to prevent an abuse is abridged by the proposition.

The suggestion in the proclamation as to maintaining the political framework of the States on what is called *reconstruction,* is made in the hope that it may do good without danger of harm; it will save labor and avoid great

*** It must not be forgotten, that on purely political questions the Supreme Court is bound to follow the decisions of the executive or legislative departments of government.**

confusion; but why any proclamation now upon this subject? This question is beset with the conflicting views that the step might be delayed too long or be taken too soon. In some States the elements for resumption seem ready for action, but remain inactive, apparently for want of a rallying-point — a plan of action. Why shall A adopt the plan of B, rather than B that of A; and if A and B should agree, how can they know but that the general government here will reject their plan? By the Proclamation *a plan is presented,* which may be accepted by them as a rallying point, and which they are assured in advance will not be rejected here. This may bring them to act sooner than they otherwise would.

The objections to a premature presentation of a plan by the National Executive consists in the danger of committal on points which could be more safely left to further developments. Care has been taken to so shape the denouement as to avoid embarrassment from this source, saying that on certain terms certain classes will be pardoned with rights restored.

It is not said that other classes or other terms will never be included, saying that reconstruction will be accepted if presented in a specified way. It is not said it will never be accepted in any other way. The movements by State action for emancipation in several of the States not included in the Emancipation Proclamation, are matters of profound gratulation; and while I do not repeat in detail what I have heretofore so earnestly urged upon this subject, my general views remain unchanged, and I trust that Congress will omit no fair opportunity of aiding these important steps to the great consummation.

In the midst of other cares, however important, we must not lose sight of the fact that *the war power is still our main reliance.* To that power alone can we look yet for a time to give confidence to the people in the contested regions that the insurgent power will not again overrun them. Until that confidence shall be established, little can be done any where for what is called Reconstruction.

Hence our chiefest care must still be directed to the army and navy, who have thus far borne their harder part so nobly and well.

And it may be esteemed fortunate that, in giving the greatest efficiency to these indispensable arms, we do also recognize the gallant men, from commander to sentinel, who compose them, and to whom, more than to others, the world must stand indebted for the home of freedom, disenthralled, regenerated, enlarged, and perpetuated.

ABRAHAM LINCOLN.

December 8, 1863.

PROCLAMATION OF AMNESTY BY THE PRESIDENT.

THE following Proclamation is appended to the Message: —

PROCLAMATION.

Whereas, in and by the Constitution of the United States, it is provided that the President shall have power to grant reprieves and pardons for offences against the United States, except in cases of impeachment; and whereas, a rebellion now exists whereby the *loyal State governments* of several States *have for a long time been subverted*, and many persons have committed, and are now guilty of treason, against the United States; and whereas, with reference to said rebellion and treason, laws have been enacted by Congress declaring forfeitures and confiscation of property and liberation of slaves, all upon conditions and terms therein stated, and also declaring that the President was thereby authorized, at any time thereafter, by proclamation, to extend to persons who may have participated in the existing rebellion in any State or part thereof, pardon and amnesty, with such exceptions, and at such times, and on such conditions, as he may deem expedient for the public welfare; and,

Whereas, the congressional declaration for limited and conditional pardon accords with well-established judicial exposition of the pardoning power; and whereas, with reference to said rebellion, the President of the United States has issued several proclamations with provisions in regard to the liberation of slaves; and whereas, it is now desired by some persons heretofore engaged in said rebellion *to resume their allegiance to the United States*, and to *re-inaugurate loyal State governments* within and for their respective States,

Therefore, I, Abraham Lincoln, President of the United States, do proclaim, declare, and make known to all persons who have directly or by implication participated in the existing rebellion, except as hereinafter excepted, that a full pardon is granted to them and each of them, with restoration of all rights of property, except as to slaves, and in property cases where rights of third parties have intervened, and upon the condition that every such person shall take and subscribe an oath, and thenceforward keep and maintain said oath inviolate, and which oath shall be registered for permanent preservation, and shall be of the tenor and effect following, to wit:

I, ——, do solemnly swear, in presence of Almighty God, that I will henceforth faithfully support, protect, and defend the Constitution of the

United States and the Union of the States thereunder, and that I will, in like manner, abide by and faithfully support *all acts of Congress* passed during the existing rebellion *with reference to slaves,* so long and so far as not repealed, or modified, or held void by Congress, or by decree of the Supreme Court, and that I will in like manner *abide by and faithfully support all proclamations of the President,* made during the existing rebellion, *having reference to slaves,* so long and so far as not modified or declared void by the Supreme Court. So help me God.

The persons excepted from the benefits of the foregoing provisions are all who are or shall have been civil or diplomatic officers, or agents of the so-called Confederate Government; all who have left judicial stations under the United States to aid rebellion; all who are or shall have been military or naval officers of said so-called Confederate Government above the rank of colonel in the army and of lieutenant in the navy, and all who left seats in the United States Congress to aid the rebellion.

All who resigned commissions in the army or navy of the United States and afterwards aided the rebellion, and all who have engaged in any way maltreating colored persons, or white persons in charge of such, otherwise than lawfully as prisoners of war, and which persons may have been found in the United States service as soldiers, seamen, or in any other capacity.

And I do further proclaim, declare, and make known, that, *whenever,* in any of the States of Arkansas, Texas, Louisiana, Mississippi, Tennessee, Alabama, Georgia, Florida, South Carolina, and North Carolina, *a number of persons,* not less than one tenth in number of the votes cast in such States at the Presidential election of the year of our Lord one thousand eight hundred and sixty, having taken the oath aforesaid, and not having since violated it, and being qualified a voter by the election law of the State existing immediately before the so-called act of secession, and excluding all others, *shall reëstablish a State government which shall be republican, and in no wise contravening said oath, such shall be recognized as the true government of the State, and the State shall receive these under the benefit of the constitutional provision, which declares that the United States shall guarantee to every State in this Union a republican form of government, and shall protect each of them against invasion, on application of the legislature, or the executive,* where the legislature cannot be convened, *and against domestic violence;* and I do further proclaim, declare, and make known, that any provisions which may be adopted by such State government in relation to the freed people of such States which shall recognize and declare their permanent freedom, provide for their education, and which may yet be consistent, as temporary arrangement, with their present condition as a laboring, landless, and homeless class, will not be objected to by the National Executive.

And it *is suggested, as not improper, that in constructing a loyal State government in a State, the name of the State, the boundary, the subdivisions, the constitution, and the general code of laws, as before the rebellion, be maintained,* subject only to the *modifications* made necessary by the *conditions hereinbefore stated,* and such others, if any, not contravening said conditions, and which may be deemed expedient by those framing the new State government.

To avoid misunderstanding, it may be proper to say that this proclamation, so far as it relates to State governments, has no reference to States wherein loyal State governments have all the while been maintained.

As for the same reason it may be proper further to say, that *whether members sent to Congress from any State shall be admitted to seats, constitutionally rests exclusively with the respective Houses, and not to any extent with the Executive;* and still further, that this proclamation is intended to present the people of the States wherein the national authority has been suspended and loyal State governments have been subverted, *a mode in and by which the national authority and loyal State governments may be established within such States, or in any of them;* and while the mode presented is the best the Executive can suggest, with his present impressions, it must not be understood that no other possible mode would be acceptable.

Given under my hand at the City of Washington, the eighth day of December, A. D. one thousand eight hundred and sixty three, and of the Independence of the United States of America the eighty-eighth.

ABRAHAM LINCOLN.

MILITARY GOVERNMENT

OF

HOSTILE TERRITORY

IN TIME OF WAR.

PREFACE TO MILITARY GOVERNMENT.

The following pages on "Military Government of Hostile Territory in Time of War," were written early in 1864, in answer to a letter of the Hon. J. M. Ashley, M. C., of Ohio, to the Secretary of War (dated December 24, 1863), which enclosed the draft of a bill for a military provisional government over insurrectionary States, proposed by Mr. Ashley for consideration by the "Special Committee of the House on the Rebellious States." In that letter he requested the Secretary "to make any suggestions he might have to make," or, "if he had not time to make any, to submit the bill to the Solicitor of the War Department for his opinion." This communication, with the proposed bill, were accordingly referred, as requested, by the Secretary of War. A copy of the letter, and of my reply, are hereto appended.

The subjects discussed are of great and growing importance. Clear and just views of the rights, powers, and obligations of the Government are necessary to a wise and consistent administration of affairs in the insurrectionary districts, during their transition from open hostilities to their peaceful restoration to the Union. A careful regard, in the beginning, to the proper limitations of authority in the respective departments of this government, will be necessary in order to avoid embarrassment and confusion in the end; and a just appreciation of the war powers of the President will tend to relieve patriotic citizens from apprehension, even if Congress should, for the present, omit further legislation on these subjects.

The following chapters are only a development of the principles stated in the "War Powers," pages 54 to 57.

W. W.

Washington, D. C., March 24, 1864.

MILITARY GOVERNMENT.

CHAPTER I.

WAR — ITS MEANS AND RESULTS.

JUSTIFIABLE war may, by the law of nations, be rightfully continued until the purposes for which it was commenced have been accomplished. The overthrow and destruction of armies, the capture of enemies, the seizure of property, and the occupation of hostile territory, are but preliminary measures. In our civil war, the final result should be the complete reëstablishment of lawful government on foundations strong enough to insure its continued supremacy without danger of subversion or of renewed assault. To attain that result, after active hostilities shall have ceased, order must be restored, and domestic tranquillity must be maintained. To preserve order, some means must be devised for restraining lawless aggressions in hostile districts, and for securing non-combatant citizens in the enjoyment of civil rights; otherwise, the country would be plunged into anarchy; successful campaigns would result only in waste of blood; conquest, however costly, could not be made permanent or secure, and legitimate government could not be successfully restored.

SOME FORM OF GOVERNMENT IS NECESSARY TO SECURE A CONQUEST.

Though it is a legitimate use of military power to secure the possession of that which "has been acquired by arms, yet it is difficult, by aid of any moderate number of troops, to guard and oversee an extended territory; and it is practically impossible for any army to hold and occupy all sections of it at the same moment. Therefore, if the inhabitants are to be permitted to remain in their domiciles unmolested, some mode must be adopted of controlling their movements, and of preventing their commission of acts of hostility against their conquerors, or of violence against each other. Stragglers from our army must be protected from murder; commissary's supplies must be guarded from capture by guerillas, and non-combatants must be secured in their social rights, and punished for their crimes. The total disorganization produced by civil war requires, more even than that produced by foreign war, the restraints of martial law. In countries torn by intestine commotions, neighbors become enemies; murders, robberies, destruction of property, and all forms of lawless violence are common, and, in the absence of military rule, would go unrestrained. Hence, to secure peaceful possession of such territories, some form of government must of necessity be established, whereby these crimes can be prevented or punished. Firm possession of a conquered province can be held only by establishing a government which shall control the inhabitants thereof.

Since war destroys or suspends municipal laws in the country where hostilities are carried on, no government is left there but such as is derived from the laws of war. All crimes must be restrained or punished by belligerent law, or go unwhipped of justice. Hence every case of wrong must be dealt with by *force of arms*, or must be disposed of by tribunals acting under sanction and authority of military power.

WHY GOVERNMENT IS ESSENTIAL TO THE SECURITY OF A CONQUEST.

The necessity of provisional or temporary government will become apparent by observing the condition of a people who have been overpowered by arms.

Suppose, by way of illustration, that in one of the border slave States in time of profound peace, by some sudden and unforeseen catastrophe, all the officers of civil government were to perish; that the judges, sheriffs, juries, and all courts of justice were to withdraw from that region; that the jails and penitentiaries were to be set open, and the escaped criminals were to reappear amid the scenes of their former crimes; that the officers of the United States had fled; that all public property had been seized by violence, and appropriated to private uses; that all restraints of law or of force were taken from wicked and unprincipled men; that "might made right"; that debts could not be collected; that obligations the most solemn could not be enforced; that men and women could be shot, hung, or murdered in cold blood, if they differed in opinion on any question of religion, of politics, or of settlement of accounts; that private malice could be gratified by the midnight burning of a neighbor's house, and that injuries too foul and too horrid for mention could be perpetrated without means of redress; that all the laws of civilized society and the most sacred rights of humanity could be violated every hour of the day or night, with no protection for the innocent, no punishment for the guilty.

Such a state of things would *inevitably result in civil war.* Clans and associations would be formed; the whole people would sleep on their arms; revenge would inflame them; havoc and slaughter would be widespread; burning villages and smoking towns, devastated lands and general ruin would demonstrate to all observers that *order* is essential to the social *existence* of a community, and that peace can be maintained only by some government of laws.

If the absence of government in time of peace would be followed by such calamitous results, they could not be avoided or escaped by a population already engaged in civil broils, if unprotected by military force, or military administration. In the rebellious States now occupied by our armies, we find a population split into factions, part slave, part freemen; traitors fighting against loyal men; non-combatants hostile to friends of our government; officers attempting to collect the revenue and to enforce the blockade in deadly encounters with swindlers and freebooters; banditti and guerillamen with their secret allies, murdering in cold blood our sick or wounded soldiers; robbers, plunderers, cutthroats, incendiaries, and assassins wreaking their inhuman passions even upon defenceless women and children; never was there a society, whose shattered and revolutionary condition more imperiously demanded a firm and powerful provisional government, following after the cessation of active hostilities. To withdraw, and so to lose control of conquered territory, either by military occupation of our armies in force, or by provisional government, would be to throw away all that has been gained by war, and basely to violate an obligation under the laws of war to the people who shall have been coerced into submission to our power.

MILITARY GOVERNMENT A MILD FORM OF HOSTILITIES — A CONCESSION — ITS TENDENCY.

The maintenance of a provisional military government is an economical mode of continuing hostilities against a subjugated people, by dispensing with the unnecessary use of force.

To grant a government of any kind to a conquered people, while engaged in active hostilities, is a concession, a boon, a benefit, not an unjustifiable assumption of rights. The law of war justifies the use of *brute force* as the means of governing a public enemy. The judges under that law are military officers and sometimes common soldiers, without aid of law-books, counsellors, juries, codes, statutes, or regulations other than their own *will.* From their decrees there is no appeal; judge, jury, and executioner too often stand embodied in a single individual at the but-end of a Sharp's rifle.

In the civil war brought upon southern rebels by their own choice, to permit them to be governed by rules, regulations, statutes, laws, and codes of jurisprudence; to give them *jurists* able and willing to abide by standing laws, and thus to restore (as far as is consistent with public safety and the secure tenure of conquest) the blessings of civil liberty and a just administration of laws — most of which are made by those on whom they are administered — is an act of magnanimity worthy of a great people.

Such a government, though founded on and administered by military power, surely tends to restore the confidence of the disloyal by giving them rights they could not otherwise enjoy, and by protecting them from unnecessary hardships and wrongs. It cannot fail to encourage and support the friends of the Union in disloyal districts, by demonstrating to all the forbearance and justice of those who are responsible for the conduct of the war.

THERE MUST BE A MILITARY GOVERNMENT OR NO GOVERNMENT.

When the country can no longer be governed by the magistrate, it must be handed over to the soldier.

When law becomes powerless, force must be applied. When civil tribunals fall, military tribunals must rise.

Foreign territory acquired by the United States, by conquest or by treaty, does not, by force of the Constitution, become entitled to self-government,* nor does the *conquest* of public enemies within the domain of the United States confer upon them the right of self-government; for none but military control of the conqueror can exist in a hostile region. There being in the belligerent district in the South no power or authority of the enemy which can be recognized as legitimate by the United States, our military power must be the basis on which our control over the affairs of the inhabitants living there must finally rest. By conquest, the local government and the courts of justice are deprived of their power, because the former is hostile, and the latter derive their authority from a public enemy. No local tribunal, civil, judicial, political, or military exists in a conquered district whose authority is recognized as lawful by the conqueror, except such as is established by him.† Hence the only government that can be organized while war lasts, is one whose authority is derived from the military power of the conqueror, and by the right of conquest. But as he is clothed

* 3 Story, Comm. 1318. Am. Ins. Co. *vs.* Canter, 1 Peters, 511, 542, 516.

† By the Act of July 17, 1862, it is made the duty of the President to seize the estate, etc., of all persons acting thereafter as *governors* of States, *members of legislatures*, or of *conventions*, or *judges of courts*, of the so-called Confederate States; and of *any person* holding *any office* under either of the said States. Such persons cannot therefore be *recognized* by our government otherwise than as criminals.

only with military authority, he can establish no government other than one of a military character. Therefore, if he finds it expedient to administer civil or municipal codes of law, they must be adopted and applied as military law, following therein, as far as practicable, the rules and forms of civil jurisprudence.

THE RIGHT TO ERECT MILITARY GOVERNMENTS IS AN ESSENTIAL PART OF THE WAR-POWER, AND IS FOUNDED IN NECESSITY AND SANCTIONED BY AUTHORITY.

Thus it has been shown that justifiable war ought to be prosecuted until the object for which it was commenced has been attained. That object is the restoration of the authority of the United States over all the territory and inhabitants thereof, a result which can be accomplished with the least injury to ourselves and to our enemies by substituting, as far as safety will permit, a temporary government over them by military law, instead of continuing the use of mere force.

Reason and experience alike demonstrate the necessity of that mode of regulating a hostile community while passing through the intermediate state from open and general warfare to the reëstablishment of peaceful institutions. No government other than that authorized by the law of war is practically useful, or can lawfully exist, until peace is so far restored that the enemy will voluntarily submit to the laws of Congress.

The right to exercise control by armed force in time of war over hostile regions is a necessary part of the power of making and prosecuting war. If the people of a belligerent locality can be lawfully captured and held as prisoners of war, and can thus be subjected to the orders of a commanding officer, it would be unreasonable to suppose that the same captives could not be held subject to the same orders, if permitted to go at large within the limits in which the military power of that officer was supreme.

Absolute necessity is the foundation and justification on which the right to enforce military government rests. That right has been used or practically acknowledged by most of the modern civilized nations. It is a right founded on reason, indispensable in practice, and is sanctioned by the authority of writers on international law, by jurists in Europe, and by the Supreme Court of the United States.

Wheaton, Law of Nations (Lawrence's ed.). 99.
Halleck, Intern. Law, 778.
Fleming *vs.* Page, 9 How. S. C. R. 615 (Appendix, 76).
Cross *vs.* Harrison, 16 " 190 (Appendix, 80).
Leitensdorfer *vs.* Webb, 20 How. 177 (Appendix, 86).
Am. Ins. Co. *vs.* Canter, 1 Peters, S. C. R. 542.
U. S. *vs.* Gratiot, 14 Peters, S. C. R. 526.
Also, see cases in the Appendix.

CHAPTER II.

THE CONSTITUTION AUTHORIZES THE PRESIDENT TO ESTABLISH MILITARY GOVERNMENTS.

Whenever the President is called on to repel invasion or to suppress rebellion by force, if the employment of military government is a useful and proper means of accomplishing that object, the Constitution confers on him the power to institute such government for that purpose.

The power of the President to establish military governments is derived from the Constitution, Art. II., Sec. 1, Cl. 1, and is a legitimate exercise of his authority as Commander-in-Chief.

Art. IV., Sec. 4, also provides that, "The United States shall guaranty to every State in this Union a republican form of government; and shall protect each of them against invasion, and, on application of the Legislature, or of the Executive (when the Legislature cannot be convened), against domestic violence."

A condition of public affairs like that now existing in certain rebellious States, renders a military government thereof indispensably necessary to enable the United States to perform this guaranty of the Constitution. The authority, therefore, to institute such a government for that purpose belongs to the President, because he is bound to see the laws enforced; and also, under Art. I., Sec. 8, Cl. 18, to Congress, because it is bound to pass all laws necessary and proper to enable the President to execute his duties.

The topics now under consideration do not require any examination of the nature or extent of the right or duty of Congress, or of the President as an *executive* officer, to carry the Art. IV., Sec. 4, into effect. The erection and maintenance for a time, by executive authority, of a provisional government in any State or Territory as a "necessary and proper means" of carrying the guaranties of the Constitution into effect, may be the subject of explanation in a future essay.

The right of Congress is beyond question to establish temporary territorial or provisional governments over those parts of the country which, having been engaged in civil war against the United States, have by force of arms been coerced into submission to our government.*

It is not necessary in this place to make further explanations of Articles I. and IV., it being sufficient for our present purpose to refer to the powers conferred by the second Article.

The Constitution, Article II., Sec. 2, Cl. 1, provides that, "The President shall be Commander-in-Chief of the Army and Navy of the United States, and of the Militia of the several States when called into the actual service of the United States."

This clause confers by necessary implication, upon the Commander-in-Chief of the Army and Navy, the right in time of war to subject public enemies to military government and regulation; for no limits to the power of the President, acting as a military commander, are prescribed in the Constitution. The laws of war, by which alone his operations should be regulated, establish his right to erect such government, and to maintain it by force of arms. The war powers of the

* See *post*, Ch. VI.

President are interpreted and controlled only by the rules of belligerent law.*

As the authority to call into active service the Army and Navy, to capture or kill an adversary in battle, to seize and destroy his property, and to occupy and hold his lands by force, has been confided, without limitation, to the President, when the occasion for these measures occurs, would it not seem inconsistent to withhold from him the right to *keep* what he has acquired by arms, and to hold in his control (while war lasts) the enemy whom he has overthrown?

If it be said that the power thus claimed is not granted to the President *in express terms*, it may with equal correctness be said that the authority to carry on war, to suppress insurrections or to repel invasions, or to make captures on land or sea, is not conferred upon him in express terms. The Constitution enables the President to use war powers in no other way than by authorizing him under certain circumstances to call into service and to take command of the Army and Navy. But Congress is empowered to provide for "raising and maintaining armies," and to "make rules for captures on land and sea." Hence no one can doubt that when an army is raised, and captures are to be made, the President, being placed in command, has the right to employ these forces so as to accomplish the purpose for which they were organized, and therefore has the right to make captures, as unquestionably as he would have

* See cases subsequently cited.

Fleming *vs.* Page, 9 How. 615.
Cross *vs.* Harrison, 16 How. 90.
Leitensdorfer *vs.* Webb, 20 How. 177.
Wheaton, 99; War Powers, 54.

if that right had been conferred on him in plain words by the Constitution.

There can be no reason to doubt that the army is placed under the supreme command of the Chief Magistrate for all purposes for which offensive or defensive war may be justly waged.

If he has the authority to commit any act of hostility for suppression of rebellion or repelling of invasion, he has equal right to commit *all* acts of hostility which may in his judgment be required to secure success in his military operations; and he has therefore the same right to erect a military government in hostile territory, under circumstances justifying it, as to perform any other military act.

The erection of such government over the territory and persons of a public enemy in time of war is an act of war, is in fact continuing against them a species of hostility without the use of unnecessary force. It is a mode of retaining a conquest, of continuing custody and supervision over an unfriendly population, and of subjecting malcontent non-combatants to the will of a superior force so as to prevent them from engaging in hostilities or inciting insurrections or breaches of the peace, or from giving aid and comfort to the enemy. Large numbers of persons may thus be held in subjection to the moral and physical force of comparatively few military men. Contributions may be levied, property may be confiscated, commerce may be restrained or forbidden, and an unfriendly population may be held in subjection by military government, for the same reasons which would justify the repression of their open hostilities by force of arms. If the Constitution allows the President to go to war, and to conquer the public enemy, the greater power must include the less; the power to make a conquest must include the authority to keep and maintain possession of it, while war continues.

No one would doubt our right to occupy a hostile district of country by military posts, or by soldiers stationed in commanding positions, or to enforce upon all its inhabitants the rigid rules of martial law.

How, then, can the right be questioned to hold the same territory by a *small* number of soldiers, administering the same law, under the same authority, whether these military men be called by their ordinary titles, or be styled provost marshals or military governors?

If the humanity of the conqueror allows the rigid rules of martial law to be relaxed, and permits the forms of local jurisprudence to be continued under the same authority, so far as it may be done consistently with the security of the conquest, on what principle can his right to do so be denied?

DUTY OF THE CONQUEROR TO GOVERN THOSE WHOM HE HAS SUBJUGATED.

In view of the necessity of securing the ends for which war is waged, and the consequences following from the absence of government over conquered territory, it is undoubtedly the right and duty of the conqueror to erect and maintain, during war, *a provisional military government* over districts which have been subjected to his power.

This right is recognized and confirmed by the acknowledged laws of war, and by the decisions of the Supreme Court of the United States; the propriety and necessity of its enforcement have been shown by our experience in New Mexico and California, and in the States now in rebellion.

CHAPTER III.

DISTRIBUTION OF POWERS UNDER MILITARY GOVERNMENT.

Military governments control and regulate a great variety of public, private, civil, criminal, judicial, legislative, and military affairs. Their powers may be concentrated in a single officer, acting as a military governor, or they may be distributed among several persons acting under authority of the Commander-in-Chief, who may appoint one as commander, another as governor, a third as chief justice, and others as collectors of customs, in the same department.

Among the various modes of instituting military governments, one is by a proclamation of martial law, and by authorizing or appointing courts martial, courts of inquiry, and military commissions to carry that law into execution over belligerent districts. These institutions are best adapted to localities whose inhabitants are too hostile to admit of milder forms of administration.

The character of the laws, and the organization of the tribunals now *authorized by the statutes* to administer such government, will next be considered.

DIFFERENT KINDS OF LAW OF WAR.

Martial Law consists of a system of rules and principles regulating or modifying the rights, liabilities, and duties, the social, municipal, and international relations in time of war, of all persons, whether neutral or belligerent.*

* See Military Arrests, p. 10. War Powers, p. 166.

Military law is that part of the martial law of the land designed for the government of those who are engaged in the military service.

Of the rules and principles of martial law, many have as yet not been reduced to the form of statutes or regulations, although they are familiar in the practice of courts martial. The 69th Article of War refers to and adopts them as part of the martial law. They may be styled the "*lex non scripta*," the custom of war, the *common law of the army*.

In the United States, martial law is modified by military laws made by Congress as articles of war, by general regulations for the government of the army, by all statutes on military subjects which the Constitution empowers Congress to pass, and by all lawful orders of the President, as Commander-in-Chief, and of the Secretary of War, or officers acting under them.

Martial law, thus modified, is, when in force under the Constitution, administered within or without the United States by various *military tribunals*, including courts martial, military commissions, and courts of inquiry.*

MILITARY TRIBUNALS — HOW AUTHORIZED — THEIR CHARACTERISTICS.

The war courts now established by statutes, and recognized by judicial decisions, are called *courts martial*, *courts of inquiry*, and *military commissions*.

The Constitution, Art. I., Sect. 8, Clause 14, gives Congress power "to make rules for the government and regulation of the land and naval forces."

The 16th clause declares that Congress shall have

* See Benet on Military Law and Courts Martial, 11.
Dehart on Military Law and Courts Martial, 3.

power to "provide for organizing, arming, and disciplining the militia; and for governing such part of them as may be employed in the service of the United States."

To provide for disciplining and governing militia in the service, means *to make laws, rules, or regulations* for their discipline and government. The power to make them would be inoperative, unless means could be employed to administer them. Congress, therefore, has power to provide *means* as well as rules for governing. No uncertainty is left upon this question; for the 18th clause of the same section gives Congress power "to make all laws which shall be necessary and proper to carry into execution the foregoing powers, and all other powers vested by the Constitution in the Government of the United States, or in any department or officer thereof."

In the execution of this authority, Congress has provided for governing the army by erecting military courts, which are not merely necessary and proper, but are the only practical means yet found for carrying into execution the rules and regulations so enacted. Such courts are therefore sanctioned as positively as if established by express language in the Constitution.

POWER OF THE PRESIDENT TO ESTABLISH COURTS OF WAR.

Not only has Congress power to create tribunals to administer "rules and regulations for governing the army and the navy," but there exists another independent power to create and establish courts with jurisdiction over a wider range of subjects and of persons. That power is vested by the Constitution in the President, as Commander-in-Chief of the army and navy, when in actual service in time of war, and is a branch of the power to erect and maintain military governments.

Military courts are a usual and essential part of the machinery of military government; the right to institute the one necessarily implies the right to organize the other, and the jurisdiction of such courts embraces offences not declared punishable by any law of Congress, and persons out of the reach of any but military process.

How far it may be within the province of Congress to control the operations of war courts instituted by the President, need not be here discussed.

As has been said, one class of courts of war may be instituted by laws of Congress, and another class may be created by the President. Both are under his control as military chief of the forces, while at the same time he is bound to execute the laws of the land.

The right of the Commander-in-Chief, as well as the right of Congress, to create military courts, has been sanctioned by repeated decisions of the United States.*

DO COURTS OF WAR EXERCISE JUDICIAL POWER?

As the proceedings of war courts in some respects resemble those of courts of law, it has been questioned whether they exercise any part cf the judicial power which is vested by the Constitution in "one Supreme Court and in such other inferior courts as CONGRESS may from time to time ordain and establish." — Constitution, Art. III., Sect. 1.

It has been decided by the Supreme Court of the United States, that military tribunals exercise no part

* See authorities in the Appendix.

of the *judicial* power, but only a portion of the military power of the Executive. And it has also been determined that the sentences or other lawful proceedings of courts martial of the United States are not the subject of appeal or revision in any judicial courts of the States or of the United States.*

WOULD JUDICIAL COURTS BE USEFUL AS WAR COURTS?

If it be said that judicial courts ought to employed for the administration of the laws of war, in order thereby to preserve the safeguards of civil liberty, the answer is that the whole system of judicial courts would be worse than useless in armies moving from place to place. Their organization is incompatible with the administration of military rights and remedies, by reason of local jurisdiction, jury trials, territorial limitations of process, and slowness of procedure, to say nothing of the inexperience of learned jurists in military affairs.

* Vallandigham's Case. (Appendix, 88).
Dynes *vs.* Hoover, 20 How. 81, 82. (Appendix, 84)

CHAPTER IV.

DIFFERENT KINDS OF MILITARY TRIBUNALS.

I. COURTS MARTIAL.

Courts martial have been recognized or established by express laws of Congress.

The Act of February 28, 1795, provided for calling out the militia and also for the organization of courts martial, designating the officers of whom they should be composed, prescribing punishments by these tribunals for persons who should fail (in the instances specified in Sect. 5) to obey the orders of the President. These courts derived their authority, not from any State law, but only from the statutes of the United States.*

It is, however, not questioned that either of the States may pass laws providing for the trial of such delinquents by State courts martial.†

The act of April 10, 1806, enacts articles of war, regulates (Article 64) the mode of organizing *general courts martial;* gives (Art. 65) the power of appointing them to general officers commanding an army, or colonels commanding a separate department, and institutes inferior courts martial (Art. 66); limits

* Commonwealth *vs.* Irish, 3 S. & R. 176.
S. C. 5 Hall's Law Jour. 476.
Meade *vs.* Dep. Marsh. Va. Dist. 5 Hall L. J. 536.

† Houston *vs.* Moore, 3 S. & R. 169.
Martin *vs.* Mott, 12 Wh. R. 19.

and requires confirmation of sentences (Arts. 65, 67), and provides (Art. 69) for the appointment of prosecuting officers usually called Judge Advocates. This act regulates the oaths of officers composing the court; the oath of the Judge Advocate, the punishment of the accused for standing mute; it provides for challenges, punishes misbehavior in court, contempts, or unbecoming conduct of persons convicted; it lays down rules relating to testimony and oaths of witnesses, and depositions, and designates (Sect. 99) such crimes or misconduct as are punishable by courts martial.

The Act of Aug. 5, 1861, gives power to commanders of divisions or separate brigades to appoint general courts martial in time of war.

The decisions of these tribunals are required to be reported to, and to be reviewed by, some superior officer who may confirm, modify, or set them aside. But the final judgments of courts martial are not liable to be reviewed or reversed by any *judicial* court of the United States.*

When a court martial has once acquired jurisdiction of the person and the subject-matter, that jurisdiction is exclusive of civil courts for that offence. But the same transaction may constitute an offence against municipal as well as military law, and, in such cases, the offender is liable to punishment by both.

II. MILITARY COURTS OF INQUIRY.

The Act of April 10, 1806, provides the manner of constituting such courts, their powers and proceedings. It recognizes the right of organizing them by the gen-

* Dynes *vs.* Hoover, 20 How. (Appendix, 84).
Vallandigham's Case. (Appendix, 88).

erals or commanding officers; power is conferred upon these courts to summon, to compel attendance, and to examine witnesses; the right of the accused to cross-examine witnesses is secured; and the mode of authenticating proceedings is prescribed.

But courts of inquiry being liable to abuse, are prohibited in all cases, except when demanded by the accused, or ordered by the President of the United States.

The Act of March 3, 1863, Sect. 25, gives power to every Judge Advocate of a court of inquiry to issue process to compel the attendance of witnesses, like that which State, Territorial, or District Courts issue in places where said court of inquiry is held.

These and other statutes show that this class of military courts is fully recognized by the laws of the United States.

III. MILITARY COMMISSIONS, INSTITUTED BY THE COMMANDER-IN-CHIEF, OR UNDER STATUTES.

Military commissions were first made familiar to the people of this country by General Orders No. 287, issued by General Scott at the head-quarters of the army, National Palace of Mexico, Sept. 17, 1847.

During the occupation of Mexico by our army many crimes were committed by hostile individuals against soldiers, and by soldiers against the Mexicans, not punishable by courts martial as organized under the Articles of War; and, as General Scott wrote in his order, "A supplemental code is absolutely needed. That *unwritten* code is martial law, as an addition to the *written* military code prescribed by Congress in the Rules and Articles of War, and which unwritten code all armies in hostile countries are forced to adopt, not only for their own safety, but for the protection of the unoffending inhabitants and their property about the theatres of military operations, against injuries on the part of the army, contrary to the laws of war. . . . For this purpose it is ordered that all offenders in the matters aforesaid shall be promptly seized, confined, and reported for trial before military commissions to be duly appointed, etc."

These commissions were appointed, governed, and limited, as nearly as practicable, as prescribed for courts martial; their proceedings to be recorded, reviewed, revised, disapproved, or confirmed, and their sentences executed, all as nearly as might be as in the cases of the proceedings and sentences of courts martial, "provided that no military commission shall try any case clearly cognizable by any court martial, and provided also that no sentence of a military commission shall be put in execution against any individual belonging to this army, which may not be according to the nature and degree of the offence, as established by evidence, in conformity with known punishments in like cases in some one of the States of the United States of America."

"The administration of justice, both in civil and criminal matters, through the ordinary courts of the country, was nowhere and in no degree to be interrupted by any officer or soldier, except" in certain specified cases.

Martial, military, and civil or municipal law were administered in Mexico by General Scott, under such military commissions, with the exception above stated. But courts of this description were instituted *under the general war power of the Commander-in-Chief*, — a power which was fully conceded by the Supreme Court of the United States, — not under the authority of Congress. Congress has, however, recognized in express terms "military commissions," in the act of March 5, 1863, Chap. 75; and having authorized the appointment of a Judge Advocate General, required all proceedings of such commissions to be returned to him for revision and record. This Act, Section 30, gives military commissions, equally with courts martial jurisdiction, in time of war, in case of "murder, assault and battery with intent to kill, manslaughter, mayhem, wounding by shooting or stabbing with an intent to commit murder, robbery, arson, burglary, rape, assault and battery with intent to commit rape, and larceny, when committed by persons who are in the military service of the United States, and subject to the articles of war."

Spies are also, by the same Act, Section 38, punishable with death by sentence of a military commission.

The several statutes above cited show that Congress, in pursuance of its powers under the Constitution, has recognized and established courts martial, courts of inquiry, and military commissions.

Courts of the same denomination, but exercising a much broader jurisdiction of persons and subjects, have been organized and established by the President of the United States, under the war powers delegated to him by the Constitution, as Commander-in-Chief of the army and navy; and the binding authority of such courts has been admitted and solemnly asserted by the Supreme Court of the United States. Tribunals instituted by the war power of the President are those through which it is most usual to apply the laws of war in enemy's country, while hostilities are in progress, and for a certain length of time after a declaration of peace.

All these tribunals constitute usual and necessary parts of the machinery of warfare, and are the essential instruments of that military government by which alone the permanency of conquest can be secured.

IV. COURTS OF CIVIL JURISDICTION UNDER MILITARY AUTHORITY.

In the preceding pages it has been shown that the right of the President, as Commander-in-Chief of the army, to organize and administer government in all its branches by military power, in time of war, over belligerent districts of country recovered from a public enemy, and his right to subdivide and delegate those powers to different persons acting under his orders, are sanctioned by the Constitution and laws of Congress, by the decisions of the Supreme Court, and by our practice in former wars.

The same rights have been exercised during the present civil war. President Lincoln has appointed as Governor of the State of Louisiana, Brigadier-General Geo. F. Shepley; as Judge of the Provisional Court of the same State, Hon. Charles A. Peabody;* as Military Commander of the department containing Louisiana, Maj.-Gen. B. F. Butler; and General Butler has appointed to act under him a Sequestration Committee.

The commissions and orders under which they have acted are as follows: —

COMMISSION AS MILITARY GOVERNOR.

WAR DEPARTMENT, WASHINGTON CITY,
June 3, 1862.

HON. GEORGE B. SHEPLEY, &c. &c.

SIR: — You are hereby appointed Military Governor of the State of Louisiana, with authority to exercise and perform, within the limits of that State, all and singular, the powers, duties, and functions pertaining to the office of Military Governor (including the power to establish all necessary offices and tribunals and suspend the writ of *habeas corpus*), during the pleasure of the President, or until the loyal inhabitants of that State shall organize a civil government in conformity with the Constitution of the United States.

By the President.

SEAL OF U. S.

E. M. STANTON,

Secretary of War.

* The President has more recently appointed as a Judge of the District Court of the United States for the Eastern District of Louisiana, Hon. Chas. A. Duvall, whose nomination has been confirmed by the Senate. He has decided many important prize cases.

EXECUTIVE ORDER, ESTABLISHING A PROVISIONAL COURT IN LOUISIANA.

EXECUTIVE MANSION,
WASHINGTON, October 20, 1862.

The insurrection which has for some time prevailed in several of the States of this Union, including Louisiana, having temporarily subverted and swept away the civil institutions of that State, including the judiciary and judicial authorities of the Union, so that it has become necessary to hold the State in military occupation; and it being indispensably necessary that there shall be some judicial tribunal existing there capable of administering justice, I have, therefore, thought it proper to appoint, and I do hereby constitute a Provisional Court, which shall be a Court of Record for the State of Louisiana, and I do hereby appoint CHARLES A. PEABODY, of New York, to be a Provisional Judge to hold said Court, with authority to hear, try, and determine all causes, civil and criminal, including causes in law, equity, revenue, and admiralty, and particularly all such powers and jurisdiction as belong to the District and Circuit Courts of the United States, conforming his proceedings, so far as possible, to the course of proceedings and practice which has been customary in the Courts of the United States and Louisiana — his judgment to be final and conclusive. And I do hereby authorize and empower the said Judge to make and establish such rules and regulations as may be necessary for the exercise of his jurisdiction, and to appoint a Prosecuting Attorney, Marshal, and Clerk of the said Court, who shall perform the functions of Attorney, Marshal, and Clerk, according to such proceedings and practice as before mentioned, and such rules and regulations as may be made and established by said Judge. These appointments are to continue during the pleasure of the President, not extending beyond the military occupation of the city of New Orleans, or the restoration of the civil authority in that city and in the State of Louisiana. These officers shall be paid out of the contingent fund of the War Department, compensation as follows: . . . . Such compensations to be certified by the Secretary of War. A copy of this order, certified by the Secretary of War, and delivered to such Judge, shall be deemed and held to be a sufficient commission. Let the seal of the United States be hereunto affixed.

ABRAHAM LINCOLN.

By the President:

WILLIAM H. SEWARD, *Secretary of State.*

SEQUESTRATION COMMISSION.

GENERAL ORDERS No. 91.

HEAD-QUARTERS, DEPARTMENT OF THE GULF,
NEW ORLEANS, November 9, 1862.

The Commanding General being informed, and believing, that the district west of the Mississippi River, lately taken possession of by the United States troops, is most largely occupied by persons disloyal to the United States, and whose property has become liable to confiscation under the acts of Congress and the proclamation of the President, and that sales and transfers of said property are being made for the purpose of depriving the Government of the same, has determined, in order to secure the rights of all persons as well as those of the Government, and for the purpose of enabling the crops now growing to be taken care of and secured, and the unemployed laborers to be set at work, and provision made for the payment of their labor, —

To order, as follows: —

I. That all the property within the district to be known as the "District of Lafourche," be and are hereby sequestered, and all sales or transfers thereof are forbidden, and will be held invalid.

II. The District of Lafourche will comprise all the territory in the State of Louisiana lying west of the Mississippi River, except the parishes of Plaquemines and Jefferson.

III. That

Major JOSEPH M. BELL, Provost Judge, President,
Lieut. Col. J. B. KINSMAN, A. D. C.,
Capt. FULLER (75th N. Y. Vols.), Provost Marshal of the District,

be a commission to take possession of the property in said district, to make an accurate inventory of the same, and gather up and collect all such personal property, and turn over to the proper officers, under their receipts, such of said property as may be required for the use of the United States army; to collect together all the other personal property, and bring the same to New Orleans, and cause it to be sold at public auction to the highest bidders, and, after deducting the necessary expenses of care, collection, and transportation, to hold the proceeds thereof subject to the just claims of loyal citizens and those neutral foreigners who in good faith shall appear to be the owners of the same.

IV. Every loyal citizen or neutral foreigner who shall be found in actual possession and ownership of any property in said district, not having acquired the same by any title since the 18th day of September last, may have his property returned or delivered to him without sale, upon establishing his condition to the judgment of the Commission.

V. All sales made by any person not a loyal citizen or foreign neutral, since the 18th day of September, shall be held void, and all sales whatever, made with the intent to deprive the Government of its rights of confiscation, will be held void, at what time soever made.

VI. The Commission is authorized to employ in working the plantation of any person who has remained quietly at his home, whether he be loyal or disloyal, the negroes who may be found in said district, or who have, or may hereafter, claim the protection of the United States, upon the terms set forth in the memoranda of a contract heretofore offered to the planters of the parishes of Plaquemines and St. Bernard, or white labor may be employed at the election of the Commission.

VII. The Commissioners will cause to be purchased such supplies as may be necessary, and convey them to such convenient depots as to supply the planters in the making of the crop; which supplies will be charged against the crop manufactured, and shall constitute a lien thereon.

VIII. The Commissioners are authorized to work, for the account of the United States, such plantations as are deserted by their owners, or are held by disloyal owners, as may seem to them expedient, for the purpose of saving the crops.

IX. Any persons who have not been actually in arms against the United States since the occupation of New Orleans by its forces, and who shall remain peaceably upon their plantations, affording no aid or comfort to the enemies of the United States, and who shall return to their allegiance, and who shall, by all reasonable methods, aid the United States when called upon, may be empowered by the Commission to work their own plantations, to make their own crop, and to retain possession of their own property, except such as is necessary for the military uses of the United States. And to all such persons the Commission are authorized to furnish means of transportation for their crops and supplies, at just and equitable prices.

X. The Commissioners are empowered and authorized to hear, determine, and definitely report upon all questions of the loyalty, disloyalty, or neutrality of the various claimants of property within said district; and further, to report such persons as in their judgment ought to be recommended by the Commanding General to the President for amnesty and pardon, so that they may have their property returned; to the end that all persons that are loyal, may suffer as little injury as possible, and that all persons who have been heretofore disloyal may have opportunity now to prove their loyalty and return to their allegiance, and save their property from confiscation, if such shall be the determination of the Government of the United States.

By command of MAJOR-GENERAL BUTLER.

GEO. C. STRONG,
A. A. G., Chief of Staff.

JURISDICTION OF COURTS APPOINTED BY MILITARY AUTHORITY TO ADMINISTER JUSTICE.

Military courts, being lawfully established by virtue of the war power of the President, as a part of his military government over the territory of a public enemy, with jurisdiction over all persons and things within the district limited in his commission to the judge, have the right to make and enforce rules for the creation and service of process, and for all other proceedings before them. Their judgments may be rendered subject to appeal, if so directed by the President. The orders and decisions of the judges will be final and conclusive upon all subjects, matters, and persons over whom they have, by the terms of their commissions, exclusive and final jurisdiction. From such decisions and judgments there is no appeal to any judicial court of the United States.* They must be forever recognized by all departments of government as valid and conclusive.

DOES THE CONSTITUTION PROHIBIT SUCH PROCEDURES?

The question may be asked whether courts administering municipal or local laws, condemning criminals without previous indictment, trial by jury, limitation of place in which trial shall be held, and without right of appeal, are not within the prohibitions of the Constitution.

The clauses referring to these subjects are as follows: —

Amendment, Art. V.

"No person shall be HELD *to answer* for a capital or otherwise infamous crime unless on a presentment or indictment of a Grand Jury, *except* in cases arising in the land or naval forces; or in the militia when in actual service in time of war or public danger," etc.

Amendment, Art. VI.

"In all *criminal prosecutions* the accused shall enjoy the right to *a speedy and public trial by an impartial jury* of the State and district wherein the crime shall have been committed, which district shall have been previously ascertained by law," etc.

Amendment, Art. VII.

"In suits at common law, where the value in controversy shall exceed twenty dollars, the right of trial by jury shall be preserved; and no fact tried by a jury shall be otherwise reëxamined in any court of the United States, than according to the rules of the common law."

* Dynes *v.* Hoover, 20 How. (See Appendix.)
Vallandigham's Case. (See Appendix.)

To obtain a correct view of the meaning and application of the fifth, sixth, and seventh articles of the Amendment above cited, it will be necessary to observe that the citizens owing allegiance to the Government of the United States are by civil territorial war divided into classes of persons having different rights and liabilities.

First, the inhabitants of that section of the country which upholds that Government; and, second, the inhabitants of that section of country who have become public enemies; also, there are two classes of loyal citizens, — first, those who are engaged in the military service; and, second, those who are not.

Military courts may be in two different conditions: —

First, ordinary courts organized and acting under provisions of statutes, and administering the laws of war upon persons engaged in our military service; and, second, courts established by the war power of the Commander-in-Chief, and administering the domestic government of territorial public enemies in a hostile district of country held by our military power.

None of these provisions of the Constitution have any application to *military courts or the proceedings thereof.* They relate only to *judicial power* conferred thereby on judicial courts.

The fifth article expressly excludes cases arising in the land and naval forces, among our own citizen soldiers and seamen.

Art. 6th secures a jury trial in open court in the State and district where the crime was committed, and refers only to a judicial proceeding relating to crimes in the ordinary judicial courts.

Art. 7th refers only to proceedings in common law courts.

These regulations of procedures in common law and other ordinary courts apply to tribunals of a character totally different from *military courts.* The Constitution sanctions courts military, and courts judicial, and it requires the latter to be constituted according to these amendments, while the former are under no such restrictions.

The Supreme Court recognize this distinction, and say, in the case of Dynes *vs.* Hoover,* "These provisions show that Congress has the power to provide for the trial and punishment of military and naval offences in the manner then and now practised by civilized nations, and that the power to do so is given without any connection between it and the third article of the Constitution, defining the judicial power of the United States; indeed, that the two powers are entirely independent of each other."

Thus it is evident that whoever is subject to the jurisdiction of courts martial, etc., can claim none of the benefits of these Articles of Amendment, and that citizens of the United States who have been declared by our Government *public enemies* of the country, have no rights guaranteed to them under any provisions of our Constitution.

THE RIGHTS OF REBELS. — WHAT THEY CLAIM.

To form correct opinions in relation to the rights of persons inhabiting that part of the country now subjected to the government *de facto* of the so-called Confederate States, it is proper to ascertain what rights they claim.

Having founded new governments within the terri-

* 20 Howard, Rep. 79. (See Appendix.)

tory over which our national sovereignty extends, under the asserted right of revolution; having ratified those governments, both confederate and state, by popular conventions, by legislative acts of secession, by submission, by profession of allegiance, and by all other known modes of expressing assent and adherence thereto, they have publicly withdrawn from and disclaimed all allegiance to the United States. They demand that we should treat them as an independent nation. They not only assert no right to protection under our constitution, but wage open, barbarous, offensive war against the inhabitants of the loyal States and against our government. They seek recognition from and alliance with foreign countries, and if successful in arms, they will be entitled to compel the United States to submit to them as conquerors. Our territory, our government, and our population will then be subjected to their control. Their laws and their institutions will then be forced upon us, and nothing but the overthrow and destruction of the public enemy can prevent this result.

They have already been recognized by leading European powers as BELLIGERENTS. They have demanded and have received from our government, the concession of many *belligerent rights*; as for instance, the exchange of prisoners of war captured on land; the release of confederate seamen condemned for piracy; and the recognition of flags of truce, and the blockade of seaports, under the law of nations.

The claim, so far as it can be ascertained, of the confederate *de facto* government, as against the United States, is, 1st, The concession of full belligerent rights, and, 2d, Their recognition as an independent nation. No demand of any right under our constitution or our laws has ever been made by the confederates. Those who deny their liability to perform the obligations imposed on subjects of the United States, have not fallen into the absurdity of claiming the privileges of subjects. The confederates claim only such rights as the law of war, which is a part of the law of nations, secures to them. That claim this government is bound to concede, whenever it determines to treat them, not as subjects, but as belligerents.

Have the insurgents admitted liability on their part to regard our laws or constitution in carrying on war against us? Have they not forsworn their allegiance to this government, and can they claim protection while denying allegiance? Can an enemy justly assert any right under a constitution he is fighting to destroy? The insurgents deem themselves public enemies to the United States in open war, and admit their liability to abide by the stern rules of belligerent law. They demand no privilege under a constitution which, by commencing war, they have violated in every clause.

Is it not remarkable that persons who profess to adhere to our government, should set up pretensions on behalf of our adversaries which our adversaries themselves disclaim?

RIGHTS CONCEDED TO INSURGENTS.

Whoever makes war against a nation renounces all right to its protection. The people of the United States have founded a government to secure the "general welfare," by preventing enemies, foreign or domestic, from destroying the country. They did not frame a constitution so as to paralyze the power of self-defence. They have not forged weapons for their adversaries, or manacles for themselves.

The Constitution, in fact, guarantees no *rights*, but only

declares the *liabilities*, of public enemies, — if they are invaders, that they shall be repelled; if they are insurgents, that they shall be put down by force; if they are rebels, banded together in territorial civil war, then that civil war shall be fought through, and conquest and subjugation shall reëstablish lawful government. Any other result must be a destruction of the country, and therefore an overthrow of the Constitution.

In the enforcement of these hostile measures against public enemies, the most liberal concession demanded by the code of civilized warfare, is that traitors should be deemed belligerents; but, while enjoying the immunities, they must be subject to the liabilities, of war.*

Therefore, whether the Articles of Amendment of the Constitution, previously cited, apply to martial proceedings or not, is immaterial in determining the rights of a hostile people engaged in civil war against the United States.

The appeal to arms and the laws of war was forced upon us, because the insurrectionary districts refused to submit to the Constitution. They cannot, therefore, justly complain that under the laws of war they are no longer sheltered by that constitution which they have spurned.

ARE THE INHABITANTS OF INSURRECTIONARY STATES PUBLIC ENEMIES?

Whether persons inhabiting insurrectionary States are in law to be deemed "public enemies," is a *political* question, which, like similar questions arising under our form of government, is to be determined, *not* by judicial courts of law, but by the Legislative and Executive Departments.†

* See the Prize Cases, 2 Black's R. 638. War Powers, 141.

† Some of the consequences flowing from the *status* of a public enemy, have been stated in a previous publication. (See War Powers, 8th Ed. pp. 236–244.)

Among those subjects which, as the Supreme Court of the United States has already decided, are finally to be determined by the political departments of government, are the following, viz: —

Questions of boundary between the United States and foreign countries.*

"The question like this," says Chief Justice Marshall, "respecting boundary of nations, is, as has been truly said, more a political than a legal question; and, in its discussion, the courts of every country must respect the pronounced will of the legislature." Taney C. J. says: "The legislative and executive branches having decided the question, the courts of the United States were bound to regard the boundary determined on by them as the true one." †

Questions as to the sovereignty of any foreign country or its independence.

"To what sovereignty any island or country belongs is a question which often arises before courts."

"And can there be a doubt that when the *executive* branch of the government, which is charged with our foreign relations, shall, in its correspondence with a foreign nation, *assume a fact* in regard to the sovereignty of any island or country, it is conclusive on the judicial department? And in this view it is not material to inquire whether the Executive is right or wrong. It is enough to know that, in the exercise of his constitutional functions, he *has decided* the question. Having done this, under the responsibilities which belong to him, it is obligatory on the people and government of the United States."

"In the cases of Foster *vs.* Nelson, and Garcia *vs.* Lee, this Court have laid down the rule *that the action of the*

* Foster & Elam *vs.* Nelson, 2 Pet. 307.

† United States *vs.* Percheman, 7 Pet. 51.
United States *vs.* Arredondo (1832), 6 Pet. 711.
Garcia *vs.* Lee, 12 Pet. 516, 517, 520, 522.

political branches of the government, in a matter that belongs to them, is conclusive."*

Questions as to the recognition of State governments in the Union.

Whether the government of Rhode Island *was the duly constituted* government of that State, was a question which belonged to the political and not to the judicial power, so that the Circuit Court of the United States had not the power to try and determine this question, so far as the United States was concerned.

Congress has delegated to the President, by the Act of Feb. 28, 1795, the power to decide for the purposes of that act, whether a government organized in a State is the duly constituted government of that State, and, after he has decided this question, the courts of the United States are bound to follow his decision.†

Questions as to the status of foreign nations whose provinces or dependencies are in *revolution* — *foreign invasion* of our own country — and *insurrection, or rebellion, or civil war, at home, and the status of those engaged therein*, are political questions determinable by the executive and legislative branches of our government.‡

* Williams *vs.* Suffolk Ins. Co. 13 Peters, S. C. R. 420 (McLean J.) See also Gelston *vs.* Hoyt, 3 Wheaton, 246, United States *vs.* Palmer, 3 Wheaton, 610.

† Luther *vs.* Borden, 7 Howard, S. C. R. 40, 42, 43, 44.

‡ Luther *vs.* Borden, 7 Howard, 40, 44. Lawrence's Wheaton, 514. Martin *vs.* Mott, 12 Wheaton, 29, 30. Law Reporter, July, 1861, 148. The "Tropic Wind," Op. of Judge Dunlop. The prize cases "*Hiawatha*" and others. 2 Black. War Powers, 8th ed. 141 & 215. See also charge of Nelson J. on the trial of the officers, etc., of the Savannah, p. 371. In this case the rebel privateer put in as a defence his commission to cruise under the confederate flag: and the same defence was made in Philadelphia by other persons indicted for piracy. In both cases it was held that the courts must *follow the decision of the executive and legislative departments* in determining the political status of the Confederate States. See also Smith's Trial, p. 96. Santissima Trinidad, 7 Wheaton, 305. Upton's Maritime Warfare and Prize, 2d ed., pp. 44 to 107.

Therefore, it will be the province of the political departments of our government to decide, among other questions, —

1. Whether the Confederate States shall have the status of belligerents.

2. Whether they have the status of *public enemies*.

3. Whether local governments to be formed within the territory now in rebellion shall be recognized.

4. Whether and when a state of *peace* shall be declared or recognized.

5. Whether the Confederate States shall be recognized by receiving their commissioners, or by acknowledging their independence.

On these and similar questions the courts are bound to follow the decisions of the President and of Congress.

THE PRESIDENT.

The action of the Executive Department has stamped as "public enemies" all persons residing in the insurrectionary States.

The President issued a proclamation on the 15th April, 1861, which declares that the laws had been opposed and their execution obstructed for some time past, in certain States, by combinations too powerful to be suppressed by the ordinary course of judicial proceedings. He called out 75,000 of the State militia in order to suppress said combinations.

On the 19th of April, 1861, he proclaimed a *blockade* of the ports within certain States, in pursuance of the statutes of the United States and *the laws of nations* in such case provided, and gave warning that vessels breaking or attempting to break that blockade should be *captured* and *condemned as lawful prize*. He also declared that any persons who, under pretended authority of said States, should molest any United States vessel, should be deemed pirates. This blockade was, by a subsequent proclamation of April 27, 1861, extended to other States.

By the proclamation of May 10, 1861, he suspended the privilege of the writ of habeas corpus in the islands on the coast of Florida.

On the 16th of August, 1861, in pursuance of an Act of Congress, he declared "that the inhabitants of the States of Georgia, South Carolina, Virginia, North Carolina, Tennessee, Alabama, Louisiana, Texas, Arkansas, Mississippi, and Florida (excepting the inhabitants of Western Virginia, etc.), *are in a state of insurrection against the United States, and that all commercial intercourse between the same and the inhabitants thereof, with the exceptions aforesaid, and the citizens of other States, and other parts of the United States, is unlawful, and will remain unlawful until such insurrection shall cease, or has been suppressed.*" He then declares *forfeiture* of goods, or conveyances thereof, *going to* said States, and, after fifteen days, of *all vessels belonging in whole or in part to any inhabitant* of any of said States (except as aforesaid), wherever found.

On the 1st of July, 1862, he again declared the same States in *insurrection and rebellion*, so that the taxes could not be collected therein, in pursuance of the Act of 1861, Chapter 45.

On the 25th of the same month, he gave a further warning under the provisions of the sixth section of the Act of July 17, 1862, requiring rebels to "*return to their proper allegiance to the United States*, on pain of forfeitures and seizures," as provided for in said Act.

The proclamation of Sept. 22, 1862, was made by the President as an Executive officer and as Commander-in-Chief of the Army and Navy, "that the *war* will be prosecuted hereafter as heretofore for the purpose," etc.;

that slaves in *States* which should be *in rebellion* on the first day of the following January should be free, and that he would, by subsequent proclamation, designate such States; and at that date (January 1, 1863), the President did designate such States, and did declare "*that all persons held as slaves within said States*, etc., are and hereafter shall be free," and "that the executive government of the United States, including the military and naval authorities thereof, will recognize and maintain the freedom of said persons."

From an examination of these proclamations issued by President Lincoln, by virtue of his executive power and as a military chief, it cannot be doubted that in the most solemn and formal manner he has recognized the *inhabitants* of the insurrectionary States as in *civil war*, and therefore *as public enemies*. His proclamation characterizes these hostilities as "the war now prosecuted;" he requires the rebels to "return to their proper allegiance to the United States," admitting that they have renounced such allegiance; in all his proclamations, excepting the first, he treats *the inhabitants* of the rebellious States as *in simili statu* (with specified exceptions only), and in the proclamation of Jan. 1, 1863, no exceptions are made of any class of persons within the designated districts.

The Executive Department has thus definitely settled the question that all inhabitants of the designated States are *public enemies*, — First, by proclamations depriving them of slaves, of ships, and of property used in commerce; by a blockade and a declaration of *non-intercourse;* by claiming against them the *rights of war;* and by asserting that the existing hostilities are "WAR." Second, by extending to the insurgents the usual rights and privileges of a belligerent public enemy; as by release of captured pirates (under the order of the President issued from the State Department) as prisoners of war,* by exchange, *by cartel*, of prisoners of war captured on land, by claiming the right of retaliation, and by various other acts, which are legitimate in the conduct of the war, but irreconcilable with the assumption that the United States are not engaged in war, but only in enforcing the laws against certain criminals who have violated certain statutes by engaging in insurrection or rebellion.

If these acts and these proclamations do not show that the Executive Department has *declared* and *determined* the *status* of the inhabitants in insurrection to be that of *public enemies*, it would be difficult to conceive of any course of executive proceedings that would have had that effect.†

CONGRESS.

The action of the Legislative Department, which has been in harmony with that of the President, has in like manner definitively pronounced the inhabitants of insurrectionary States to be public enemies. In the war of 1812, between the United States and Great Britain, the Act of July 6, 1812, and the Act of February 4, 1815, indicated the character and extent of legislation necessary to record the decision of the Legislative Department, that Great Britain was at that time a public enemy.

But since the present rebellion commenced, Congress has enacted laws far more stringent and comprehensive than either of those above cited, against the inhabitants of the rebellious States. The four chief acts which re-

* See War Powers, 8th ed. p. 215.

† The effect of the President's Message and Proclamation of Amnesty of Dec. 8, 1863, upon the persons, property, and political rights of the inhabitants of rebellious states, far transcends in importance that of either of his previous executive acts.

cord the decision of Congress on the question whether rebels are *public* or private enemies, are, —

1. The Act of July 13, 1861, ch. 3.
2. " " " May 20, 1862, ch. 81.
3. " " " July 17, 1862, ch. 195.
3. " " " March 12, 1863, ch. 120.

In the extraordinary but brief session of the 37th Congress, which assembled on the 4th of July, 1861, and lasted but thirty-three days, statutes of the highest importance were passed, and among them none will hereafter attract more attention than the Act of July 13, 1861, ch. 3. Means were thereby provided for collecting the revenue in rebellious districts by the use of military and naval forces, the President was authorized to close ports of entry, and it was enacted, in the fifth section,—

"That whenever the President, in pursuance of the provisions of the second section of the act entitled 'An act to provide for the calling forth the militia to execute the laws of the Union, suppress insurrections, and repel invasions, and to repeal the act now in force for that purpose,' approved February 28, 1795, shall have called forth the militia to suppress combinations against the laws of the United States, and to cause the laws to be duly executed, and the insurgents shall have failed to disperse by the time directed by the President, and when said insurgents claim to act under the authority of any State or States, and such claim is not disclaimed or repudiated by the persons exercising the functions of government in such State or States, or in the part or parts thereof in which said combination exists, nor such insurrection suppressed by said State or States, then in such case it may and shall be lawful for the President, by proclamation, to *declare* that *the inhabitants of such State, or any section or part thereof* where such insurrection exists, are in a state of insurrection against the United States; and thereupon *all commercial intercourse* by and between the same and the citizens thereof, and the citizens of the rest of the United States, shall cease and be unlawful so long as such condition of hostility shall continue; and *all goods and chattels, wares and merchandise coming from* said State or section into the other parts of the United States, and all *proceeding to* such State or section, by land or water, shall, together with the vessel or vehicle conveying the same, or conveying persons to or from such State or section, be *forfeited* to the United States."

Also, in the sixth section, it was enacted, —

"That from and after fifteen days after the issuing of the said proclamation, as provided in the last foregoing section of this act, any ship or vessel belonging in whole or in part to any citizen or inhabitant of said State or part of a State whose inhabitants are so declared in a state of insurrection, found at sea, or in any port of the rest of the United States, shall be forfeited to the United States."

By the Act of May 20, 1862, ch. 81, further provisions were made interdicting commerce between loyal and disloyal States, and new forfeitures and penalties were prescribed.

By the Act of July 17, 1862, ch. 195, a new punishment for the crime of treason was declared, penalties were prescribed against all persons who should engage in, or give aid or comfort to the rebellion or insurrection, and they were declared to be disqualified from holding office under the United States. By Section fifth it was enacted, —

"That, to insure the speedy termination of the present rebellion, it shall be the duty of the President of the United States to cause the seizure of all the estates and property, money, stocks, credits, and effects of the persons hereinafter named in this section, and to apply and use the same and the proceeds thereof for the support of the army of the United States; that is to say, —

"First. Of any person hereafter acting as an officer of the army or navy of the rebels in arms against the government of the United States.

"Secondly. Of any person hereafter acting as president, vice-president, member of Congress, judge of any court, cabinet officer, foreign minister, commissioner, or consul of the so-called confederate states of America.

"Thirdly. Of any person acting as governor of a State, member of a convention or legislature, or judge of any court of the so-called confederate states of America.

"Fourthly. Of any person who, having held an office of honor, trust, or profit in the United States, shall hereafter hold an office in the so-called confederate states of America.

"Fifthly. Of any person hereafter holding any office or agency under the government of the so-called confederate states of America, or under any of the several states of the said confederacy, or the laws thereof, whether such office or agency be national, state, or municipal in its name or character. *Provided*, That the persons, thirdly, fourthly, and fifthly above described, shall have accepted their appointment or election since the date of the pretended ordinance of secession of the State, or shall have taken an oath of allegiance to, or to support the constitution of the so-called confederate states.

"Sixthly. Of any person who, owning property in any loyal State or Territory of the United States, or in the District of Columbia, shall hereafter assist and give aid and comfort to such rebellion; and all sales, transfers, or conveyances of any such property shall be null and void; and it shall be a sufficient bar to any suit brought by such person for the possession or the use of such property, or any of it, to allege and prove that he is one of the persons described in this section."

Section sixth provided that if any persons other than those above named, had engaged in, or aided the armed rebellion, and should not within a limited time *return to their allegiance*, their property should be liable to seizure and condemnation.

Section seventh provided proceedings for confiscation of such property, real and personal, —

"And if said property, whether real or personal, shall be found to have belonged to a person engaged in rebellion, or who has given aid or comfort thereto, the same shall be condemned as *enemies' property*, and become the property of the United States."

"Slaves escaping, and taking refuge within the lines of the army, and all slaves captured from, or deserted by, those engaged in rebellion, and coming under control of the government of the United States, and all slaves of such persons found or being within any place occupied by rebel forces, and afterwards occupied by forces of the United States, shall be deemed captives of war," etc.

The Act approved March 12, 1863, ch. 120, § 1, provides that agents may be appointed by the Secretary of the Treasury to collect all abandoned and captured property in any State or Territory designated as in insurrection by the proclamation of July 1, 1862, —

"*Provided*, that such property shall not include any kind or description which has been used, or which was intended to be used, for waging or carrying on war against the United States, such as arms, ordinance, ships, steamboats, or other water craft, and the furniture, forage, or other military supplies or munitions of war."

Section fourth of the same statute, provides, —

"That all property coming into any of the United States not declared in insurrection as aforesaid, from within any of the states declared in insurrection, through or by any other person than any agent, duly appointed under the provisions of this act, or under a lawful clearance by the proper officer of the Treasury Department, shall be confiscated to the use of the government of the United States. And the proceedings for the condemnation and sale of any such property shall be instituted and conducted under the direction of the Secretary of the Treasury, in the mode prescribed by the eighty-ninth and ninetieth sections of the act of March 2, 1799, entitled, 'An act to regulate the collection of duties on imports and tonnage.' And any agent or agents, person or persons, by or through whom such property shall come within the lines of the United States unlawfully, as aforesaid, shall be judged guilty of a misdemeanor, and on conviction thereof shall be fined in any sum not exceeding one thousand dollars, or imprisoned for any time not exceeding one year, or both, at the discretion of the court. And the fines, penalties, and forfeitures accruing under this act, may be mitigated or remitted in the mode prescribed by the act of March 3, 1797, or in such manner, in special cases, as the Secretary of the Treasury may prescribe."

From these statutes it is seen that the Legislative Department has recognized "certain districts of country, not only as in a state of insurrection and rebellion," but as "*carrying on a war*" against the United States. Commercial intercourse has been interdicted between the insurrectionary and the loyal States, and property found *in transitu* is made liable to seizure and confiscation, for the use of the United States, and property of persons engaged in the rebellion is to be seized and confiscated as ENEMIES' property. The *inhabitants (that is to say* ALL *the inhabitants) of the insurrectionary States, or parts of States, are declared to be in a state of insurrection against the United States, and any ship or vessel, belonging in whole or in part to any citizen or inhabitant of such State, whose inhabitants are so declared in insurrection, found at sea, or in any part of the rest of the United States, shall be forfeited to the United States.*

Thus belligerent rights derived from the acknowledged existence of civil territorial war, have been plainly asserted and exercised by Congress, and the insurrectionists have been treated as a *public enemy* in every form and manner known to legislation, and in language far more stringent than that used by Great Britain when, by the Non-intercourse Act, our revolutionary war was changed, by act of Parliament, into a public territorial war.*

THE SUPREME COURT.

Has the Supreme Court thus far followed the decisions of the political departments of government on the question as to the *status* of rebels as public enemies? — that is to say, enemies within the sense of international law?

This question will be answered by reference to the cases which have arisen since the beginning of the war.

By far the most important decisions on this subject were made in March, 1863, and are commonly known as "The Prize Cases." †

In these opinions the judges recognize the insurrectionists as public enemies, following, as was their duty, the decision of the Political Department of the government.

How could judgment, condemning these vessels as lawful prize, be sustained if the belligerents were not admitted to be *public enemies?* Though a vessel, captured while trading with an enemy, may be lawful prize, irrespective of the character of the trader, whether friendly, neutral, or hostile, to whom it belongs, yet it is because his vessel may aid a *public enemy*, that it becomes liable to capture. No property of a friendly or neutral power can be lawfully captured because it might aid a criminal, a robber, or a pirate, or an *insurgent*, while acting merely as a *private* or personal

* See Act 16 Geo. 3, 1776.

See dissenting opinion in The Prize cases. War Powers, 153.

† The opinion of the Court, together with that of the dissenting Judges, may be found by reference to the 2d Vol. Black's S. C. Reports, or to the 8th ed. of the War Powers, pages 140 to 156, and an analysis of these opinions may be found in the same volume, pages 238 to 243.

enemy of the United States. The law of prize has no application to the case of personal or private enemies, and cannot be invoked to justify a capture of private property, unless there exists a *public enemy* and a *state of war*.

Blockades, under the law of nations, can lawfully exist only when there is a *public enemy* to the country which proclaims and enforces them.

The Circuit Courts of the United States, having adjudged the inhabitants of States declared in rebellion to be public enemies, have therefore decided that they are not entitled to sue in any of the national courts.*

Doubtless the disability to sue in courts of the United States, and all other disabilities resulting from the *status* of a public enemy, may be removed. But it is for the President and Congress to determine what sound policy and public safety shall require.

It is a matter of congratulation that there is no want of harmony between the different departments of Government, and that the Supreme Court has not gone beyond its legitimate functions in time of civil war; but has, by following the decisions of the political departments on political questions, given the best evidence that, even in revolution, it will not be necessary for the safety of the country to overthrow its judiciary.

Thus it has been shown that the question whether the inhabitants of the States in insurrection are "*public enemies*," and entitled to the rights, or subject to the liabilities of belligerent law, is to be decided, not by the

* See Bouneau *vs.* Dinsmore, 24 Law Rep. 381.
S. C. 19 Leg. Inst. 108.
Israel G. Nash (of North Carolina) Complt. *vs.* Lyman Dayton *et al.* (decided by Nelson, Judge of the U. S. Circuit Court of Minnesota.)
See also U. S. *vs.* The Isaac Hemmett, Legal Jour. 97.
U. S. *vs.* The Allegheny, ib. 276.

judicial, but by the *political* departments of this Government. That the Executive and Legislative departments have formally and finally decided that the rebels are a *public enemy*, and are subject to *the laws of war*. That the Judicial Department has submitted to and followed that decision; and that the question as to the *political status* of rebellion, is now no longer open for discussion. That whatever rights, other than the rights of war, may be conceded to the inhabitants of rebellious territory, will be bestowed on them from considerations of policy and humanity, and not from admission of their claims to rights under our Constitution.*

---

* Messrs. Fishback and Baxter claimed recognition as United States Senators from the State of Arkansas, a State declared by proclamation of the President to be in rebellion. Since the publication of the first edition the Senate, on the 29th of June, 1864, resolved that they were not entitled to seats therein, — yeas, 8; nays, 25.

CHAPTER V.

DELEGATION OF AUTHORITY.

Judicial authority cannot be delegated, and as the commander of a department, or other officer who presides over a military tribunal while determining a case of civil jurisdiction, acts in a *quasi* judicial capacity, a question has been made whether the right to hold such courts can be delegated by the President to his officers. Although such proceedings of the war courts as complaints of parties, pleadings, examination of witnesses, deliberations and decisions of judges, in many respects resemble those of judicial courts, yet, as they are not deemed judicial within the true meaning of the Constitution, no valid objection arises from that source, to the delegation of the power to hold military courts, to such officers as may be appointed by the President.

This, and nearly all the war powers, must be exercised through officers acting under the Commander-in-Chief; for his authority must be exerted at the same time in different and distant places; and as he cannot be omnipresent, that authority which could not be delegated would become comparatively useless. The practice of the Government has, from the beginning, been in accordance with this view of constitutional law.

The power of the President is in part delegated to his Secretary of War, whose acts are deemed in law to be the acts of the President.* The commanders of military

* Wilcox *vs.* Jackson, 13 Pet. R. 498.
Opinion of Wm. Wirt, Att'y Gen. (July 6, 1820).
U. S. *vs.* Eliason, 16 Pet. S. C. R. 291

departments are clothed with authority transferred to them by the Commander-in-Chief. Therefore, if that authority is not limited so as to prevent it, they have the right, while in the enemy's country in time of war, to organize military courts martial and commissions, and to administer all other belligerent laws. Tribunals so organized may exercise all functions properly conferred upon them, and their decisions are not only valid, but are not subject to reversal by any judicial court; but only by the final action of the President.

So also, if a military governor is placed over such hostile district, clothed with the powers of the Commander-in-Chief, he may himself administer the laws of war over those subjected thereto within his precinct, and may establish courts military and civil, with jurisdiction over all persons and things therein. And whether he acts on his own discretion in so doing, under general orders, or under special orders in each case, he is, according to military law, responsible only to his superior officer.

Although no *civilian*, or *civil* or *merely executive* officer, has a right to institute a military court, unless deriving special authority to do so from some law of Congress or from military orders, there seems to be no reason why any of the war powers, in time of actual service, may not be delegated to military men by the President, or by any other military officer who possesses them; and no reason for making any distinction between the different classes of powers which may be so delegated.

CHAPTER VI.

HOW MILITARY OR PROVISIONAL GOVERNMENTS MAY BE CREATED AND REGULATED BY CONGRESS.

The right and duty of administering purely military government belongs to the war-making power, which is usually subject only to the rules of the belligerent law. When that power is regulated by any treaties, constitution, or statutes of the invading country, then military governments established under it must be conducted in accordance with the laws of war, as modified by such legislative, constitutional, or treaty restrictions. Thus, wherever in the United States such a government shall be instituted by the Commander-in-Chief, his administration of it may, to a certain extent, and with certain limitations, be regulated by acts of Congress.

The right of the United States to acquire territory by purchase, treaty, or annexation, necessarily implies the existence in Congress of the power to establish some form of government over *regions* thus *added to the country.* Conquest itself confers on the conqueror authority to make laws for the conduct of people subjected to his power. The right of the government when conqueror in civil territorial war to make rules and regulations relating to conquest and captures may, by the Constitution of the United States, be exercised by the Legislative Department.

A provisional government, partaking in a high degree of a martial character, may be ordained and established over *subjugated districts* in time of *civil* war, by laws of Congress, and may be administered by civilians or by military persons, appointed by the President, according to the requirements of the statutes.

It is also the duty of Congress to pass all laws which are proper and fit to aid the President in carrying into effect his obligation to suppress rebellion and enforce the laws, to secure domestic tranquillity, and to guaranty to each State a republican form of government.* And as the creation and administration of military or provisional governments is an essential means of accomplishing these objects, it would seem for this reason also to be the duty of Congress, in aid of the Commander-in-Chief, and without interfering with his military operations, to erect governments over the subjugated districts, clothed with powers adequate to administer the laws of war, subject to the Constitution and the statutes of the United States, and to such orders as the President may from time to time issue, not inconsistent therewith. Governments thus established rest not alone upon the military power of the President as Commander-in-Chief of the army and navy, but upon the war powers of Congress, and should be so organized as to endure until the people of these districts shall be again permitted to resume self-government, and be again clothed with their former political rights.†

Therefore, although the President may, while engaged in hostilities, and in the absence of laws restricting his authority, enforce belligerent rights against a public enemy, Congress also may establish rules and regulations which, without interfering with his powers

* Constitution, Art. 1, Sect. 8, Ch. 18. See *ante*, p. 269.

† The model of our territorial governments, in time of peace, is the Ordinance of 13th July, 1787.

See 3 Story, Com. on Const. 1312.

Webster's Speeches, Jan. 1830, pp. 360–364.

as commander of the army, it will be his duty to administer.

In a province to be subdued by soldiers, the only means by which the will of Congress, or the will of the head of the army can usually be carried into execution, is by force of arms. In one sense, all government, whether provisional or *quasi* civil, established under such circumstances, must assume a military character. In that view it can be controlled by Congress only through use of the military power of the army. Yet the President is bound to execute all laws which Congress has a right to make; and so far as the Legislature has the *authority* to interfere with or control the President by laws or by regulations, or by imposing upon him the machinery of provisional governments, so far he is bound to administer them according to statute.

LIMITS OF POWER. CONFLICT BETWEEN THE WAR POWERS OF THE PRESIDENT AND THE LEGISLATIVE POWERS OF CONGRESS.

Though the Executive, Legislative, and Judicial departments of our government are to a certain extent independent of each other, yet no one of these departments is without some control over the others. The legislature can make no law without the concurrence of the President, unless passed by two-thirds of the voters in both houses; and laws, when made, are void if pronounced unconstitutional by the Supreme Judicial Court. The judiciary, in deciding purely political questions, are bound to follow the decisions of the Legislative or Executive departments, and are in other respects controlled by the action of the coördinate branches of the government. The Executive can make treaties only by concurrence of the Senate; and most of the appointments to high offices must, to be valid, be made with its advice and consent. The President cannot declare war; but Congress can. Congress cannot carry on war; but the President can. Congress may make rules and regulations concerning captures, and for the government and regulation of the land and naval forces, when in service, binding upon the President, whose duty it is to see *all* constitutional laws faithfully executed, while he is made the supreme commander of the army and navy.

Questions may therefore arise as to the limitation of the respective powers of the Commander-in-Chief in conducting hostilities, and the powers of Congress in controlling him, by virtue of this legislative right to make rules and regulations for the government of military forces, and respecting captures on land and sea.

To determine how far Congress may interfere with and govern the military operations of the Executive, when the war power is employed in enforcing *local government* by martial law, without derogating from his power as Commander-in-Chief of the army, will require careful consideration, inasmuch as such government can be in fact maintained and enforced only by military, and not by legislative authority.

HOW THESE GOVERNMENTS MAY BE TERMINATED.

Military governments may be terminated by the commanding general at his will, by withdrawal of the officers who administer it.

As it is in the power of the Legislative Department to declare war, and to provide or withhold the means of carrying it on, Congress also may, after hostilities shall have ceased, declare or recognize peace, terminate military or provisional governments, or may regulate them and cause them to be modified or wholly withdrawn, whether originally erected by its own authority or by the war power of the President, and may institute civil territorial governments in their place.

Or the people of the district, having formed a new government for themselves, by permission of the United States, may be admitted into the Union as a State, and thus the military government will be displaced.

But military governments are not of necessity terminated by a declaration of peace between belligerents, or a cession of territory in dispute, but may be continued long after war ceases, by presumed assent of the President and of Congress.

"The right inference," says Mr. Justice Wayne, in delivering the unanimous opinion of the Supreme Court,* "from the inaction of both the President and of Congress, is, that it (the military government) was meant to be continued until it had been legislatively changed. No presumption of a contrary intention can be made. Whatever may have been the cause of delay, it must be presumed that the delay was consistent with the true policy of the Government." "California and New Mexico were acquired by conquest confirmed by cession. During the war they were governed as conquered territory, under the law of nations, and in virtue of the belligerent rights of the United States as the conqueror, by the direction and authority of the President as Commander-in-Chief. By the ratification of the treaty of Guadalupe-Hidalgo, on the 20th of May, 1848, they became a part of the United States, as ceded conquered territory. The civil governments established in each during the war, and existing at the date of the treaty of peace, continued in

* Cross *vs.* Harrison, 16 How. 193.

operation after that treaty had been ratified. California, with the assent and coöperation of the existing government, formed a constitution which was ratified by its inhabitants, and a State government was put in full operation in December, 1849, with the implied assent of the President, the officers of the existing government of California publicly and formally surrendering all their powers into the hands of the newly-constituted authorities. The constitution so formed and ratified was approved by Congress, and California was, on the 9th of September, 1850, admitted into the Union as a State. New Mexico also formed a constitution, and applied to Congress for admission; the application was not granted, but on the 9th of September, 1850, New Mexico, and that part of California not included within the limits of the new State, were organized into territories, with new territorial governments, which took the place of those organized during the war, and existing on the restoration of peace." *

Such governments, founded only in and sustained by war power, are, when peace is officially recognized, entirely within the control of Congress.

When the enemy have laid down their arms, and make no further opposition to the execution of our laws, there can exist no reason why the President should not obey and enforce the rules and statutes of Congress, regulating his own conduct and the military governments and military tribunals established by him. No reason could be offered to explain why he should not make complete and unquestioning submission to the will of the people. His refusal to do so would subject him to impeachment.

* Halleck, Int. Law, 828, 829.

There seems to be less danger to civil liberty from the use of military governments and tribunals as temporary instruments for carrying on war and of securing conquest, than from any other use of military forces.

CHAPTER VII.

It has been shown in the foregoing chapters, that the President has authority to establish military governments over enemy territory in time of war, —

1st. Because such governments are necessary to the successful prosecution of hostilities, and to secure the objects for which war has been waged.

2d. Because the Constitution, by making him Commander-in-Chief of the army, confers on him the right to use all proper means of warfare, including war-governments and war-courts; and

3d. Because the Supreme Court have recognized this authority, and have given to it the sanction of law by their decisions.

The next question will relate to the character and extent of the powers to be exercised by military governments.

JURISDICTION OF MILITARY GOVERNMENTS.

To such military governments as are established by the Commander-in-Chief, in time of war, he may delegate more or less power, according to the object for which he has instituted them.

In the District of Columbia, a military governor has been appointed for the performance of certain limited duties essential to the regulation of the police of the forces stationed within the defences of Washington, the treatment of persons under arrest and in prison, and other important specific duties. In the mean time, the sessions of the Supreme Court of the United States, and of the local courts, and of Congress, and the business of all the departments of the Government, are undisturbed.

In districts of country declared to be in rebellion, whose inhabitants are "public enemies," such governments have been commissioned with powers to administer local, municipal, civil, and criminal law, and with jurisdiction embracing all persons and all questions which may arise therein.

There is no other necessary limit to the jurisdiction of a military governor, than there is to that authority under which he received his appointment. The existence of state or municipal governments, or of military, civil, or ecclesiastical tribunals, established before the war began, in the rebellious districts, does not affect the jurisdiction of such governments or courts as may be erected therein by the war power of the United States. Since these sections of country have become hostile — the inhabitants thereof being now public enemies — no authority of such enemies, executive, judicial, or military, can be recognized by the conqueror as rightful or legitimate. No legislature, no judiciary of a public enemy, can be permitted to retain or exercise any jurisdiction or control over persons or property found in that region which is within the military occupation of our army.

The enemy's courts and legislatures derive their right to ordain and enforce laws from a government at open war with our own, — one which we refuse to recognize, and we might as well acknowledge the independence of the seceding States, and surrender to their army, as to subject ourselves, or to allow others, to pay obedience to their laws, their courts, or their jurisdiction.

A public enemy has no jurisdiction, either by courts instituted by him, or by any civil, military, or judicial officers appointed by him, to exercise authority in any locality which is held by our military power. But all persons and all subjects who are found there, are under our military control, whether that control be exercised by soldiers in the field, or by military governors, who may call to their aid military tribunals, or may even allow civil tribunals to proceed under military authority.

The only limitations to the jurisdiction of such military power over persons and property, are such as are derived from the laws of war; though in the United States further limitations may be prescribed by laws of Congress.

Hence, aliens residing in belligerent districts, non-combatants, whether neutral, friendly or hostile, persons engaged in hostility, persons belonging to the invading country, and accompanying the army, are alike within the jurisdiction of a military government, and of military courts duly established therein.

CHAPTER VIII.

THE LAW ADMINISTERED BY MILITARY GOVERNMENTS.

As the powers of a *de facto* government belong to the conqueror by the laws of war, he may suspend, modify, or abrogate all municipal laws of those whom he has conquered; he may disregard their former civil rights and remedies; he may introduce and enforce a new code of laws, military and municipal, and may carry them into effect by new military tribunals, having abolished all courts and offices held under the authority of his enemy.*

It has been held by the Supreme Court that "the laws, whether in writing or evidenced by the usage and customs of the conquered or ceded country, *continue in force till altered* by the new sovereign."†

While they continue in force, it is by the express or implied permission of the new sovereign, and until altered by him. They are recognized only as an expression of the will of the conqueror.‡ If the law should conflict with the will of the conqueror, the LAW must yield;

* Halleck, Int. Law, pp. 830–831, and cases there cited.
Bowyer, Universal Public Law, ch. 16, 158.
Fabrigas *vs.* Mostyn, 1 Cowper, 165.
Gardner *vs.* Fell, 1 Jacob & Walker, 27.
Flemming *et al. vs.* Page, 9 How. 603.
Am. Ins. Co. *vs.* Canter, 1 Peters, 542.
Cross *et al. vs.* Harrison, 16 How. 164.
Heffter, Droit Int'l, sect. 185.

† Strother *vs.* Lucas, 12 Peters, 436, and authorities there cited.

‡ For the operation of transfers of territory upon the laws and rights of

otherwise the conqueror would be subjected to the rule of those whom he has subjugated.

But the local laws of a conquered country may be changed not only by the law-making power of the conquering country, but by virtue of the BELLIGERENT rights of the conqueror.*

All these propositions follow from the fact that the power of a public enemy to make or administer law is terminated by the conquest of that territory by a different law-making and law-administering power, viz., that of the conqueror.

The local laws of a conquered country of which our army holds military occupation, have no force or effect whatever, except by our permission. When such local laws agree with those of the invading country, such laws may be, and usually are, adopted and sanctioned because they do so agree therewith. Thus rules governing the rights of property, the relations of persons,

the inhabitants of the territory ceded or conquered, see, among other authorities, the following, viz: —

Vattel, B. B. ch. 13, sects. 199, 201.
4 Com. Dig. Ley. (C.)
Calvin's Case, 7 Coke, 176.
Blankard *vs.* Galdy, 2 Salk. 411; S. C. 2 Mod. 222.
Mostyn *vs.* Fabrigas, Cowp. 165.
Hall *vs.* Campbell, Cowp. 204, 209.
Anon. 2 P. Williams, 76.
Ex parte Prosser, 2 Br. C. C. 325.
Elphinstone *vs.* Bedreechund, Knapps P. C. R. 338.
Ex parte Anderson, 5 Ves. 240.
Evelyn *vs.* Forster, 8 Ves. 96.
Sheddon *vs.* Goodrich, 8 Ves. 482.
2 Ves. Jr. 349.
Att'y Gen'l *vs.* Stewart, 2 Meriv. 154.
Gardiner *vs.* Fell, 1 Jac. and W. 77.
8 Wheaton, 589; 12 Wheaton, 528–535.
6 Pet. 712; 7 Pet. 86, 87; 8 Pet. 444–465.
9 Pet. 133, 734, 749.

* Cross *vs.* Harrison, 16 How. 199.

and the laws of crimes in the respective countries of the belligerents are often so nearly alike that the administration of them is permitted to remain unchanged even in war. But no law or institution established by law is permitted to survive, which is in conflict with those of the conqueror.

In all cases, the will of the conqueror governs. Hence, in a ceded or subjugated territory, all laws violating treaty stipulations with foreign nations, or granting rank and titles or commercial privileges in conflict with the institutions of the conqueror, are abrogated.*

It has been asserted that the municipal laws of a belligerent territory remain in force, "*proprio vigore*," until altered by military orders; but, although such laws may have been tacitly adopted, or the enforcement thereof may have been permitted, it is not because these laws retained any validity "*proprio vigore*." Their only validity was derived from the tacit or express sanction and adoption thereof by the will of the commander-in-chief of the invading army.

In case of conquest of a foreign country, the question has been asked, what laws, if any, of the invading country are *ipso vigore*, and without legislation extended over the territory acquired in war?

The suppression of the present rebellion is not the conquest of a *foreign* country. The citizens of the United States residing in the districts in rebellion are not *alien* enemies, though they are *public* enemies; and it is important, in several points of view, to observe the dis-

* Halleck, Int. Law, 833, 834, and authorities there cited:
Bowyer, Univ. Pub. Law, ch. 16.
Campbell *vs.* Hall, 1 Cowper, 205.
Fabrigas *vs.* Mostyn, 1 Cowp. 165.
Gardner *vs.* Fell, 1 Jacob and Walk. 27, 30, note.
Att'y Gen'l *vs.* Stewart, 2 Merivale, 159.

tinction between enemies who are subjects of a foreign government, and are therefore called "*alien enemies*," and those who are denizens and *subjects* of the United States, and being engaged in civil war, are called "*public enemies.*"

An alien owes no allegiance or obedience to our government, or to our constitution, laws, or proclamations. A citizen subject is bound to obey them all. In refusing such obedience, he is guilty of crime against his country, and finds in the law of nations no justification for disobedience. An alien, being under no such obligation, is justified in refusing such obedience. Over an alien enemy, our government can make no constitution, law, or proclamation of obligatory force, because our laws bind only our own subjects, and have no extra-territorial jurisdiction.

Over citizens who are subjects of this government, even if they have so far repudiated their duties as to become enemies, our constitution, statutes, and proclamations are the supreme law of the land. The fact that their enforcement is resisted does not make them void. It is not in the power of armed subjects of the Union to repeal or legally nullify our constitution, laws, or other governmental acts.

The proclamation of the President, issued during the present rebellion, in executing the powers conferred on him by the Constitution; the Acts of Congress, in executing its powers; and the decisions of the Supreme Court of the United States, are all, in one respect, "like the Pope's bull against the comet;" the proclamation, the laws, and the decisions are alike resisted and spurned by our adversaries; neither can be enforced until the enemy is overthrown. But when the soldiers of the Union shall have routed and dispersed the last armed force of the rebellion, and when the supremacy of our military power is undisputed, the constitution, the laws of Congress, the proclamation, and the decisions of the Supreme Court, will at the same time, *pari passu*, be acknowledged and enforced. It is, therefore, idle to speculate upon the legal validity and operation of the proclamation liberating enemies' slaves, in districts not yet secured in our military possession. It would be equally useless to attempt to determine the validity and operation of our constitution, laws, and decisions of courts in these rebellious districts. Neither of them will be enforced upon the enemy until they have been subjugated. When that event takes place, whether it be the result of battles or of returning sanity of repentant madmen, the army of the United States will then have actual possession of every portion of the United States, and of every slave who may be found therein; and the rights of the slave to his freedom under the constitution, the statutes passed, and the proclamations issued by the Government during the war, will be secured to him at the same time that other rights under the same Constitution and proclamations will be secured to the other inhabitants of the country.

And there can be no doubt that in civil war the laws of the United States, rightfully extending at all times over the whole country, are to be enforced, so far as applicable, in time of war, over the belligerent territory as fast as it comes under our military control; and that in case of complete conquest, the constitution and laws of the Union will be restored to full operation over all the inhabitants thereof. At the same time, the laws of war will have swept away all local hostile authorities, and all laws, rights, and institutions resting solely thereon.

The Commander-in-Chief has the right, during war, to treat their local laws as inoperative, or to adopt some and reject others; to permit the holding of courts by local authorities acting under military power of the conqueror, or to forbid them, and to substitute military courts of his own. Having all the rights of war over the subjugated inhabitants, he has all the powers of a government *de facto* and *de jure*, and can therefore impose upon them whatever laws or regulations may suit his pleasure, in accordance with the laws of war. The LAWS OF WAR are the only laws required by the Constitution to be laid by military power upon public enemies in time of civil war. Congress may modify by legislation the hardship of belligerent rights.

But whatever may be done or omitted by the President or by Congress, the laws and municipal institutions of the conquered inhabitants are "swept by the board." Whatever law is rightfully administered, is law expressly declared or tacitly permitted by the will of the conqueror.*

JUDICIAL COURTS OF THE UNITED STATES.

The courts judicial, as established by laws of Congress in the seceded States, having been closed by civil war, may be reëstablished whenever the districts over which they have jurisdiction shall be permanently reduced under the power of the United States.

When the officers of such courts, either by engaging

* For authorities on this question, see
Halleck, Int. Law, 832.
Calvin's Case, Coke's Rep. part 7.
Gardner *vs.* Fell, 1 Jacob and Walker, 22.
Cross *vs.* Harrison, 16 How. 165.
Collet *vs* Lord Keith, 2 East. 260.
Blankard *vs.* Guldy, 4 Mad. 225.

in rebellion or otherwise, have become in law public enemies, their right to exercise judicial or other functions under authority of the United States ceased, and their offices were vacated. If new appointments were to be made now, it is obvious that the authority of courts would be enforced only by military power; their jurisdiction would be very limited; such juries as they could summon would probably be hostile to the Union, and the powers of judges, under present laws, would be be totally inadequate to meet the demands of these turbulent times. Hence it would be worse than useless to erect *judicial* courts before *peace* is completely restored. It would tend to bring the judiciary into contempt. Therefore it can hardly be deemed advisable to interfere with the stern, effective, but necessary government of hostile people by military power, until Congress shall by legislative act *recognize* a state of peace.

APPENDIX.

The most important cases decided by the Supreme Court of the United States, in relation to the subjects discussed in the foregoing pages, are: —

Fleming *vs.* Page, 9 How. 614.
Cross *vs.* Harrison, 16 How. 189.
Jecker *vs.* Montgomery, 18 How. 112.
Dynes *vs.* Hoover, 20 How. 79.
Leitensdorfer *vs.* Webb, 20 How. 177.
Vallandigham's case. Appendix, 88.

From these cases, for more convenient reference, the following passages have been extracted.

FLEMING *vs.* PAGE, 9 Howard's S. C. Rep. 614.

Mr. Chief-Justice TANEY delivered the opinion of the Court:

The question certified by the Circuit Court turns upon the construction of the Act of Congress of July 30, 1846. The duties levied upon the cargo of the schooner Catharine were the duties imposed by this law upon goods imported from a foreign country. And if at the time of this shipment Tampico was not a foreign port, within the meaning of the Act of Congress, then the duties were illegally charged, and, having been paid under protest, the plaintiffs would be entitled to recover in this action the amount exacted by the collector.

Tampico was subject to the sovereignty and dominion of the U. S.

The port of Tampico, at which the goods were shipped, and the Mexican State of Tamaulipas, in which it is situated, were undoubtedly, at the time of the shipment, *subject to the sovereignty and dominion of the United States.* The Mexican authorities had been driven out, or had submitted to our army and navy, and the country was in the exclusive and firm possession of the United States, *and governed by its military authorities, acting under the orders of the President.* But it does not follow that it was a part of the United States, or that it ceased to be a foreign country, in the sense in which these words are used in the Acts of Congress.

Tampico was *governed* by our military authorities.

The country in question had been conquered in war. But the genius and character of our institutions are peaceful, and the power to declare war was not conferred upon Congress for the purposes of aggression or aggrandizement, but to enable the general government to vindicate by arms, if it should become necessary, its own rights and the rights of its citizens.

A war, therefore, declared by Congress, can never be presumed to be waged for the purpose of conquest, or the acquisition of territory: nor does the law declaring the war imply an authority to the President to enlarge the limits of the United States by subjugating the enemy's country. The United States, it is true, may extend its boundaries by conquest or treaty, and may demand the cession of territory as the condition of peace, in order to indemnify its citizens for the injuries they have suffered, or to reimburse the Government for the expenses of the war. But this can be done only by the treaty-making power or the legislative authority, and is not a part of the power conferred upon the President by the declaration of war. His duty and his power are purely military. *As commander-in-chief, he is authorized to direct the movements of the naval and military forces placed by law at his command, and to employ them in the manner he may deem most effectual to harass and conquer and subdue the enemy. He may invade the hostile country, and subject it to the sovereignty and authority of the United States.* But his conquests do not enlarge the boundaries of this Union, *nor extend the operation of our institutions and laws beyond the limits before assigned to them* by the legislative power.

Powers of the President as Commander-in-Chief to govern the army and employ it, — to invade, to subjugate, not to extend the limits of Union.

It is true that, when Tampico had been captured, and the State of Tamaulipas subjugated, other nations were bound to regard the country, while our possession continued, as the territory of the United States, and to respect it as such. For, by the laws and usages of nations, conquest is a valid title, while the victor maintains the exclusive possession of the conquered country. The citizens of no other nation, therefore, had a right to enter it without the permission of the American authorities, nor to hold intercourse with its inhabitants, nor to trade with them. As regarded all other nations, it was a part of the United States, and belonged to them as exclusively as the territory included in our established boundaries.

Tampico *ours*, — as against foreign countries.

But yet it was not a part of this Union. For every nation which acquires territory by treaty or conquest holds it according to its own institutions and laws. And the relation in which the port of Tampico stood to the United States while it was occupied by their arms, did not depend upon the laws of nations, but upon our own Constitution and Acts of Congress. The power of the President, under which Tampico and the State of Tamaulipas were conquered and held in subjection, was simply that of a military commander prosecuting a war waged against a public enemy by the authority of his government. And the country from which these goods were imported was invaded and subdued, and occupied as the territory of a foreign hostile nation, as a portion of Mexico, and was held in possession in order to distress and harass the enemy. While it was occupied by our troops, they were in an enemy's country, and not their own: the inhabitants were still foreigners and enemies, and owed to the United States nothing more than the submission and obedience, sometimes called temporary allegiance, which is due from a conquered enemy when he surrenders to a force which he is unable resist. But the boundaries of the United States, as they existed when war was declared against Mexico, were not extended by the conquest; nor could they be regulated by the varying incidents of war, and be enlarged or diminished as the armies on either side advanced or retreated. They remained unchanged. And every place which was out of the limits of the United States, as previously established by the political authorities of the government, was still foreign, nor did our laws extend over it. Tampico was therefore a foreign port when this shipment was made.

Again, there was no Act of Congress establishing a custom-house at Tampico, nor authorizing the appointment of a collector; and, consequently, there was no officer of the United States authorized by law to grant the clearance and authenticate the coasting manifest of the cargo, in the manner directed by law, where the voyage is from one port of the United States to another. The

Collection of duties by military authority.

person who acted in the character of collector in this instance, acted as *such under the authority of the military commander, and in obedience to his orders; and the duties he exacted and the regulations he adopted were not those prescribed by law, but by the President in his character of commander-in-chief.* The custom-house was established in an enemy's country, *as one of the weapons of war.* It was established, not for the purpose of giving to the people of Tamaulipas the benefits of commerce with the United States, or with

An act of hostility.

other countries, *but as a measure of hostility, and as a part of the military operations in Mexico;* it was a mode of exacting contributions from the enemy to support our army, and intended also to cripple the resources of Mexico, and make it feel the evils and burdens of the war. The duties required to be paid were regulat-

Contributions may be levied.

ed with this view, and were nothing more than *contributions levied* upon the enemy, which *the usages of war justify when an army is operating in the enemy's country.* The permit and coasting manifest granted by an officer thus appointed, and thus controlled by military authority, could not be recognized in any port of the United States as the documents required by the Acts of Congress, when the vessel is engaged in the coasting trade, nor could they exempt the cargo from the payment of duties.

This construction of the revenue laws has been uniformly given by the Administrative Department of the government in all cases that have come before it. And it has, indeed, been given in cases where there appears to have been stronger ground for regarding the place of shipment as a domestic port. For after Florida had been ceded to the United States, and the forces of the United States had taken possession of Pensacola, it was decided by the Treasury Department, that goods imported from Pensacola before an Act of Congress was passed erecting it into a collection district, and authorizing the appointment of a collector, were liable to duty. That is, that, although Florida had by cession actually become a part of the United States, and was in our possession, yet, under our revenue laws, its ports must be regarded as foreign until they were established as domestic by an Act of Congress, and it appears that this decision was sanctioned at the time by the Attorney-General of the United States, the law officer of the Government. And, although not so directly applicable to the case before us, yet the decisions of the Treasury Department in relation to Amelia Island and certain ports in Louisiana after that province had been ceded to the United States, were both made upon the same grounds. And in the latter case, after a custom-house had been established by law at New Orleans, the collector at that place was instructed to regard as foreign ports Baton Rouge and other settlements still in the possession of Spain, whether on the Mississippi, Iberville, or the sea-coast. The Department, in no instance that we are aware of, since the establishment of the Government, has ever recognized a place in a newly-acquired country as a domestic port from which the coasting trade might be carried on, unless it had been previously made so by Act of Congress.

The principle thus adopted and acted upon by the Executive Department of the government has been sanctioned by the decisions in this Court and the Circuit Courts whenever the question came before them. We do not propose to comment upon the different cases cited in the argument. It is sufficient to say that there is no discrepancy between them. And all of them, so far as they apply, maintain that under our revenue laws every port is regarded as a foreign one unless the custom-house from which the vessel clears is within a collection district established by Act of Congress, and the officers granting the clearance exercise their functions under the authority and control of the laws of the United States.

In the view we have taken of the question, it is unnecessary to notice particularly the passages from eminent writers on the laws of nations which were brought forward in the argument. They speak altogether of the rights which a sovereign acquires, and the powers he may exercise in a conquered country, and they do not bear upon the question we are considering. For in this country the sovereignty of the United States resides in the people of the several States, and they act through their representatives, according to the delegation and distribution of powers contained in the Constitution. And the constituted authorities to whom the power of making war and concluding peace is confided, and of determining whether a conquered country shall be permanently retained or not, *neither claimed nor exercised* any rights or powers in relation to the territory in question, *but the rights of war*. After it was subdued, it was uniformly treated as an enemy's country, and restored to the possession of the Mexican authorities when peace was concluded. And certainly its subjugation did not compel the United States, while they held it, to regard it as a part of their dominions, nor to give to it any form of civil government, nor to extend to it our laws.

Neither is it necessary to examine the English decisions which have been referred to by counsel. It is true that most of the States have adopted the principles of English jurisprudence so far as it concerns private and individual rights. And when such rights are in question, we habitually refer to the English decisions, not only with respect, but in many cases as authoritative. But in the distribution of political power between the great departments of government, there is such a wide difference between the power conferred on the President of the United States and the authority and sovereignty which belong to the English crown, that it would be altogether unsafe to reason from any supposed resemblance between them, either as regards conquest in war, or any other subject where the rights and powers of the executive arm of the Government are brought into question. Our own Constitution and form of government must be our only guide. And we are entirely satisfied that under the Constitution and laws of the United States Tampico was a foreign port, within the meaning of the Act of 1846, when these goods were shipped, and that the cargoes were liable to the duty charged upon them. And we shall certify accordingly to the Circuit Court.

CROSS *vs.* HARRISON, 16 Howard's S. C. Rep. 189.

Constitution authorized acts of military government in collecting revenue.

"Indeed, from the letter of the then Secretary of State, and from that of the Secretary of the Treasury, we cannot doubt that the *action of the Military Governor of California was recognized as allowable and lawful* by Mr. Polk and his cabinet. We think it was a rightful and correct recognition under all the circumstances, and when we say rightful, *we mean that it was constitutional, although Congress had not passed an act to extend the collection of tonnage and import* duties to the ports of California.

Belligerent right of the President to institute military and civil government over California.

California, or the port of San Francisco, had been captured by the arms of the United States as early as 1846. Shortly afterward, the United States had military possession of all of Upper California. Early in 1847, the *President, as constitutional Commander-in-Chief of the army and navy*, authorized the military and naval commander of our forces in California *to exercise the belligerent rights of a conqueror, and to form a civil government for the conquered country*, and to *impose duties* on imports and tonnage as *military contributions* for the support of the government and of the army which had the conquest in possession. We will add, by way of note, to this opinion, references to all of the correspondence of the government upon this subject; now only referring to the letter of the Secretary of War to General Kearney, of the 10th of May, 1847, which was accompanied with a tariff of duties on imports and tonnage, which had been prepared by the Secretary of the Treasury, with forms of entry and permits for landing goods, all of which was reported by the Secretary to the President on the 30th of March, 1847. Senate Doc. No. 1, 1st Sess., 30th Congress, 1847, pp. 567, 583. *No one can doubt that these orders of the President, and the action of our army and navy commander in California in conformity with them, were according to the law of arms and the right of conquest, or that they were operative until the ratification and exchange of a treaty of peace.* . . . .

No doubt of authority.

"The plaintiffs, therefore, can have no right to the return of any moneys paid by them as duties on foreign merchandise in San Francisco up to that date. Until that time California had not been ceded in fact to the United States, but it was a conquered territory within which the United States were exercising belligerent rights, and whatever sums were received for duties upon foreign merchandises, they were paid under them."

After *treaty* California became *part of the U. S.*, a ceded conquered territory.

But *after the ratification of the treaty, California became a part of the United States, or a ceded, conquered territory.* Our inquiry here is to be whether or not the cession gave any right to the plaintiffs to have the duties restored to them which they may have paid between the ratifications and exchange of the treaty and the notification of that fact by our Government to the Military Governor of California. It was not received by him until two months after the ratification, and not then with any instructions or even remote intimation *from the President that the civil and military government, which had been instituted during the war*, was discontinued. Up to that time, whether such an intimation had or had not been given, duties had been collected under the war tariff, strictly in conformity with the instructions which had been received from Washington. . . . .

Civil and military government during the war instituted by the President.

The ratification of the treaty of peace was proclaimed in California by Colonel Mason, on the 7th of August, 1848. Up to this time, it must be remembered that Captain Folsom, of the Quartermaster's Department of the Army, had been the *collector of duties under the war tariff.* On the 9th of August he was informed by Lieut. Halleck, of the Engineer Corps, who was the Secretary of State of the Civil Government of California, that he would be relieved as soon as a suitable citizen could be found for his successor. He was also told that "the tariff of duties for the collection of military contributions was immediately to cease, and that the revenue laws and tariff of the United States will be substituted in its place." The view taken by Governor Mason of his position has been given in our statement. The result was to continue the existing government, as he had not received from Washington definite instructions in reference to the existing state of things in California.

His position was unlike anything that had preceded it in the history of our country. The view taken of it by himself has been given in the statement in the beginning of this opinion. It was not without its difficulties both as regards the principle upon which he should act, and the actual state of affairs in California. He knew that the Mexican inhabitants of it had been remitted by the treaty of peace to those municipal laws and usages which prevailed among them before the territory had been ceded to the United States, but that a state of things and population had grown up during the war, and after the treaty of peace, which made some other authority necessary to maintain the rights of the ceded inhabitants and of immigrants, from misrule and violence. He may not have comprehended fully the principle applicable to what he might rightly do in such a case, but he felt rightly, and acted accordingly. He determined, in the absence of all instruction, to maintain the existing government. The *territory had been ceded as a conquest*, and *was to be preserved and governed as such* until the sovereignty to which it had passed had legislated for it. That sovereignty was the United States, under the Constitution, by which power had been given to Congress to dispose of and make all needful rules and regulations respecting the territory or other property belonging to the United States, with the power also to admit new States into this Union with only such limitations as are expressed in the section in which this power is given. *The government* of which Colonel Mason was the executive, *had its origin in the lawful exercise of a belligerent right over a conquered territory.* *It had been instituted during the war by the command of the President of the United States.* *It was the government when the territory was ceded as a conquest, and it did not cease as a matter of course, or as a necessary consequence of the restoration of peace.* *The President might have dissolved it by withdrawing the army* and navy officers who administered it, but he did not do so. *Congress could have put an end to it, but that was not done.* The right inference from the inaction of both is, that it was meant to *be continued until it had been legislatively changed.* No presumption of a contrary intention can be made. Whatever may have been the causes of the delay, it must be presumed that the delay was consistent with the true policy of the government. And the more so as it was continued until the people of the territory met in convention to form a state government which was subsequently recognized by Congress under its power to admit new States into the Union.

Origin of this government;

How instituted.

It did not cease by restoration of peace;

Dissolved by power of President, or by Congress.

Civil government established as a war right.

Rights of citizenship not necessarily accompanied by *political* power.

Power of governing a territory—how it results.

In confirmation of what has been said in respect to the power of Congress over this territory, *and the continuance of the civil government established as a war right*, until Congress acted upon the subject, we refer to two of *the decisions of this Court*, in one of which it is said, in respect to the treaty by which Florida was ceded to the United States, "This treaty is the law of the land, and admits the inhabitants of Florida to the *enjoyment of the privileges, rights, and immunities of the citizens of the United States.* It is unnecessary to inquire whether this is not their condition independently of stipulations. *They do not, however, participate in political power,—they do not share in the government until Florida shall become a State.* In the mean time Florida continues to be a territory of the United States, guarded by virtue of that clause of the Constitution which empowers Congress to make all needful rules and regulations respecting the territory or other property belonging to the United States. *Perhaps the power of governing a territory belonging to the United States, which has not by becoming a State acquired the means of self-government, may result necessarily from the facts that it is not within the jurisdiction of any particular State, and is within the power and jurisdiction of the United States.* The right to govern may be the natural consequences of the right to acquire territory." American Insurance Company *vs.* Canter, 1 Peters, 542, 543. (See also U. S. *vs.* Gratiot, 14 Peters, 526.) . . . .

When military government in California *ceased.*

"Our conclusion, from what has been said, is, that the *civil government* of California, *organized as it was from a right of conquest, did not cease or become defunct in consequence of the signature of the treaty, or from its ratification.* We think it *was continued over a ceded conquest, without any violation of the Constitution or laws of the United States*, and that, until Congress legislated for it, the duties upon foreign goods imported into San Francisco were legally demanded and lawfully received by Mr. Harrison, the collector of the port, who received his appointment, according to instructions from Washington, from Governor Mason." . . . . .

What laws are in force after conquest.

Right of the conqueror to regulate trade.

"The second objection states a proposition larger than the case admits, and more so than the principle is, which secures to the inhabitants of a ceded conquest the enjoyment of what had been their laws before, until they have been changed by the new sovereignty to which it has been transferred. In this case, *foreign trade had been changed in virtue of a belligerent right, before the territory was ceded as a conquest*, and after that had been done by a treaty of peace, the *inhabitants were not remitted to those* regulations of trade under which it was carried on whilst they were under Mexican rule; because they had passed from that sovereignty to another, whose privilege it was to permit the existing regulations of trade to continue, and by which only they could be changed. We have said, in a previous part of this opinion, that the sovereignty of a nation regulated trade with foreign nations, and that *none could be carried on except as the sovereignty permits it to be done.* In our situation, that sovereignty is the constitutional delegation to Congress of the power 'to regulate commerce with foreign nations and among the several States, and with the Indian tribes.'" . . . .

"But we do not hesitate to say, if the reasons given for our conclusions in this case were not sound, that other considerations would bring us to the same results. The plaintiffs carried these goods voluntarily into California, knowing the state of things there. They knew that there was an existing civil government, instituted by the authority of the President as commander-in-chief of the army and naval forces of the United States, by the right of conquest; that it had not ceased when these first importations were made; that it was afterwards continued, and rightfully, as we have said, until California became a State, that they were not coerced to land their goods, however they may have been to pay duties upon them; that such duties were demanded by those who claimed the right to represent the United States (who did so, in fact, with most commendable integrity and intelligence); that the money collected has been faithfully accounted for, and the unspent residue of it received into the treasury of the United States; and that the Congress has by two acts adopted and ratified all the acts of the government established in California upon the conquest of that territory, relative to the collection of imposts and tonnage, from the commencement of the late war with Mexico to the 12th November, 1849, expressly including in such adoption the moneys raised and expended during that period for the support of the actual government of California after the ratification of the treaty of peace with Mexico. This adoption sanctions what the defendant did. It does more; it affirms that he had legal authority for his acts. It coincides with the views which we have expressed in respect to the legal liability of the plaintiff for the duties paid by them, and the authority of the defendant to receive them as Collector of the port of San Francisco."

JECKER *vs.* MONTGOMERY, 18 Howard's S. C. Rep. 112.

"As a principle applicable to the first of these inquiries, it may be averred as a part of the law of nations, — forming a part, too, of the municipal jurisprudence of every country, — "that in a state of war between two nations, declared by the authority in whom the municipal constitution vests the power of making war, *the two nations and all their citizens or subjects are enemies to each other.*" The consequence of this state of hostility is, that *all intercourse and communication* between them is *unlawful. Vide* Wheaton on Maritime Captures, ch. 7, p. 209, quoting from Bynkershoeck this passage: 'Ex natura belli commercia inter hostes cessare, non est dubitandum. Quamvis nulla specialis sit commerciorum prohibitio, ipso tamen jure belli, commercia inter hostes esse vetita, ipsæ indictiones bellorum satis declarant.' . . . . . . All citizens of States at war are *enemies* of each other.

"The same rule has been adopted, with equal strictness, by this court. In the case of The Rapid, reported in 8 Cranch, 155, the claimant, *a citizen* of the *United States*, had *purchased goods* in *the enemy's country, a long time before the declaration of war*, and had deposited them on an island, near the boundary line between the two countries. Upon the breaking out of hostilities, his agent had hired the vessel to proceed to the place of deposit, and bring away these goods. Upon her return, the vessel was captured, and with the cargo was condemned as prize of war for trading with the enemy. In applying the law to this state of facts, this Court said, and said unanimously, "That the *universal* sense of nations has acknowledged the *demoralizing effects that would result from the ad-*

All are enemies. *mission of individual intercourse. The whole nation are embarked in one common bottom, and must be reconciled to submit to one common fate. Every individual of the one nation must acknowledge every individual of the other nation as his own enemy, because the enemy of his country.* But, after deciding what is the duty of the citizen, the question occurs, What is the consequence of a breach of that duty? The law of prize is a part of the law of nations. In it, a *hostile character is attached to trade, independently of the character of the trader*, who pursues or directs it. *Condemnation to the use of the captor*, is *equally the fate of the property of the belligerent, and of the property engaged in anti-neutral trade. But a citizen or an ally* may be engaged in a *hostile trade*, and thereby *involve his property in the fate of those in whose cause he embarks.*"

Non-intercourse. Again the Court say, "If, by *trading*, in prize law was meant that signification of the term which consists in *negotiation or contract*, this *case would not come under the penalties of the rule. But the object and spirit of the rule is to cut off all communication or actual locomotive intercourse between individuals of the belligerent nations. Negotiation or contract has, therefore, no necessary connection with the offence. Intercourse inconsistent with actual hostility, is the offence against which the operation of the rule is directed.*" . .

Enemy property. "The same course of decision which has established that *property of a subject or citizen taken trading with the enemy is forfeited*, has decided also that it is *forfeited as prize*. The ground of the forfeiture is, *that it is taken adhering to the enemy, and therefore the proprietor is pro hac vice to be considered an enemy. Vide* also Wheaton on Captures, p. 219; and 1 C. Robinson, 219, the case of The Nelly."

Attempts have been made to evade the rule of public law, by the interposition of a neutral port between the shipment from the belligerent port and their ultimate destination in the enemy's country; but in all such cases the goods have been condemned as having been taken in a course of commerce rendering them liable to confiscation; and it has been ruled that, *without license from government, no communication, direct or indirect, can be carried on with the enemy*; that the interposition of a prior port makes no difference; that all the trade with the enemy is illegal, and the circumstance that the goods are to go first to a neutral port will not make it lawful. 3 C. Robinson, 22, The Indian Chief; and 4 C. Robinson, 79, The Jonge Pieter. . . . .

Non intercourse.

Trade unlawful.

DYNES *vs.* HOOVER, 20 Howard's S. C. Rep. 78.

The demurrer admits that the court martial was lawfully organized; that the crime charged was one forbidden by law; that the court had jurisdiction of the charge as it was made: that a trial took place before the court upon the charge, and the defendant's plea of not guilty; and that, upon the evidence in the case, the court found Dynes guilty of an attempt to desert, and sentenced him to be punished, as has already been stated; that the sentence of the court was approved by the Secretary; and that, by his direction, Dynes was brought to Washington; and that the defendant was marshal for the District of Columbia; and that in receiving Dynes, and committing him to the keeper of the penitentiary, he obeyed the orders of the President of the United States, in execution of the sentence. Among the powers conferred upon Congress, by the 8th section of the 1st Article of the Constitution, are the following: "to provide and maintain a navy;" "to make rules for the government of the land and naval forces." *And the 8th Amendment, which requires a presentment of a grand jury in cases of capital or otherwise infamous crime, expressly excepts from its operations "cases arising in the land or naval forces."* And by the 2d section of the 2d Article of the Constitution, it is declared that "The President shall be commander-in-chief of the army and navy of the United States, and of the militia of the several States, when called into the actual service of the United States."

Construction of 8th amendment Grand jury not required in cases, etc.

These provisions show that *Congress has the power to provide for the trial and punishment of military and naval offences, in the manner then and now practiced by civilized nations; and that the power to do so, is given without any connection between it and the 3d Article of the Constitution, defining the judicial power of the United States; indeed, that the two powers are entirely independent of each other...*

Power of Congress to make laws for punishment of military and naval offences.

"The objection is ingeniously worded, was very ably argued, and we may add, with a clear view and knowledge of what the law is upon such a subject, and how the plaintiff's case may be brought under it, to make the defendant responsible on this action for false imprisonment. But it substitutes an imputed error in the finding of the Court, for the original subject matter of its jurisdiction, *seeking to make the marshal answerable* for his mere *ministerial execution of a sentence*, which the Court passed, the Secretary of the Navy approved, and which the President of the United States, as constitutional Commander-in-Chief of the army and navy of the United States, directed the marshal to execute, by receiving the prisoner and convict, Dynes, from the naval officer then having him in custody, to transfer him to the penitentiary, in accordance with the sentence which the Court had passed upon him. . . . . .

Has no connection with the judicial power.

Marshal not liable for ministerial act in executing sentence, etc.

"But the case in hand is *not one of a court without jurisdiction* over the subject matter, or that of one which has neglected the forms and rules of procedure enjoined for the exercise of jurisdiction. It was regularly convened; its forms of procedure were strictly observed as they are directed to be by the statute; and if its sentence be a deviation from it, which we do not admit, it is not absolutely void. Whatever the sentence is, or may have been, as it was not a trial by court martial taking place out of the United States, it could not have been carried into execution but by the confirmation of the President, had it extended to loss of life, or in cases not extending to loss of life, as this did not, but by the confirmation of the Secretary of the Navy, who ordered the Court. *And if a sentence be so confirmed, it becomes final, and must be executed, unless the President pardon the offenders. It is in the nature of an appeal to the officer ordering the court, who is made by the law the arbiter of the legality and propriety of the court's sentence. When confirmed it is altogether beyond the jurisdiction of any civil tribunal whatever, unless it shall be in a case in which the court had not jurisdiction over the subject matter or charge*, or one in which, having jurisdiction over the subject matter, it *has failed to observe the rules prescribed by the statute for its exercise.* In such cases, as has just been said, all of the parties to such illegal trial are trespassers upon a party aggrieved by it, and he may recover damages from them on a proper suit in a civil court, by the verdict of a jury." . . . .

Sentence of court martial *final*.

Civil courts have no jurisdiction over the *sentence*.

Except.

Civil courts have no right to interfere with sentences of courts martial.

"*With the sentences of courts martial* which have been convened regularly, and have proceeded legally, and by which punishments are directed, not forbidden by law, or which are according to the laws and customs of the sea, *civil courts have nothing to do*, nor are they in *any way alterable by them.* If it were otherwise, the civil courts would virtually administer the rules and articles of war, irrespective of those to whom that duty and obligation has been confided by the laws of the United States, from whose decisions no appeal or jurisdiction of any kind has been given to the civil magistrate or civil courts. But we repeat, if a court martial has no *jurisdiction over the subject matter of the charge* it has been convened to try, or shall inflict a punishment *forbidden by the law*, though its sentence shall be approved by the officers having a revisory power of it, *civil courts* may, on an action by a party aggrieved by it, inquire into the want of the court's jurisdiction, and give him redress. (Harman *vs.* Tappenden, 1 East 555; as to ministerial officers, Marshall's Case, 10 Cr. 76; Morrison *vs.* Sloper, Wells, 30; Parton *vs.* Williams, B. and A. 330; and as to justices of the peace, by Ld. Tenterden, in Basten *vs.* Carew, 3 B. and C. 653; Mules *vs.* Calcott, 6 Bins. 85." . . . . .

Except.

Imprisonment in penitentiary of Dynes.

"In this case all of us think that *the court* which tried Dynes *had jurisdiction* over the subject matter of the charge against him; that the *sentence* of the court against him was *not forbidden by law;* and that having been *approved by the Secretary of the Navy* as a fair deduction from the 17th Article of the Act of April 23, 1800, and that *Dynes* having been *brought to Washington as a prisoner* by the *direction of the Secretary*, that the *President* of the United States, as constitutional Commander-in-Chief of the army and navy, and in virtue of his constitutional obligation that he shall take care that the laws be faithfully executed, *violated no law in directing the Marshal to receive the prisoner Dynes* from the officer commanding the United States steamer Engineer, for the purpose of transferring him to the penitentiary of the District of Columbia, and, consequently, that the *Marshal is not answerable in this action of trespass and false imprisonment.*"

Authority of sentence confirmed.

LEITENSDORFER *vs.* WEBB, 20 Howland's S. C. Rep. 176.

Civil government of N. Mexico overthrown by conquest

"Upon the acquisition, in the year 1846, by the arms of the United States, of the Territory of New Mexico, the *civil government* of this territory having *been overthrown*, the officer, General Kearney, holding possession for the United States, in virtue of the power of conquest and occupancy, and *in obedience to the duty of maintaining the security of the inhabitants in their persons and property, ordained, under the sanction and authority of the United States, a provisional or temporary government for the acquired country.* By this substitution of a *new supremacy*, although the former *political relations* of the inhabitants were dissolved, their private relations, *their rights vested under the government of their former allegiance, or those arising from contract or usage, remained in full force and unchanged, except so far as they were in their nature and character found to be in conflict with the Constitution and laws of the United States*, OR WITH ANY REGULATIONS WHICH THE CONQUERING AND OCCUPYING AUTHORITY SHOULD ORDAIN Amongst the consequences which would be necessarily incident to the *change of sovereignty*, would be the *appointment or control of the agents by*

Provisional government ordered by Gen. Kearney.

Duty.

How far their former rights were changed.

What law is to be administered by military power.

whom and the modes in which the government of the occupant should be administered, — this result being indispensable, in order to secure those objects for which such a government is usually established."

Conquest gives rights to change government and officers thereof in order to secure victory.

This is the principle of the law of nations, as expounded by the highest authorities. In the case of The Fama, in the 5th of Robinson's Rep. p. 106, Sir William Scott declares it to be "the settled principle of the law of nations, that the *inhabitants of a conquered territory change their allegiance*, and their relation to their former sovereign is dissolved; but their relations to each other, and their rights of property *not taken from them by the orders of the conqueror*, remain undisturbed." So, too, it is laid down by Vattel, book 3d, ch. 13, sect. 200, that "the conqueror lays his hands on the possessions of the state, whilst private persons are permitted to retain theirs; they suffer but indirectly by the war, and to them the result is that they only change masters."

In the case of the United States *vs.* Perchiman, 7 Peters, pp. 86, 87, this court have said, "It may be not unworthy of remark, that it is very unusual, even in cases of conquest, for the conqueror to do more than to displace the sovereign, and assume dominion over the country. The modern usage of nations, which has become law, would be violated, and that sense of justice and right which is acknowledged and felt by the whole civilized world be outraged, if private property should be *generally* confiscated and *private rights annulled*. The people change their allegiance; their relation to their sovereign is dissolved; but their relations to each other, and their rights of property, remain undisturbed." (*Vide* also the case of Mitchel *vs.* The United States, 9th ib. 711, and Kent's Com. vol. 1. p. 177.)

Judicial system ordained.

Accordingly, we find that there was *ordained by the provisional Government a judicial system, which created a superior or appellate court, constituted of three judges, and circuit courts, in which the laws were to be administered by the judges of the superior or appellate court, in the circuits to which they should be respectively assigned. By the same authority, the jurisdiction of the Circuit Courts to be held in the several counties was declared to embrace, 1st, all criminal cases that shall not be otherwise provided for by law; and, 2d, exclusive original jurisdiction in all civil cases which shall not be cognizable before the prefects and alcaldes* (*Vide* Laws of New Mexico, Kearney's Code, p. 48). *Of the validity* of these ordinances of the provisional government there is made *no question with respect to the period during which the territory was held by the United States as occupying conqueror*, and it would seem to admit of no doubt that during the period of their valid existence and operation, these ordinances *must have displaced and superseded every previous institution of the vanquished or deposed political power which was incompatible with them.* But it has been contended, that whatever may have been the rights of the occupying conqueror *as such*, these were all terminated by the termination of the belligerent attitude of the parties, and that, with the close of the contest, every institution which had been overthrown or suspended would be revived and reëstablished. The *fallacy of this pretension* is exposed by the fact, that the territory never was relinquished by the conqueror, nor restored to its original condition or allegiance, but was retained by the occupant until possession was matured into absolute permanent dominion and sovereignty; and this, too, under the settled purpose of the United States, never to relinquish the possession ac-

Courts established by military power. Jurisdiction, etc.

Displaced all old laws incompatible, etc.

When terminated.

How terminated.

quired by arms. We conclude, therefore, that the ordinances and institutions of the provisional government would be revoked or modified by the United States alone, either by direct legislation on the part of Congress, or by that of the territorial government in the exercise of powers delegated by Congress. That no power whatever, incompatible with the Constitution or laws of the United States, or with the authority of the provisional government, was retained by the Mexican government, or was revived under that government, from the period at which the possession passed to the authorities of the United States.

UNITED STATES SUPREME COURT. December Term, 1863.

THE VALLANDIGHAM CASE.

Ex parte, in the matter of Clement L. Vallandigham, Petitioner; on petition for a writ of certiorari to the Judge Advocate-General of the Army of the United States.

There is no analogy between the power of the United States Court to issue writs of *certiorari*, and the prerogative power by which they issue in England.
United States Courts derive such power solely from the Constitution and Congressional legislation.
Such petitions are not within the letter or spirit of the grants of appellate jurisdiction to this court.
A military commission is not a court within the meaning of Section 14 of Act of 1789.
This Court has no power to originate a writ of *certiorari*, or to review or pronounce any opinion upon the proceedings of a military commission.
Affirmative words in the Constitution, giving this Court original jurisdiction in certain cases, must be construed negatively as to all other cases.

Petitioner charged with expressing disloyal sentiments and sympathy for rebels;

The petitioner was, on May 5, 1863, arrested at his residence, taken to Cincinnati, and on the next day, arraigned before a military commission, appointed by Major-General Burnside, commanding the Military Department of Ohio, on a charge of having expressed sympathies for those in arms against the United States Government, and for having uttered in a public speech disloyal sentiments and opinions. The petitioner refused to plead, and denied the jurisdiction of the commission. A plea of "not guilty" was therefore entered by the order of the commission, and the trial proceeded. Seven members of the commission were present, and tried the charge according to military law. The prisoner called and cross-examined witnesses; had the aid of counsel, and made a written argument.

Was tried, convicted, and sentenced;

The finding and sentence were that the petitioner was guilty of the substantial charges, and that he be placed in close confinement in some fortress of the United States, there to be kept during the remainder of the war. General Burnside approved the finding and sentence, and designated Fort Warren as the place of confinement. On the 19th of May, 1863, the President, in commutation of the sentence, directed the prisoner to be sent beyond our military lines, which order was executed.

Sentence commuted.

Mr. Justice Wayne delivered the opinion of the Court in which Nelson, J., concurred. After giving a detailed statement of the facts above briefly set forth, they continue as follows: —

"It has been urged in support of the motion for the writ of *cer-*

tiorari, and against the jurisdiction of a military commission to try the petitioner, that the latter was prohibited by the 30th section of the Act of March 30, 1863, for enrolling and calling out the national forces, — 12 Statutes at Large, 736, — as the crimes punishable in it by the sentence of a court-martial or a military commission applied only to persons who are in the military service of the United States, and subject to the articles of war; and also, that by the third section of the 3d Article of the Constitution, all crimes, except in cases of impeachment, were to be tried by juries in the State where the crime had been committed, and when not committed within any State, at such place as Congress may by law have directed; and that the military commission could have no jurisdiction to try the petitioner, as neither the charge against him nor its specifications imputed to him any offence known to the law of the land; that General Burnside had no authority to enlarge the jurisdiction of a military commission by the General Order Number Thirty-eight, or otherwise. General Burnside acted in the matter as the general commanding the Ohio Department, in conformity with the instructions for the government of the armies of the United States, approved by the President of the United States, and published by the Assistant Adjutant-General, by order of the Secretary of War, on the 24th of April, 1863.* Constitutional objections stated.

It is affirmed in the thirteenth paragraph of the first section of these Instructions, that "military jurisdiction is of two kinds: first, that which is conferred and defined by statute; second, that which is derived from the common law of war. Military offences, under the statute, must be tried in the manner therein directed; but military offences which do not come within the statute must be tried and punished under the common law of war. The character of the courts which exercise these jurisdictions depends upon the local law of each particular country. In the armies of the United States, the first is exercised by courts martial; while cases which do not come within the 'rules and articles of war,' or the jurisdiction conferred by statute or court martial, are tried by military commissions."

These jurisdictions are applicable, not only to war with foreign nations, but to a rebellion, when a part of a country wages war against its legitimate government, seeking to throw off all allegiance to it to set up a government of its own.

Our first remark upon the motion for a *certiorari* is, that there is no analogy between the power given by the Constitution and laws of the United States to the Supreme Court and the other inferior courts of the United States, and to the judges of them to issue such processes, and the prerogative power by which it is done in England. The purposes for which the writ is issued are alike, but there is no similitude in the origin of the power to do it. In England the Court of King's Bench has a superintendence over all courts of an inferior criminal jurisdiction, and may, by the plenitude of its power, award a *certiorari* to have any indictment removed and brought before it; and where such *certiorari* is allowable, it is awarded at the instance of the king, because every indictment is at the suit of the king, and he has a prerogative of suing in whatever court he pleases. The courts of the United

* They were prepared by Francis Leiber, LL. D., and were revised by a board of officers, of which Major-General E. A. Hitchcock was president.

States derive authority to issue such a writ from the Constitution and the legislation of Congress. To place the two sources of the right to issue the writ in obvious contrast, and in application to the motion we are considering for its exercise by this Court, we will cite so much of the third article of the Constitution as we think will best illustrate the subject. "The judicial power of the United States shall be vested in the Supreme Court, and in such inferior courts as the Congress may, from time to time, ordain and establish." "The judicial power shall extend to all cases in law and equity, arising under the Constitution, the laws of the United States, and treaties made or which shall be made under their authority; to all cases affecting embassadors, other public ministers and consuls," etc., "and in all cases affecting embassadors, other ministers and consuls, and those in which a State shall be a party, the Supreme Court shall have original jurisdiction. In all other cases before mentioned, the Supreme Court shall have appellate jurisdiction, both as to law and fact, with such exceptions, and under such regulations, as the Congress shall make." Then Congress passed the act to establish the judicial courts of the United States,—1 Stats. at Large, p. 73, chap. 20,—and in the 13th section of it declared that the Supreme Court shall have exclusively all such jurisdiction of suits or proceedings against embassadors or other public ministers or their domestics or their domestic servants as a court of law can have or exercise consistently with the laws of nations, and original but not exclusive jurisdiction of suits brought by embassadors, or other public ministers, or in which a consul or vice-consul shall be a party. In the same section the Supreme Court is declared to have appellate jurisdiction in cases hereinafter expressly provided. In this section, it will be perceived that the jurisdiction given, besides that which is mentioned in the preceding part of the section, is an exclusive jurisdiction of suits or proceedings against embassadors or other public ministers or their domestics or domestic servants, as a court of law can have or exercise consistently with the laws of nations, and original, but not exclusive, jurisdiction of all suits brought by embassadors, or other public ministers, or in which a consul or vice-consul shall be a party, thus guarding them from all other judicial interference and giving to them the right to prosecute for their own benefit in the courts of the United States. Thus substantially reaffirming the constitutional declaration that the Supreme Court had original jurisdiction in all cases affecting embassadors and other public ministers and consuls and those in which a State shall be a party, and that it shall have appellate jurisdiction in all other cases before mentioned, both as to law and fact, with such exceptions and under such regulations as the Congress shall make.

The appellate powers of the Supreme Court, as granted by the Constitution, are limited and regulated by the acts of Congress, and must be exercised subject to the exceptions and regulations made by Congress. Durousseau *vs.* The United States, 6 Cranch. 314; Barry *vs.* Mercien, 5 How. 119; United States *vs.* Currey, 6 How. 113; Forsyth *vs.* United States, 9 How. 571. In other words, the petition before us we think not to be within the letter or spirit of the grants of appellate jurisdiction to the Supreme Court. It is not in law or equity within the meaning of those terms, as used in the third article of the Constitution. Nor is a military commission a court within the meaning of the 14th section of the Judiciary Act

A military commission not a court, within the meaning of the Judiciary Act.

of 1789. That act is denominated to be one to establish the judicial courts of the United States, and the 14th section declares that all the 'before-mentioned' courts of the United States shall have power to issue writs of *scire facias*, *habeas corpus*, and all other writs not specially provided for by statute, which may be necessary for the exercise of their respective jurisdictions agreeably to the principles and usages of law. The words in the section, 'the before-mentioned' courts, can only have reference to such courts as were established in the preceding part of the act, and excludes the idea that a court of military commission can be one of them. Whatever may be the force of Vallandigham's protest, that he was not triable by a court of military commission, it is certain that his petition cannot be brought within the fourteenth section of the Act; and further that the court cannot, without disregarding its frequent decisions and interpretations of the Constitution in respect to its judicial power, originate a writ of *certiorari* to review or pronounce any opinion upon the proceedings of a military commission. It was natural, before the sections of the third articles of the Constitution had been fully considered in connection with the legislation of Congress, giving to the courts of the United States power to issue writs of *scire facias*, *habeas corpus*, and all other writs not specially provided for by statute, which might be necessary for the exercise of their respective jurisdiction, that by some members of the profession it should have been thought, and some of the early judges of the Supreme Court also, that the 14th section of the Act of 24th September, 1789, gave to this court a right to originate processes of *habeas corpus ad subjiciendum* and writs of *certiorari*, to review the proceedings of the inferior courts as a matter of original jurisdiction, without being in any way restricted by the constitutional limitation that in all cases affecting embassadors, other public ministers and consuls, and those in which a State shall be a party, the Supreme Court shall have original jurisdiction.

No *certiorari* can issue from the Supreme Court to review proceedings of a military commission.

This limitation has always been considered restrictive of any other original jurisdiction. The rule of construction of the Constitution being, that affirmative words in the Constitution declaring in what cases the Supreme Court shall have original jurisdiction, must be construed negatively as to all other cases. 1 Cranch, 137; 5 Peters, 284; 12 Peters, 657; 9 Wheaton; 6 Wheaton, 264.

The nature and extent of the court's appellate jurisdiction and its want of it to issue writs of *habeas corpus ad subjiciendum*, have been fully discussed by this court at different times. We do not think it necessary, however, to examine or cite many of them at this time. We will annex a list to this opinion, distinguishing what this court's action has been in cases brought to it by appeal, from such applications as have been rejected, when it has been asked that it would act upon the matter as one of original jurisdiction. In the case *Ex parte* Milburn, 9 Peters, 704, Chief Justice Marshall said, as the jurisdiction of the court is appellate, it must first be shown that it has the power to award a *habeas corpus*. In *Ex parte* Kaine, 14 Howard, the court denied the motion, saying that the court's jurisdiction to award the writ was appellative, and that the case had not been so presented to it, and for the same cause refused to issue a writ of *certiorari*, which in the course of the argument was prayed for. In *Ex parte* Metzger, 5 How. 176, it was determined that a writ of *certiorari* could not be allowed to examine a commitment by a district judge, under the treaty between the United States and France,

Military commission exercises special authority;

for the reason that the judge exercised a special authority, and that no provision had been made for the revision of his judgment. *So does a court of military commission exercise a special authority.* In the case before us, it was urged that the decision in Metzger's case had been made upon the ground that the proceeding of the district judge was not judicial in its character, but that the proceedings of the military commission were so; and, further, it was said that the ruling in that case had been overruled by a majority of the judges in Kaine's case. There is a misapprehension of the report of the latter case; and as to the judicial character of the proceedings of the military commission, we cite what was said by the court in the case of Ferreira. "The powers conferred by Congress upon the district judge and the secretary are judicial in their nature, for judgment and discretion must be exercised by both of them, but it is not judicial in either case, in the sense in which the judicial power is granted to the courts of the United States." 13 Howard, 48.

Not *judicial*;

Its proceedings cannot be reversed by the Supreme Court.

Nor can it be said that the authority to be exercised by a military commission is judicial in that sense. It involves discretion to examine, to decide and sentence, but there is no original jurisdiction in the Supreme Court to issue a writ of habeas corpus ad subjiciendum to review or reverse its proceedings, or the writ of certiorari to revise the proceedings of a military commission. And as to the President's action in such matters, and those acting in them under his authority, we refer to the opinions expressed by this court in the cases of Martin *vs.* Mott, 12 Wheaton, pages 19, 28 to 35 inclusive; and Dynes *vs.* Hoover, 20 Howard, page 65, &c.

For the reasons given, our judgment is, that the writ of *certiorari* prayed for to revise and review the proceedings of the military commission, by which Clement L. Vallandigham was tried, sentenced, and imprisoned, must be denied, and so do we order accordingly."